WHO'S SMILING NOW?

by

Joy Wood

DEDICATION

To John

When I saw you I fell in love, and you smiled because you knew

(Arrigo Bioto)

Chapter 1

LAURA

In her pretty white bra and matching lacy knickers, she positioned herself on the chair in front of the ornate dressing table mirror. Staring back was a young and vibrant woman approaching her twenty-first birthday, with a fabulous boyfriend and a good job. But Laura didn't see that . . . she never did. No matter how many years had lapsed, and the trauma of her disturbing childhood had faded, it was only ever the daughter of a killer that she saw.

And it never changed.

She took a deep breath in. No point in dwelling on that now when she needed to look her best for tonight. She gathered her lustrous dark hair from the nape of her neck, clasped it into a make-shift ponytail, and lifted it onto her head in a temporary bun.

Up or down?

Cohan preferred it down.

Maybe down – he'd only undo it anyway.

As she let it drop to her shoulders, a tidal wave of guilt weaved its way through her. She shouldn't even be thinking about what Cohan liked. He was a holiday fling, someone she'd met six days ago and nothing more. What she should be doing was concentrating on flying home tomorrow and seeing her boyfriend Matthew.

The short break in Spain cat-sitting for her aunt had been a fantastic escape from the daily grind of commuting into the city, and if only Matthew had come with her like he was supposed to, she'd have never found herself cheating on him. There wouldn't have been the opportunity to be unfaithful. And Matthew, with his youthful looks and boyish charm would never cheat on her. If she found him in a room naked with another woman, there'd be some sort of explanation. He was loyal, dutiful and totally reliable, yet here she was doing the dirty on him, about to meet another man and she couldn't stop herself however much she knew it was wrong. Cohan Laity was like a box of favourite chocolates, you ate plenty and enjoyed them, but you still kept delving in for more despite being full and knowing you really shouldn't. What sort of a person did that make her? She already knew the answer and dismissed it straight away. Analysing herself was not a favourite pastime.

Tomorrow Matthew would be waiting for her at the airport, full of apologies for not coming on the short break that she'd only agreed to as it was supposed to be for them both. Her dear mum would have the kettle on in their cosy family home eagerly watching at the window for them to pull down the drive so she could feed them with some calorie laden creamy concoction she'd baked.

She stared back at her reflection in the mirror. Tonight was the last time she was going to see the charismatic Cohan Laity, and the last time he'd make love to her.

It's for the best, she told herself. Attractive as she'd found him, their brief holiday fling . . . affair, or whatever she labelled it as, had reached its natural conclusion. Tonight's dinner was a fond farewell to their time together.

With a steady hand, she applied her smoky grey eye-shadow filling in the generous eyelids she'd been lucky enough to be blessed with, carefully emphasising the corner of the top eyelid with a flick of the black eye-liner pen. Lashings of black mascara completed the dark mystical look courtesy of the volumising brush which boasted *separating the lashes and coating them perfectly.*

A quick skim with a nice bronzer on her face, a touch of blusher to her cheeks, and a light pink lip gloss completed the look. She turned her head from side-to-side in the mirror to check the make-up she'd applied. Oriental most probably described her look best and fortunately for her, she'd been blessed with blemish free skin, high cheekbones and eyes so dark, they were almost black.

She'd always stood out as being slightly different, certainly unlike her brother and sister. But they were genetic children; whereas she'd been adopted by her beloved parents, their two children had become three overnight. The Foley's had already got her older sister Danielle, and in a cruel twist of fate, years later when most women would have been well past their fertile years, her mum had fallen pregnant and given birth to Teddy. But genetics had played a cruel trick and Teddy had been born with Down's syndrome. He was fifteen now and much loved by them all, although perhaps not so much by Danielle who appeared most of the time to find him tiresome whereas Laura absolutely adored him. Teddy was vulnerable and reminded her of how she was as a child, and she loved him dearly because of it.

She decided to wear her hair loose, so tipped her head upside down, flung it back up again to create lift, and gave it a quick spray to ensure the volume would stay in place. Cohan had admired her thick lustrous hair and she wanted to look her best for him. With a quick widening of her eyes to check there were no mascara blobs, she was ready.

She carefully slipped the short white dress over her head to make sure she didn't get any of the newly applied make-up around the neck, and pulled it down her body, reaching behind to zip it up. She checked herself in the full-length mirror next to the dressing table, pleased with the finished result. The bright white of the dress showed off her brown arms and legs beautifully. Although she hadn't acquired a St Tropez suntan in the short time she'd been in Spain, she certainly looked a nice healthy shade, more likely due to genetics as opposed to sunburn. One glimpse at the sun and she was instantly two shades darker.

A spray of her floral musky perfume caused another guilty twist in her tummy. Matthew had bought the perfume for her when she'd mentioned she'd ran out, and here she was, wearing it for another man. But there was little point dwelling on that when she'd already done the dirty . . . several times. Feeling guilty now would achieve nothing, especially when she was about to repeat it all over again that evening.

As she slipped her feet into the decorative sling-back silver pumps, she turned from side to side examining what she looked like from all angles, it was almost as if she was watching someone else being bad . . . it certainly didn't seem like Laura Foley.

Tonight, Cohan was taking her to a beautiful restaurant out of town *with views to die for* he'd said, which he wanted her to see before she left.

Cohan's handsome face was easy to bring to mind. Not drop-dead gorgeous as in a playboy, but he certainly had an attractiveness about him in a roguish manly way. Definitely not a pretty boy though. Her mother always said personality was more important than looks, and Cohan certainly had oodles of that. He was charming. Another of her mother's expressions fitted Cohan perfectly, *he'd be able to sell ice to Eskimos.*

Her phone pinged and she reached for it.

Be with you shortly, beautiful

The emoji face amused her. Cohan attached the same emoji to each text he sent her and never varied it like most people. She'd asked him why he never changed it and he told her it was because whenever he thought about her, she made him smile. She'd nudged him in his ribs for being cheesy and he'd playfully made a big show as if she'd hurt him by clutching his side. Since then, every text he sent her contained the same smiley face.

She squeezed her iPhone into her tiny evening purse and made her way downstairs to the window seat at the front of the house and waited for Cohan to arrive. The terraced house was part of a row on a popular street with holiday makers as it was fairly central and close to the promenade. The street was busy with various couples, some carrying beach bags and clutching towels on their way back to their houses and apartments, and others dressed up and heading to the bars and restaurants. Like her they'd no doubt be partaking in some alcohol, food and plenty of sex that evening.

Sheba, one of the cats she'd been looking after jumped on the window seat and she held her arm against him. "No you don't, you're not wrecking my efforts with cat hairs. You stay right there."

She ran her hand along his soft fur to keep him at arm's length, and thought back to her first day in Spain. Was it only six days ago? It seemed much longer.

She'd taken a taxi from the airport as her aunt had instructed, and called on the neighbour who had the key. She'd familiarised herself with the house quickly, preferring to get outside to enjoy the sunshine. Apparently, the cats were self-sufficient; basically her job was just to feed them. She checked each room but couldn't locate them, and as her tummy rumbled and the promenade beckoned, she decided to go out and see the cats later on. They had a cat flap to get in and out so they'd be fine.

The sun had been shining beautifully that first day as she made her way towards the seafront. The promenade was vibrant with the shops selling their beautiful coloured wares and she soaked up the atmosphere of the hustle and bustle of holidaymakers. She paused at a display of scarves and touched the assortment of coloured fabrics, telling herself she'd buy a couple before she went home. They'd be ideal as presents for her mum and sister. Teddy, her young brother would be pleased with any sort of present, so she'd go for a tee-shirt with a funny logo and maybe a cap. He loved his caps.

She selected a few postcards for him which she intended taking home with her, but she also had to post one to him as Teddy saved foreign stamps and spent hours consulting his wall map in his bedroom and putting a tiny pin in each country he received the card from. Only then would he file the card in his scrap book. She lost count of the times she had to go through the scrap book with him billing and cooing over the variety of cards he had.

A pretty card depicting the promenade with the stunning sea as the background was the one she decided to mail Teddy. The colour of the ocean on the card was perhaps more turquoise than it appeared that particular day, and the paving stones were a little more vibrant than they currently looked, but they'd been worn down by the thousands of feet marching along them each day, or more likely the photograph had been digitally enhanced. Whichever, she knew Teddy would be thrilled to receive it even if she most probably would be home before it arrived.

The café she chose for lunch had a lovely view overlooking the promenade and the food was relatively cheap. While she was eating a cheese salad, she texted Matthew and sent a panoramic photograph of the bay. Although she was still miffed with him that he hadn't come with her, she was softening a bit. It was a short-notice break and he was in the middle of a shutdown at the oil refinery he worked at so his boss wouldn't sanction him any leave. Seemingly production had stopped while essential repairs were carried out and it was very much hands on deck for them all, but he had asked her to let him know when she arrived and it seemed petty not to. And her intention had been to take loads of photos each day to make him envious for missing the trip.

The waitress had interrupted her, "I'm so sorry, I forgot," she said with an apologetic expression as she placed a latte down on the table.

Laura smiled, "Don't worry, thank you."

She reached in her bag for a pen and the post card she'd bought for her brother, and began to write, *Dear Teddy . . .*

"Excuse me."

The sun was obscuring her view as she looked up, so she had to put her hand over her eyes to block it out. A tall chap dressed casually in a tee-shirt, shorts and flip-flops stood alongside her table.

"Would you mind if I took this seat?" he asked nodding to the vacant one opposite her, "most of the tables seem taken?"

He looked to be about thirty and his hair was short and brown with a flicked-up fringe. His dark stubble indicating he hadn't shaved for a few days, suited him. He was certainly pleasant on the eye.

She'd glanced around at the adjacent tables. The café was much busier than when she'd first sat down. There might be tables inside, but who'd want to be cooped up on such a lovely day when they could be enjoying the sunshine?

"Please do," she reached forward and shuffled her bag of postcards a little closer to allow him some room.

He took the seat and tossed his mobile phone on the table, "Thank you."

"I'm going shortly when I've finished my coffee and written this card, so you'll have the table to yourself."

"Don't dash off on my account," he'd said, "I'm literally just taking a ten-minute breather from the office. It's too nice today to stay indoors."

"Yes, isn't it, I hope it stays like this all week."

"You're here on holiday?" he'd asked.

"Yes, I'm house-sitting for a week, or technically I should say, cat-sitting."

"Let's hope it stays fine for you then." He'd reached out his hand, "I'm Cohan by the way."

She'd offered her hand which he quickly enveloped in his larger masculine one, like a well-fitting glove.

"I'm Laura."

Chapter 2

LAURA

The honk of a car horn interrupted her thoughts about her first day in Spain. She waved eagerly at Cohan to acknowledge she'd seen him and made her way out of the front door, locking it behind her.

Her heart rate quickened as she got into his Ford Fiesta and smelt his freshly showered masculinity. His lush lips brushed her cheek tenderly causing the usual tummy flutter and an urge to say, *shall we forget dinner.*

"Hi," she smiled fastening her seat belt.

"Hi, yourself," his delicious brown eyes twinkled, "you look beautiful."

"Thank you."

"All set for our goodbye meal?" he tilted his head, almost as if he could read her mind and would happily miss dinner too.

She widened her eyes, "Yes, are you?"

"Definitely not," he scowled as if it was the biggest regret of his life, "but I'm determined tonight's going to be special."

And it would be. He'd make sure of that.

Cohan Laity had already proven he knew how to give a woman a good time.

The beautiful restaurant set on a cliff top had stunning views of the mountains. He must have had to tip the waiter heavily to get what appeared to be one of the best tables in the house. Rather than sit opposite her, he sat to the right of her around the small intimate table so they could both enjoy the view.

He ordered a glass of champagne and she covertly watched him as they leisurely perused the menu. She was going to miss him when she went home.

"What do you fancy?" he asked interrupting her mushy thoughts.

"Erm . . . maybe the salmon mousse to start, and perhaps the seafood risotto. What about you?"

"The mushroom soup, and I think I'm going for the sea bass."

"You do eat a lot of fish, I think every time we've eaten together you've had fish."

"Yes, I prefer it when I'm out, I don't cook it at home though, I can't stand the smell lingering. And it's safer for me with my nut allergy."

"That must be such a worry for you."

"It is, but I'm used to it now."

"How long have you had it?"

"Since I was a child, but it's easier these days. I always have my EpiPen when I'm out and about."

"Where is it now?" she frowned.

"In the car but I won't need it here, I've telephoned ahead. Good restaurants are vigilant, it's those you pop into on a whim you have to be careful of."

"What happens if you're given nuts by mistake?"

"My tongue starts to swell and I have trouble swallowing. It's important to then inject myself with the EpiPen and get to hospital ASAP."

"God, that sounds awful. Has it happened very often?"

"No, I can count on one hand the amount of times it has. It was more worrying when I was younger at school. My mother got a job as a helper in the canteen so she could keep her eye on what I was eating." He took a sip of his champagne, "Don't look so worried.

It's something I've learned to live with, it isn't a problem."

The waiter approached the table, "Are you ready to order?"

"Yes, I think we are," Cohan nodded.

The food had been delicious, and he'd entertained her with stories from his childhood and how he'd become the editor of the university magazine.

During coffee, he took her hand and kissed it before reaching into the inside pocket of his jacket and handing her a long thin box which, if she wasn't mistaken, contained a piece of jewellery.

"I hope you like it."

She gave him a 'I wish you hadn't look' but he dismissed it. "Open it," he urged, "I got it especially for you."

She took it from him and opened the lid. Resting on the brown velvet was the most exquisite bracelet with tiny rose gold flowers with white gold leaves linking them together. It was a classy piece of jewellery, even to her eye, and must have cost him plenty.

She shook her head, "Cohan, you really shouldn't have."

"Why not?" He removed it from the box and reached for her wrist. Her eyes fixed on his large hands as they fastened the clasp. Not neatly groomed manicured fingernails thank goodness, she hated to see that on a man, she liked what he had, clean masculine hands with blunt cut short nails.

"Perfect." He gently turned her arm from side to side, showing off the vibrancy of the new untarnished gold. "I knew it would look good on you and I wanted you to have something special to remind you of our few days together," he leaned forward and kissed her gently, "a beautiful piece of jewellery for a beautiful lady."

She turned her wrist to examine the bracelet. He had a good eye; it was extremely tasteful. It was thoughtful of him, but sophisticated men like him were most likely to be buying gifts for their lovers regularly. He most probably bought them at a discount price in bulk so he could shower each of his conquests as they were leaving.

"It's lovely, but you shouldn't have." And she meant it. She was going to have to lie if Matthew asked where it had come from.

"It's just a bracelet," he dismissed, "and I promise you, I haven't had to raid the piggy bank. I can still afford to eat, so enjoy it."

"That's a relief," she grinned back, "but I haven't bought you anything, I feel bad now."

"Don't. There's nothing I need. Well, nothing monetary anyway," he smiled playfully. He took her hand again and she turned to face his gorgeous dark chocolaty eyes. He must enjoy giving gifts as they seemed vivid and bright, which wasn't due to alcohol as he'd only had the one glass. The bottle of wine still had some remnants left, but she'd had more than enough to do justice to it.

"Tell me," his voice thickened slightly, "have you enjoyed tonight?"

"Of course I have, who wouldn't? It's been a lovely evening," she squeezed his hand, "and my gift is so pretty. Thank you."

"Well the evening isn't over yet."

"Thank God for that," she laughed, pleased that she had one more night with him.

He watched her face intensely, which she found incredibly sexy. As if he was hanging onto each of her responses. It was quite powerful. Matthew was the opposite. He had to be nudged numerous times when she was talking to him he was so easily distracted.

His stare became more intense, "I don't want you to leave."

"I don't want to go either," she said loving the fact he didn't want her to go, "but I've got to. These few days have been a sort of fairy tale, like something that happens in books, but my life is in the UK." She was saying the words out loud, but inside she felt a warm glow that he wanted more.

He widened his eyes, "You could always change your life and stay."

"I can't do that," she dismissed, "I've got to go, Matthew's waiting for me."

"That would be Matthew who couldn't be bothered to be here with you."

Although she'd been pretty peeved with Matthew, that statement wasn't entirely true so she had to defend him, "It wasn't that he couldn't be bothered, I told you the reason why he couldn't come. He had to work."

Cohan wasn't listening. He had the ability to listen carefully when she was talking about her life and things she enjoyed, that was one of the things she found so attractive about him, he seemed to want to know everything about her. But he was also direct when he wanted something. That had been apparent in the conversations they'd had. From being a child to university and his first job, he went after everything he wanted. That's why he'd be a successful author, Cohan Laity would excel at anything he did.

He raised an eyebrow enquiringly, "Can you slip back into your life so easily after what we've shared?"

"I'll have to. I've loved every moment of us being together, but it isn't real. You're here to write your book and I have a life at home. We can't ignore that."

His mouth turned downwards, like an unhappy emoji of a man. "You could stay for a while with me and we could take it from there."

She shook her head dismissively, "I can't. I've got a job to go back to, and my family."

"But surely we can work something out? Look," he screwed his face up, "I know we've only just met, and I'm possibly rushing you into something you've not considered," he paused momentarily as if giving her time to think, "to be honest, I hadn't considered it either until today, but I can't just let you go after what we've shared." His stare intensified, "If you stay and things work out between us, we could live anywhere you wanted to. We don't have to make a permanent home here."

She pulled her hand away. "Please don't do this. I'm booked on a flight home tomorrow. Matthew and my parents will be waiting. I have a life, okay maybe not the most exciting one in the world, but it's mine and one I need to get back to. My mother and father need me. Teddy can be quite a handful. I can't just disappear and make a life away from them."

"So why, if everything was fine at home," he tilted his head, "did you come looking for me?"

"I didn't *come looking for you*, as you put it. You know I wasn't looking for anything."

For the first time since she'd met him, he irritated her. He had no business talking like that, she didn't like it. She'd already said what she'd done with him was completely out of character. And it was. This wasn't really her. The closer the day came to her return home, the guiltier she felt. It was almost a relief to be going home so she could draw a line under it. As if it hadn't really happened.

"Okay then," he eased himself back on his chair, "if the mountain won't come to Muhammad, how about Muhammad coming to the mountain?"

She frowned, what on earth was he on about?

"I'll come to England," he continued, "I want to be with you, Laura, and if that's what it takes, then so be it. I'm not keen on the cold weather, but I can live with it."

Where the hell had this come from? Cohan Laity could have his pick of women. He was hot, good-looking, charismatic, and money didn't appear to be a problem. She'd dismissed their time together as a holiday fling with plenty of sex which she'd been more than willing to comply with. And that's all it was, plenty of Sangria and sex. Nothing had prepared her for any of this.

"Don't be silly," she dismissed, "you can't just up sticks and come to England."

Her tummy began to feel jittery. It was bad enough she'd been unfaithful to Matthew, but in her mind she'd separated it. A sort of, what goes on in Spain, stays in Spain. She certainly didn't need him complicating things any further. It might be wise not to go back with him for a night of sex after all, probably best to put a bit of distance between them both.

She reached for her napkin from her knee and placed it on the table. "You'll have to excuse me while I go to the ladies . . . and then perhaps we should be making our way back."

He raised an eyebrow questioningly, "To mine?"

They'd spent every evening and most afternoons at his apartment making love. It was natural he thought they would tonight. She certainly had. It had been on her mind all evening while they ate dinner, but he'd poured cold water on her libido with his suggestions.

She shook her head dismissively, "Maybe not. I think it's best if I went home tonight."

"So you're mad at me for speaking up about how I feel?"

"No, I'm not," she said, maybe a little too quickly because she was. "I'm just sorry you're making this into something it isn't, that's all."

His face took on a pained expression. "Don't do this, Laura," he warned.

"Do what?"

"Dismiss what we have together. It denigrates the last few days to casual."

It was casual but suddenly appeared to be getting completely out of hand. She hadn't expected anything like this. He'd never even hinted about having feelings for her. Okay, maybe in bed he'd muttered stuff, but that was just sex talk surely? It didn't mean anything.

"I'm not dismissing it. I've had a lovely few days with you which I'll treasure. But that's it. It was never going to be anymore than that. There'll be another Laura Foley along here next week."

His already dark eyes seemed to go a shade darker making her feel uneasy. This was a glimpse of him she'd not seen before. He couldn't possibly have developed feelings for her in the short time they'd been together.

He looked down at his watch. "I'll get the bill, but I'm not giving up. If it takes all night, I'm going to do my best to persuade you to stay. I'm not letting you go back to your previous life. You and I meeting has changed the future for us both, you just haven't accepted it," his eyes flashed with determination and something she couldn't quite recognise, "yet."

Chapter 3

LAURA

The stewardess's voice advising them to turn off all mobile devices or switch them to flight mode reminded her she hadn't done so. She reached into her bag underneath the seat in front of her and took out her phone. There was a text from Cohan.

Safe trip, gorgeous, missing you already.

Against her better judgement, she'd gone back with him to his apartment the previous evening. His declaration of wanting their relationship to continue had thrown her initially, but not enough for her to reject him. Why was that? Once he'd put pressure on her to stay, she'd been adamant in her own mind she wasn't going to go back and have sex with him, but he was appealing and extremely persuasive. He certainly had been gifted with bucket loads of charm and knew exactly how to use it.

Their lovemaking had been particularly special in light of her leaving and it being their last time together. He'd been passionate and loving, tender and giving. She still ached in places, reminding her of their epic night. His intensity made her consider he might be in love with her, but she quickly dismissed it as no more than infatuation. It had only been six days, you couldn't know anybody properly in that time. And if it had been as much as six weeks, he'd be seeing her very differently, that was for sure.

Thankfully, he hadn't harassed her further about staying after they'd left the restaurant, so he must have got the message. She was still puzzled about him wanting to prolong things between them though. It wasn't as if he'd had loads to drink, he'd had very little because of having to drive.

Anyway, it was all irrelevant now as she was on the flight heading home. Her tummy began to churn with agitation, which wasn't down to a fear of flying, it was more to do with her betrayal. The right thing to do would be to tell Matthew. Explain that she'd only agreed to meeting Cohan for a drink as they'd got on so well in the café. It was just a friendly thing; she hadn't expected it to turn into anything sexual. She'd been lonely and mad as hell with him that he hadn't been able to join her. But how could she say all that? It sounded feeble. Nobody forced her into taking her clothes off and indulging in fabulous sex with a man she hardly knew. Even now she couldn't believe how easy it had been. Matthew would be devastated, and selfishly she couldn't afford to lose him. He was her childhood dream of a life-long man, who would love her unconditionally. He was her future. She couldn't allow anything to jeopardise that. And he'd never understand her being unfaithful. He had really old-fashioned views on loyalty and commitment. His brother Chris had been badly let down days before his wedding by his fiancée who'd been having sex with a work colleague, and Matthew had been such a support to him, cajoling him along when things were particularly tough. Chris had taken on a mortgage with his future wife and couldn't manage it on his own, so Matthew had moved into the flat with him to help financially as well as emotionally. She loved Matthew for that. Privately they'd vowed to always be honest with each other and that had been her intention when she said it, but clearly it had been easier said than done. If she confessed to Matthew about what had happened in Spain, he wouldn't forgive her despite how much he cared for her. He was all about fidelity. His own mother had left his father following an affair and was now living in France with her second husband. Although he loved his mother dearly, he'd confessed some of that love had died when she'd been unfaithful to his father. One night after too much Gin, he admitted he'd never quite felt the same about her because of what she did even though his dad had found happiness with his second wife.

As the plane began to taxi towards the runway, she looked away from the small window as she didn't like to see it take off the ground. She always feared it wouldn't. Once they were airborne, she reached in her bag for the soft eye mask so she could try and make up for some of the sleep she'd missed during the night. She rested her head back and her mind began drift to a familiar theme.

She'd been christened Georgina Laura and until she was nine years of age and adopted, she was known as Georgie. But the 1st day of June, 2007 was imprinted on her mind forever. Her young life as she knew it, changed dramatically. Overnight she became an orphan. It made her shudder to think she could have ended up in a children's home, but fate had dealt her a better second hand than the horrendous first one, and she got a new life with an adoptive family. Many years had now lapsed and it was much longer in years than her previous life, but her old life and particularly her genetic father, Frank Milton was constantly on her mind. And despite the heinous crime he committed and the terrible pain he'd inflicted, she missed him terribly.

Her biological mother labelled her a daddy's girl, amongst other things that is – she definitely wasn't the most maternal of women, and to say her parents' marriage was volatile, was putting it mildly.

As a child, she'd known instinctively her family life was different from the other kids at school. Their dads held down regular jobs and took them out at weekends to the park, swimming, and for ice cream, whereas Frank Milton was far too busy for family life and spent his time stealing, gambling and smoking pot. But she loved him unconditionally. No matter what he did, her love for him never wavered. And with the passage of time, she recognised that she most probably romanticised what he was really like to the point she couldn't tell fact from fiction. But he occupied her thoughts on a daily basis even now after all this time.

From as far back as she could remember, maybe aged four or five, she used to trail around with him. Her mother used to do some sort of casual work when she could get it and on the days when she wasn't at school, she was with her daddy. She knew how to amuse herself while he supped ale in the pub with the locals; she soon learned how to sit quietly with her Coke and bag of crisps while he swapped stories with the bar flies, no doubt picking their brains for any snippets of information on vulnerable families he could rob next. She quickly cottoned on how to use her cuteness to distract a shop assistant, while her father nicked chocolates and goodies for them both to go to the park and eat.

The family home was a chaotic affair. She would spend endless hours listening to her mummy and daddy arguing. She would sit on the stairs and hear the shouting, the name calling, the slaps and although she didn't quite know then what was going on, she now realised it was the making-up sex.

Her mother was no doubt worn down by her father. She didn't seem to be around much, but Georgie was never quite sure what she got up to. Not having food in the house was a regular occurrence; there were times when she'd have to go to bed hungry, and the house was always cold, but she didn't understand at her age it was because they couldn't afford to heat it. All she perceived was she was always freezing and despite asking her mum frequently to have the fire on, it was always *no, put another jumper on.*

Her daddy used to leave the house each day, and when she'd beg him to take her with him, he'd tell her she had to go to school because she was clever and going to make lots of money one day. At the time she couldn't equate how being clever meant getting lots of money but she used to agree as Daddy said it so it must be right. He used to read to her fabulous adventure stories when she was very young and tell her she was the prettiest and brightest girl in the world and when she grew up, all the men would want to marry her because she was smart and beautiful, and she would have lots of lovely babies of her own one day.

Sometimes her daddy would be gone for days, it was hard to tell how long he'd be. *Just expect me when you see me,* was his favourite expression. During those times, she pined for him. Her mother wasn't attentive and would just send her to bed early to be rid of her. But Daddy had a magic way of helping her cope when he had to go away. He'd bought her a tin of brightly coloured ribbons from the market and every time he had to go away, he would tie some around Fred, her teddy bear's neck with a big bow. Each was a different colour. Sometimes there were as many as seven coloured ribbons around the bear's neck. He would tell her to remove one each day when she woke up, and before she'd removed every single one, he'd be back. There had been occasions when she'd got down to just one ribbon around the bear's neck, but Daddy never let her down (not with the ribbons, that is), he always came back before the last one. If she got down to the only one, she was always excited as she knew he would be home later that day.

And when he did arrive home, she loved it as he'd be laden down with special food like crumpets, cakes, biscuits, chocolates, and bottles of vodka for him and Mummy. Even now, after the passage of time, thinking about those times brought a smile to her face. A warmth spread through her as she recalled the familiar sound of the front door opening and him coming into the hall and singing at the top of his voice, "Hey there, Georgie girl." As soon as she heard it, she'd rush towards him and he'd scoop her up and swing her around until she was dizzy. "How's my favourite girl?" he would ask and she'd fill him in with what had been happening in her little life, keen to embellish stories about school achievements which weren't really her, they were Mia Steer the class favourite, but for a time she could talk herself up to please her daddy.

Sadly, her young life as she knew it all came to an abrupt end one morning when she'd heard Mummy and Daddy yet again shouting at each other in the kitchen. Her mother sent her up to her bedroom with a slice of toast in her hand. She'd laid on her bed until she'd eaten her toast and pulled the covers over her head to shut out their bickering. She must have dozed off and when she awoke, the house was quiet. She assumed her daddy had gone out and headed for the kitchen to find her mummy. The sight she had to witness in that tiny kitchen was something no child should. Her mummy was laid in the middle of the kitchen floor, her great big bulbous eyes wide open and staring at the ceiling, with a huge great carving knife jutting out of her chest. Even after the passage of time, she hated the colour red. It reminded her of her mother's blood, like a puddle running along the tiled kitchen floor.

She screamed out loud, but nobody was there to hear. She ran from the kitchen, down the hall and forced the front door wide open. Stood on the door-step about to ring the bell was Ann, the lady from church who had been visiting most weeks and bringing them food parcels.

The hours that followed were harrowing for a little girl. Seeing her mummy dead, was an image she couldn't erase. Ann had called the police and she'd been taken to the old lady next door by a police officer. *Who would do that to Mummy* she kept asking, but nobody answered. She'd begged them to find her daddy, knowing everything would be alright once he came home.

Tell him to hurry back to Georgie girl, she'd sobbed to the female police officer.

But Daddy never came back. Ann from church took her home with her to stay temporarily until social services could place her.

That was the first day of the rest of her life.

Frank Milton was eventually arrested in the north of England where he'd been hiding and Georgie girl never saw her daddy again. He'd died in custody awaiting trial, some sort of fracas with another inmate, the irony being he'd met his death the same way he'd killed her mother – with a knife plunged into his heart.

Did he think about her as he took his last breath?

After a period of time fostering her, Ann Foley from the church and her husband Ian became her legally adoptive parents, and their children, Danielle and

Teddy her adoptive siblings. Her name had been changed when she went to live with them, they were forced to. The murder case was well known in and around the area they lived in. It was easier to just switch her Christian and middle name around and she became Laura to the rest of the world. It took a while getting used to it at school, but eventually she did and Laura suited her well. And the success she'd made of her young life such as her academic achievements, passing her driving test first time at seventeen, and acquiring her prestigious job in the centre of London was all down to Laura Foley, but she had to give credit to her adoptive parents. Even though she was academically able, without their support, she'd never have amounted to anything.

The Foleys had been exactly the parents she was sure most of the other children at school had. Ann dressed her in pretty clothes, listened to her reading after school, fed her healthy and nutritious food, most of which she'd never even tasted before, and gave her endless cuddles and love. Ian Foley took her to church, read with her, taught her right from wrong, and above all made her believe she could achieve anything in life. She rubbed along with Danielle and adored Teddy. Her young life as she'd known it, had changed for the better.

But occasionally, just occasionally, however much she tried to suppress her, Georgie girl crept back in. Over the years she'd read endless literature about alter ego to try and understand why she still lurked, hidden away deep within her. Experts believe there is inherently both good and evil parts residing beneath everyone's personality, and an alter ego literally really means a 'second I' where the person uses a different personality in a different role. That seemed a likely analysis and one she could identify with.

Thankfully nobody in her adoptive family knew Georgie girl existed. It was as if she'd been wiped out just like her genetic parents, but the truth was, she'd never truly gone away, Laura just worked hard to keep her hidden. She had to. Georgie was a deviant, the daughter of a killer. But it suited her on occasions to blame her for negative decisions in her life, such as right now being unfaithful to Matthew. It made it much easier to pin the blame on her alter ego, because Laura Foley would never dream of doing anything like that.

Her whole life was mapped out. Without Matthew there wouldn't be a future. He was everything she could possibly want to live a normal life with a husband that loved her and, eventually, children of her own. So things had worked out just as her daddy had told her it would. And the best thing was, her adoptive mum and dad adored Matthew too, he was already part of the family.

Her heart skipped a beat.

She missed him and couldn't wait to see him.

Chapter 4

DANIELLE

Danielle leant against the kitchen sink watching her mum whipping the Yorkshire pudding mix in an old cream mixing bowl.

"Why are you going to all this trouble, Laura's only been gone a week? I can't imagine she'll be expecting a full Sunday roast with all the trimmings the minute she gets back."

"I know, but it's the only time we get to eat as a family and Matthew's coming too." She lifted the whisk in and out of the mixture checking its consistency. "Remember though," she warned, "not a word about the proposal."

"I'm not going to say anything," Danielle dismissed, "if he wants to make the big announcement on her twenty-first, let him. What if she says no, though, what happens then?"

"Of course she isn't going to say no. She loves Matthew, she's been with him long enough now to know he's the one for her."

"Yeah, all the more reason not to tie herself down. She's never been with anyone else, how does she know if he's even the right one?"

"Don't be saying things like that. Matthew's lovely, he's just right for her. And all the trouble he's gone to. Not many men would invite his future mother-in-law to show them the ring before he bought it. And he wouldn't have bought it, you know, if I'd have said it wasn't right."

"Yeah maybe," Danielle answered, fiddling with her new red acrylic nails, "or is it that he can't make decisions himself? I still think it's a bit naff asking her to marry him in front of everyone, and at her twenty-first party too. Why doesn't he take her somewhere romantic and propose?"

"He was intending to ask her in Spain but it couldn't be helped he had to work."

"Still," she shrugged, "he could make more of an effort and take her somewhere nice. Can you imagine when she's asked in years to come, where did your husband propose to you, and she says at my parents' house on my twenty-first birthday."

"It isn't about where," her mother said, placing the bowl down on the work-top, "it's about the intention and declaration of love. It's not all hearts and flowers in a relationship; it's about good solid love for each other. Your trouble is, you have your head in the clouds with all this social media celebrity nonsense. It isn't like that in real life, which you'll find out yourself one day when you meet somebody, you'll see."

The back door opening interrupted them and her father entered with Teddy, her younger brother following closely behind.

"Mind the door," her dad warned, but it was too late, Teddy had let it slam. Teddy gave his usual toothy grin which he did frequently when he was in trouble for something he shouldn't have done. He was fifteen and always looked cumbersome, almost as if his shoes were three sizes too big. Because he had Down's syndrome, he didn't have an awareness of what others thought. He irritated her to death most of the time, always following Dad or Laura around like a lapdog, and trying on occasions to smooch up to her, but she'd learnt many tricks over the years to deflect him.

Her dad lifted a carrier bag of muddy vegetables onto the draining board. "Have you got enough?" he asked her mum, "Teddy's just dug these up from the allotment."

"Oh lovely, well done, Teddy," Mum squealed putting on the praise voice she always seemed to reserve for him, "I've got enough for today, but we'll have these in the week. I'll do some of your favourite sausages with them. You'd like that, wouldn't you?"

Teddy pulled a face, "I'd rather have a McDonald's."

"Well you can't live on those," her mum replied sharply, "you'll end up overweight and spotty."

"Don't care," he grunted and reached in his pocket to look at his pay-as-you-go phone their mum had reluctantly allowed him to have. He shook his head, "Laura's not back yet."

"She'll be here soon enough," her mum reassured, "so you'd better go and get out of those clothes and wash your hands and face while you're at it."

He looked down at his hands, "Not dirty," he challenged, holding them up.

"If you've been on the allotment, they'll be dirty I can assure you. Just because you can't see dirt, it doesn't mean there isn't any there. So go on, get yourself cleaned up. And I'll be checking mind."

Danielle decided to leave them to it. There was a copy of Hello magazine in her bedroom waiting to be read. Sitting around with them would come soon enough when she'd have to endure them fawning over Princess Perfect about her trip.

Her dad stopped her, "Hang on young lady, where you dashing off to?"

"My room, why?"

"Don't you think you should be lending your mother a hand?"

"She's fine Ian," her mother chipped in, "she has offered."

And she had. Okay maybe not with much conviction as she didn't want to damage her nails, but she had asked. Her dad gave her a disapproving look as she left the kitchen as if to say he didn't believe it one bit.

God, I wish he'd give me a bloody break.

She closed the bedroom door and lay down on the bed. Thank God she was going out tonight and could legitimately get away. Oh how she wished she had a different life, with modern parents like her bestie Nikki. Her mum and dad were ace. She loved spending time at their house. None of the religious mush her mum and dad spewed out and expected everyone to live an extemporary life, Nikki's parents were well chilled.

It was rare she'd ever invite any of her friends home; she did when she was younger, but not anymore. The house was chaotic and Teddy was always creeping around and constantly doing the unexpected. They were all used to him as a family, but others weren't, so she found it easier to avoid friends visiting the house.

Tonight she was going to McCawbers wine bar in town and hoping to make some headway with Jed. Thankfully there were a few of them going, she didn't want it to just be her and Nikki on their own as she was fearful Nikki might cop off with Jed. Although she denied fancying him and reckoned her ethos was sister-ship and not going after a friend's potential catch, Nikki was ever so pretty and she worried Jed might go for her instead. Not that she wasn't pretty herself, she knew she was attractive even though she had to work at it. Her hair extensions alone cost hundreds of pounds and keeping up with her nails and brows every couple of weeks made a serious dent in her salary. Thankfully living at home helped. She only had to pay a minimal amount of money; Dad insisted both her and Laura contributed to the household expenses. If she could afford a flat, she'd jump at the chance, but it was unlikely on her current salary and she wasn't a saver. Every spare penny went on looking good.

She flicked through her magazine trying to take her mind off work the following day and having to face Juliet Fleck's wrath because she'd forgotten to pass a telephone message on. Why the hell don't people just use mobiles rather than ringing a bloody switchboard? It was the twenty-first century. Hopefully she'd get out of that job soon when she had the so called *experience* every decent advertising agency wanted. Since finishing her degree, she hadn't expected her first job with the prestigious *Justin Credible* advertising and marketing agency to be reception duties and pushing the latest designer coffee pods into a machine boasting intense coffee with a mild roasted finish, and distributing them around the office. She could do so much more if she had the chance. Why couldn't someone recognise her potential?

The glossy photographs of Meghan Markle began to blur as her eye lids became heavy. She rested the magazine down and closed them, giving her an opportunity to bring her favourite daydream to mind, where she was a big name with her own advertising company dealing only with A-list celebrities. She'd have plenty of money to do as she liked, when she liked, and not have to answer to anyone. Images of her own place in central London came to mind, maybe in Chelsea, and she'd pay an interior designer to make it look sophisticated and desirable so everyone wanted to visit. She'd have a patio so groups of friends could sit outside indulging themselves with endless bottles of prosecco and wine, and she'd have a bedroom with a walk-in wardrobe so she could have all her designer clothes colour-coded with her range of shoes and handbags laid out so she could select them easily. And the best bit was, she'd be alone and wouldn't have to suffer Princess Perfect and Teddy on a daily basis with her mum and dad fawning over them as if she didn't exist.

Yes, one day she was going to be successful.

They'd all notice her then.

Chapter 5

LAURA

Laura breathed a sigh of relief to be home as the aeroplane taxied towards the terminal building. Spain was well and truly behind her now. She thought about the gifts she'd brought her brother Teddy. He'd be thrilled to bits with them. When she'd been adopted into the family, Teddy was only six years younger, and she developed a closeness with him that she never had with Danielle.

Teddy would be eagerly waiting to see her and he'd patiently listen to her descriptions of Spain. She'd have to embellish them slightly, tell a few tales about the cats she'd barely seen as she'd spent most of the time with Cohan. She could easily do that. And she'd bought him some postcards to add to his collection which he'd love.

She glanced down at the pretty bracelet on her wrist that Cohan had given her. Nobody would be any the wiser she hadn't bought it herself. She'd wear it and remember him with fond memories.

Him and Georgie girl.

Matthew was waiting as she came through customs and warm heat flooded through her when she spotted his face searching for her at arrivals. His boyish grin made her heart flip. She rushed towards his open arms and hugged him tightly. He smelled the same – clean, salty skin and citrusy. His lips felt warm and familiar as she kissed him back.

He pulled away and rested his forehead on hers. Their noses touched. "God I've missed you," he said.

"I've missed you too." She was about to say more when he put his finger firmly on her lips.

"Before you say anything, I promise you, I'll never let you down again. I'm so sorry I couldn't be there with you. I've regretted it every single day. It was awful not being with you."

"It was awful you not being there."

"That's never going to happen again, I'm going to make sure of it."

And he would do just that. Matthew was a man of his word. His stupid boss that wouldn't allow him leave because of a shut-down, better look out. Without any shadow of doubt, he would be an asset to the company in a few years. He had an invisible 'future leader' tattoo on his forehead and if you cut him open, figuratively speaking, he'd have *conscientious* running through him like a stick of rock. She didn't doubt that in years to come, he would be a senior member at the company.

"Come on, then," he kissed her quickly again, "I've not got long on the car park and they charge a bloody fortune if you go over."

He took her case from her with one hand and reached for hers with the other. Her much smaller hand fitted in his perfectly. It felt right, just how it was meant to be. He dragged her case along as they made their way to the car park.

She looked sideways at him, and he met her glance with a gorgeous I love you wink.

This was her life – the only one she wanted. Spain was a holiday with a bit of romance thrown in . . . but that was for Georgie girl.

Best to forget all about it now.

Laura was home.

During the car journey, she filled Matthew in on Spain with the things she could tell him about, but he seemed pre-occupied.

"Anyway, enough about me. How've you been while I was away?"

"Fine," he slowed the car down and indicated right towards Sandown Woods. Once he'd turned, he increased his speed down the leafy lane. It was a journey they've done many times as Matthew loved to watch the sun set, but it wasn't appropriate right now as they needed to get home.

"Why we going here?" she frowned.

"I need to show you something."

"Can't it wait, we're nearly at mine?" she breathed out, "you know Mum, she'll be chomping at the bit for us to get there."

"It'll only take a minute." He pulled the car into a spot overlooking the lake, applied the handbrake and cut the engine.

"Go on, then, be quick," she urged knowing her mum would be at the window waiting.

His sudden paleness concerned her. She repeated the question more gently, "What is it?"

"I've found a lump."

"Where?"

"In one of my balls. I found it last night when I was in the shower." He started to undo his belt and unzip his fly.

She glanced around the immediate area of their car but they were on their own. Not many people out and about early on a cold Sunday morning. He reached for her hand and placed it on his testicle. His expression was anxious, but expectant also, as if he was secretly hoping she couldn't feel anything at all.

"Can you feel it?"

It was hard to miss. There was definitely a hard lump. And it felt exactly like the ones on the testicle and breast prosthesis the nurse had brought in when they had a lesson at college on breast and testicular awareness. She could remember clearly feeling for the small pea-sized lump then, which was exactly the same as she was feeling right now.

"Yeah," she nodded, and pulled her hand away. No point in denying it. He must be worried sick so she needed to offer some reassurance, "It's not necessarily anything to worry about, it might be a cyst or something."

"But it could be worse than that. It could be cancer."

"Hey," she touched his arm, "you're jumping ahead a bit. It could be anything. You'll have to go and see a doctor. Ring in the morning and make an appointment. It might be something and nothing. Does it hurt?"

"A bit."

"That's good then. I've read that if you get a lump that hurts, it's often not cancer."

He didn't look convinced. His skin had gone a ghastly white colour and tiny beads of sweat were becoming evident on his upper lip.

She put her hand on his face and gently turned it so he was looking directly into her eyes.

"Don't be running away with ideas. See what the doctor says first. He'll organise some tests if he's worried. My guess is he'll give you some antibiotics or something."

A tiny bit of colour returned, "You reckon?"

"I'm sure of it," she reassured, "ring first thing in the morning and insist you're seen tomorrow some time. Bypass those receptionists; you know what they're like."

"Yeah, I will." He seemed chirpier, "I'll ring in work and tell them an emergency has cropped up to make sure I can get in first thing."

"Yes, do that."

Matthew never said another word as he drove the rest of the way to her place, but he clung onto her hand between gear changes. An uneasy tightness crushed her chest and a ditty sprung to mind she'd chanted many times as a child with her skipping rope. Like one of those tunes you heard on the radio that you kept repeating over and over in your mind until you were sick to death of it.

Do something bad and you will find,
Karma's lurking right behind.

Chapter 6

DANIELLE

Monday mornings sucked. Danielle always arrived at the office earlier than most because of the buses. If she caught the one into the city she'd prefer to, then she'd end up ten minutes late for work, but by getting the earlier one, she was thirty minutes too early. There were no benefits, not to her anyway. It wasn't as if she could leave any earlier at the end of the day.

The office door opened as she was hanging her coat up, and her no-nonsense boss, Juliet Fleck appeared, as always completely immaculate with her salon style dyed grey hair. While most people with a bob-hairstyle had one side of their hair that didn't go quite the way you would want it to and flicked outwards instead of under, that didn't happen to Juliet. Her bob was perfect. Both sides of her hair were completely symmetrical and her long fringe almost covered her heavily made up eyes. Piss-holes in the snow sprang to Danielle's mind with her heavy seventies look eye-shadow.

"Ah Danielle, good, you're already here. Be a love and go on reception until Kirsty gets here, would you? She's got a scan this morning but she'll be here after that."

No *please* from Juliet. She had a way of telling you what to do with a smile on her face which disguised a look of, *don't argue with me, I'm the boss and that's what you're doing*.

Danielle took a deep breath in before answering. She kept her voice light, "I've got a few bits to do myself this morning. Michelle has asked me to chase up a couple of suppliers first thing."

"That'll have to wait," Juliet dismissed, "you can do that later when Kirsty gets here. Tell Michelle I've asked you to do reception."

Juliet glared through her piss-hole eye make-up, no doubt waiting for a compliant acknowledgement. How was she ever going to get on if she was always the gofer? Oh, how she'd love to tell her to get stuffed. But she didn't. Instead she nodded.

"Thank you," Juliet replied curtly and turned towards the door.

There was nothing to be gained by protesting. She didn't want Juliet bringing up Friday again and the message she'd omitted to pass on. What the hell all the fuss was about she just didn't get. Juliet had rambled on about how potential clients had to be encouraged to sign up with their agency, and without new clients, they'd all be out of a job. She reckoned, because she hadn't received the message from Hermione Mawer, a prolific author, and consequently not returned her call, she'd gone with another agency to facilitate her book launch event in central London.

Yeah right.

Danielle didn't believe that for a minute, it was just Juliet, *over-egging the pudding*, as her mum would say.

She reached for her new Michael Kors handbag from her desk and headed for lavish reception area yet again. She hated reception duties. It was a bright and cheery enough environment, and beautifully decorated, but was the dumping ground for everyone and everything. The doors were constantly opening with staff and potential customers calling in with endless queries and messages to pass on, and the phone was continuously ringing. Mobiles phones should negate the need for a reception she always thought, but Juliet reminded her, *reception is the shop window, and every client has to be welcomed as if they were the only one.*

Twenty minutes later she was still fuming about the injustice of it all. Alice Butler from advertising was the first early caller to reception.

"Morning, Danielle. I'm interviewing today," she handed over a sheet of A4 paper, "you wouldn't believe how many people have applied who clearly have little or no experience for the job. If they read the job spec in the first place, it's obvious they don't meet the requirements, but do they read it," she sighed, "no they don't. Can you text me as each one arrives and I'll ring down when I want you to send them up?"

"Course I will. Are the candidates you've got any good on paper at least?"

"They seem to be, but who knows. The job has been re-advertised as nobody was suitable last time, so we'll have to see." She frowned, "Hey, why are you on reception again anyway?"

"Don't ask," Danielle dismissed glancing down at the interview candidates, "only four?"

Alice rolled her eyes, "Yes, thank God, I can't face any more than that on a Monday morning. Anyhow, are you alright, you look a bit pale?"

"I'm fine," Danielle placed the list near the telephone ready to tick each candidate off when they arrived, "nothing a week in the sun wouldn't cure. Anyway, good luck with the interviews."

"Thanks. See you later."

Danielle reached in her handbag for some Nurofen. Alice was perceptive, she wasn't firing on all cylinders at all, her head was throbbing from the previous evening. Jed had proven elusive. The only impression she'd made was a significant dent in her purse, and the effect of all the cocktails she'd consumed were starting to take their toll.

She made her way to the seated waiting area of reception to the water dispenser and drew a cup of water. On her way back to the desk, the front door of the agency burst open. A man rushed in clutching a Starbucks coffee cup, and by the look of it most of the contents were down the front of his taupe-coloured jacket.

"Oh, goodness," Danielle put her water down and grabbed a box of tissues from the desk. "Can I help?"

He handed her the coffee cup still containing a few dregs and started brushing the lapel of his jacket with the back of his hand. "It wasn't entirely her fault," he blew out a breath, "she was rushing, and to be honest I wasn't concentrating on where I was going. The lid can't have been that secure."

Danielle stared at his jacket. The stain seemed to be spreading the more he tried to brush it. It needed cold water on it and, with a bit of luck, it should come out. Her mother had rescued many a designer garment of hers that way when she'd spilt some sort of alcoholic beverage down the front of it.

The man was shaking his head with frustration, easing the lapel from his chest to see if the coffee had caught his shirt. He certainly was nice on the eye, maybe late twenties, early thirties, much taller than her with a slender frame and dark wavy hair cut short but flicked cutely at his neck. His complexion was a nice bronze colour, as if he'd just returned from a holiday in the sun.

"I could try and give it a gentle wipe to save it staining, if that would help?" she said tentatively.

A relieved expression passed over his friendly open face, "Would you? Do you mind?"

"No, of course not. As long as you're happy to leave it with me, are you here to see someone?"

"Yes, I'm here to see Juliet Fleck." He glanced at his watch, "Fortunately it's not made me late. Are you absolutely sure, I don't want to put you to any trouble. You're probably busy enough as it is?"

"It's no trouble, honestly. I'm almost certain there's some stain remover around here somewhere. Shall I let Juliet know you're here and while you're having your meeting, I'll see what I can do?"

"That is kind of you . . . er . . ."

"Danielle."

He held out his hand. "Pleased to meet you, Danielle," his eyes crinkled kindly, "and thank you in advance for helping me. Not the best start to a Monday morning."

The warmth of his hand was more than enough to set her pulse racing, but the way he held onto it and smiled appreciatively, speeded it up twice as fast. He didn't seem in a rush to let it go either. Eventually he did to use both hands to pull his jacket off his shoulders to remove it. The movement was innocuous enough, but somehow watching him take off an article of clothing had an effect on her equilibrium, and she was sure he must be able to see her heart thumping through her blouse.

To deflect from the stupidity of the heat travelling up from her neck to her face, she made her way around the side of the reception desk to put some space between them. It wasn't until she had the phone in her hand to let Juliet know he'd arrived, she realised she hadn't asked his name.

"Sorry, I forgot to ask your name."

"Cohan," his lips curved at the edges displaying a beautiful set of even teeth, "Cohan Laity."

Danielle lifted his jacket to her face and inhaled the fragrance of him. It was a subtle blend of woods, balms, and citrus, with a sensuality which gave a kick to her libido. How gorgeous was he? She managed to gently wipe the lapels with a stain remover and damp cloth to get the coffee marks out. At the back of a store cupboard she'd found an old hairdryer someone must have left for freshening up their hair for a night out after work, and used it to dry the jacket off. It was as good as new when she'd finished. He was sure to be pleased . . . *how pleased* she fantasised. An hour later, Kirsty was back from her scan, full of excitement about the new baby and showing her pictures of what looked like a balloon with a brick attached to it. How could anyone get excited about that?

"We aren't going to find out the sex," Kirsty droned, as if she was remotely interested in her stupid pregnancy, "my mum wants to know, but Mark and I feel we want to wait for the delivery day. It's more special that way."

Danielle handed the pictures back and was about to say something appropriate when the door opened and Juliet came in accompanied by the gorgeous Cohan Laity.

"I'll be out for lunch," Juliet told Kirsty, "but I'll be back at two thirty as I've got another client due then."

Kirsty smiled at them both. "Okay, have a lovely lunch."

Danielle hovered not sure what to do about his jacket. He'd need it if he was going outside. Best to say something, she'd done a good job so there couldn't be any grief from Juliet.

"I've got your jacket," she smiled at Cohan and reached for it from the back of the chair she'd rested it on.

"That is so kind of you, Danielle, thank you." The warmth in his eyes made her wish she could do much more for him than remove a stain. He took the jacket from her, "It's as good as new."

Juliet, no doubt wanting to make an impression, joined in, "Yes, thank you Danielle, Mr Laity said how you'd offer to help," she looked at Cohan as he pulled the jacket on, "and I can't see any coffee stains at all."

Cohan ignored Juliet and smiled warmly at her, "I'm delighted, I have another meeting at four today so at least I'll look reasonably presentable for that. I'm not sure a coffee-stained jacket would have cut it somehow."

His smile had her heart-rate up another notch, if that was even possible, he was so bloody hot. She'd have washed and pressed his whole wardrobe for that sort of praise from him.

"You're welcome." Her smile faded slightly, almost bereft he was leaving, "Have a nice lunch." She desperately wanted to detain him somehow so quickly added, "And I hope you impress whoever you're trying to at your next meeting."

He threw back his head and laughed. "If only you knew who I was meeting you'd see how funny that is."

Juliet was looking daggers. "Right," she smiled her cosmetically pumped lips at Cohan, "Shall we make a move?"

Cohan hesitated, fixing his lovely chocolate brown eyes on her. "I've had a thought. With you being so kind and sorting my jacket out, maybe you'd like to join us for lunch, Danielle?" he turned to Juliet, "if that's alright with you, that is?"

Eek! It wouldn't be alright, not one bit. But Juliet would want whatever business he might be putting their way, so would have to suck it up. Danielle was a teeny bit in love with him already for getting one over on her.

Better try the turning him down card though, she needed her job after all.

"That is kind of you, but you really don't owe me anything. Anyone would have tried to help. And I do have some work to get on with . . . but thank you anyway."

"But surely you have a lunch break?" he persisted, "we're only going to be an hour or so at the most." His eyes seemed to be willing her to say yes.

Should she? She looked enquiringly at her boss. "If you're sure?" she asked politely, knowing there was no way out for Juliet now. Saying no would make her look petty, particularly when a potential new client had suggested it.

"Of course," Juliet answered, no doubt through gritted teeth. "Do you need to get your coat? We'll wait for you."

Danielle went into her office and grabbed her jacket wishing she'd worn her navy suit as it showed her figure off better than the grey one she was currently wearing which wasn't quite as fitted at the waist as she preferred. No point in dwelling on that now though. Getting one over on stuck up Juliet was great, she'd live on it for weeks. And she was determined to enjoy every second of her lunch with the gorgeous Cohan Laity. Who knows where that could lead to?

Yes! she cheered inwardly.

Chapter 7

LAURA

Laura sat at the dressing table and sprayed her hair. She needed plenty of hairspray otherwise the time she'd spent with her curling wand was wasted.

A tap on the door made her turn. Danielle walked in looking stunning in a black pant suit. The trousers were wide and complemented by some classy stiletto heels which, if she wasn't mistaken could well be Louboutin'. Her hair was piled glamorously on top of her head courtesy of a trip to the hairdresser that afternoon. "Can I pinch some of your hairspray, I've run out?" she asked.

Laura handed over the can she had in her hand. "Help yourself. You look nice."

Danielle took the hairspray and opened the wardrobe door to stand in front of the full-length mirror. She sprayed a generous amount on her head and handed it back.

"You're not wearing that dress, are you?" she asked with a disapproving expression, as if Laura was wearing a black bin bag.

Laura glanced down at her black fitted dress which enhanced her waist and was decorated prettily at the collar with white pearls, "Yes, why what's the matter with it?"

"Isn't it from about five years ago?"

"Christmas actually, I've only worn it once so I thought I might as well get some use out of it. It cost a fortune from Monsoon."

Danielle turned back to the mirror and was peering closer at her face, rubbing her finger down the side of her nose as if blending in some foundation. "I doubt anything costs a fortune from Monsoon. Do you want to borrow something of mine . . . it is your twenty-first?"

"So?" Laura smoothed a non-existent crease out of the material, "I happen to like this dress."

A distasteful frown spoilt Danielle's perfectly-groomed eyebrows, "Rather you than me."

Laura stared back into the dressing table mirror and ran her fingers through her hair to loosen the curls. "We aren't all potential fashion models trying to look like we've just stepped out of Vogue."

Danielle's eye widened, "Clearly not."

Laura ignored the sarcasm. "Anyway, you've made enough of an effort for both of us." She couldn't help but appreciate how stunning Danielle looked. She had a talent with make-up and clothes. "I love your pant-suit, it looks fabulous."

"Yes, well, it should do, this really did cost a fortune."

"Wouldn't you rather save it for a club or something? Nice as it is, it's a bit glam for tonight."

"Yeah, I know, but I want to raise my game."

"Well you've definitely done that. What's so special about tonight?"

"I've invited someone," she reached for some hand cream off the dressing table and sat down on Laura's bed, "just casual though. I told him to call in for a drink if he was at a bit of a loose end."

Laura reeled back, "Who?"

"Just a chap I met at work," Danielle shrugged rubbing the cream into her hands, "he's Juliet's latest client. He came into the agency when I was covering reception and someone had spilt coffee all over him. I cleaned his jacket and he invited me for lunch with him and Juliet."

"Really? From what you've said about her, I bet she wasn't pleased with you joining them?"

"No, she wasn't, but he insisted and was lovely to me over lunch. The following day, he rang the office and asked me out for a quick drink after work."

"You must have made an impression then?"

"I don't know how," Danielle dismissed, "Juliet hardly let me get a word in."

"So what happened in the evening?"

"We had a really good night, even though it was only a couple of hours," Danielle's face softened, "he's one of those men who's actually interested in what you have to say. He wanted to know all about me and the family, I've never been out with anyone like that. Most blokes are too busy trying to get my knickers off rather than taking time to find out what makes me tick."

"He sounds nice, then. How come you've invited him tonight though? Seems odd to have him at a family do when you hardly know him."

"Yeah, I know," she placed the hand cream back on the dressing table, "but when he asked me to go out with him tonight and I said I couldn't as it was your twenty-first party, he looked almost disappointed, so I casually said to call in for a drink. I didn't think for a minute he'd say yes, but he seemed quite keen." She shrugged, "He still might not come, although he did take the address."

Laura gave a knowing grin, "Sounds like you really like him?"

"I do actually," Danielle admitted, "so I hope he does come."

"That nice, is he?" Laura asked standing up and moving in front of the full-length mirror. "This is a first, you gushing over a bloke. We're not likely to be on the look-out for wedding outfits soon are we?"

"I wouldn't go that far, but he's definitely got potential. If he does come, you'll see how drop-dead gorgeous he is."

"You better play it down if you introduce him to Mum then, 'cause she'll be checking out hats before you know it."

Danielle laughed, "Yeah, too right. Anyway, I'll have to see how it goes. Just because I like him, doesn't mean he feels the same way about me," she paused, her expression seemed more relaxed than usual, "we definitely have a connection though."

"I hope he does come, I can't wait to meet him. What's his name . . . ?"

The bedroom door opening interrupted them. Teddy came in looking grown-up in his smart new black polo shirt and chinos Mum had insisted he had for the party.

"Teddy," Danielle snapped sharply, "how many times have we told you to knock before you come in. Either one of us could have been naked."

Teddy screwed his face up. In his world, naked was disgusting. "Dad says you've got to hurry up, Laura, some of your friends are here."

"Come on then," Laura winked at Danielle, "let the party begin. What time are you expecting Mr Gorgeous?"

"He didn't say a time," she shrugged, "if he comes, he comes."

"Fingers crossed he does then. I'm intrigued. Maybe the iceberg's finally melting?" she teased.

Teddy frowned, "Where's there an iceberg?"

"Nowhere, Teddy," Laura dismissed, "it's an expression. Come on."

The party was more of an intimate bash with family and a few friends from college so Laura was surprised Danielle would invite a stranger to it. Ed, her boss from work, had arrived and was throwing back copious amounts of alcohol which seemed to be the norm for him these days. Ed was a great bloke, and a fantastic boss, but he'd lost his way since his wife had left and taken his son to live across the country. She made a mental note to have a word with him again about his drinking, but not tonight. He wouldn't hang around that long anyway, but it was nice of him to call in.

There were plenty of people milling around from church she'd grown up with that her mum and dad had invited. Their lives were church, and when they were younger, her, Danielle, and Teddy had to go dutifully every Sunday. But her and Danielle had rejected religion when they were old enough to do so and their parents' didn't push it, but Teddy was still involved. He really didn't have much choice.

Guests were filling their plates with the tasty buffet food her mum had made, and everyone seemed to be getting on well, chatting and mixing, while her dad was keeping busy making sure all the glasses were topped up. People had been generous and arrived clutching gifts which she'd deposited in the dining room to open later. It seemed a bit naff to open them in front of everyone.

Laura went into the kitchen to look for Matthew. For some reason he seemed a bit jittery and was drinking much more than he normally did. Maybe it was relief as the GP had given him a course of antibiotics for the swelling in his testicle. It had relaxed both of them as he'd got himself into a bit of a state imagining the worse.

God knows where he'd disappeared to. The last time she saw him he was huddled in the corner with his brother, Chris. She'd ask him later what was going on as they'd stopped talking when she'd approached them, almost as if they were talking about her.

She found her dad at the kitchen sink washing glasses by hand despite having a dishwasher. He'd set himself up as barman, glass washer, and bouncer for the evening. No chance of a riotous party with him around.

"Have you seen Matthew, Dad?"

"No, I haven't." His eyes drifted towards the door, "He might be in the garden."

The smell of cigarette smoke permeated into the kitchen causing her to cough. "I hope he's not smoking, I'll be cross if he's started again."

"You and me too if your mother's with him, she doesn't need much persuading to have a crafty one."

"Laura," her mum peeked around the back door, "can you come here a minute."

She followed her mum into the pretty garden decorated with all the fairy lights around the fence. Both Mum and Dad had gone to a lot of trouble to make sure tonight was a memorable birthday for her. As a child living with her biological parents, Georgie girl's birthdays invariably came and went. She always got a card from the budget shop down the high street, and if she was lucky there might be some money in the envelope, *to spend when they went into town*, her mother would say, which was total bull as they never went into town, and more often than not, the money would mysteriously disappear within days, anyway. Just the same way her piggy bank was always empty and it wasn't her taking the coins out. She couldn't ever bring an image to mind of having birthday presents wrapped in bright paper and bows to unwrap.

"Hurry up, Laura," Teddy called from the trellis at the bottom of the garden. He was standing next to a small table with what looked to be twenty-one candles flickering on a huge cake. He beamed as she walked towards him and everyone began to sing Happy Birthday.

She grinned and waited uncomfortably for them all to finish and when they had, she grabbed Teddy's hand, counted to three and they blew the candles out together. Everyone clapped, and the moment was captured by the endless phones flashing to take photos.

Matthew cleared his throat. "Can I have your attention for a minute longer please?"

Why was Matthew speaking publicly? It wasn't like him at all. He wasn't looking at her, either, which seemed odd.

He carried on, "I'd like to take this opportunity to thank you all for coming tonight to celebrate Laura's birthday, and thank her mum and dad for the fabulous party."

Everyone clapped. Dad gave his usual courteous nod, while Mum smiled as if she was the Queen and they'd just sung the national anthem to her.

Aw, that's nice of Matthew thanking Mum and Dad, they'll love that.

"I've also got a surprise for the birthday girl," he smiled lovingly at her and held his arm out, "come here, Laura," he beckoned.

He'd already got her tickets for a Cold Play concert as a present so she had no idea what was coming, maybe a short break away to make up for letting her down in Spain? She made her way towards him with a puzzled expression on her face.

He put his arm around her and she nestled into him. "As you all know, Laura and I have been going out for what seems like forever," he winked at her, "and we've known each other since the year dot. Well, tonight I want to ask her a question. A very special question actually."

He dropped down on one knee to cheers from the crowd, "I love you, Laura, and I want us to spend the rest of our lives together. Will you marry me?"

Oh my God!

The solitaire diamond he was clutching in the black velvet box glistened at her. She put her hand over her mouth to try and control the shock and flood of tears emerging. She couldn't. They began to escape down her cheeks despite trying hard to swallow them back. Matthew's eyes looked hopeful, but at the same time, anxious.

She nodded her head up and down vigorously, and managed a croaky squeal, "Yes!"

Loud applause followed as he placed the perfectly fitting ring on her finger and stood up to kiss and hug her. Everyone crowded round them, and it was a blur accepting all the warm embraces and congratulations. It all fitted together now and explained why Matthew had been looking shifty with his brother earlier, he'd been nervous, and Danielle offering to lend her something of hers to wear earlier so she looked nice for the proposal, a definite first her being helpful.

Her dad wrapped his arms around her and hugged her tightly. She savoured his warmth for a few seconds before breaking away.

"Thank goodness it's finally out in the open," her mum laughed, hugging her, "it's been killing us keeping this a secret. Let me have a look at the ring." Laura held out her hand and her mother took it. "It's beautiful. You are a lucky girl, Laura."

"I know I am," she replied, fighting back more tears, "really lucky."

Matthew hugged her mum and shook her dad's hand. "Welcome to the family, son," her dad joked.

"Don't be daft, Ian," her mum playfully slapped him on the arm, "he's been part of our family since he met Laura."

Matthew grinned warmly at them both, "Well, I'm glad to officially be accepted by you both, it means a lot."

Laura held onto him and smiled proudly. He was now her fiancé, *how exciting was that?*

She had a future to look forward to she'd always wanted, with a wedding to plan which her mother would love. Matthew was being treated for a cyst rather than anything sinister which was a huge relief. So tonight had been an ace twenty-first birthday – all was well.

Alongside Matthew, she stood at the front door and said goodbye to a couple of early leavers.

"Sorry we're going so early," her friend Katy said giving her a hug.

"Don't worry," Laura reassured, "what time's your flight tomorrow?"

"Seven a.m.," her boyfriend Mike chipped in.

"Well, you definitely need an early night then. Thanks for coming, and for the gift, that really was thoughtful of you both."

"Don't be daft," Katy said, "it'll be wedding gifts next. Congratulations again," she hugged Matthew and smiled, "see you when we get back."

"Yeah," Laura nodded, "see you soon. Safe trip, and have a fabulous time."

After they waved them off, Matthew reached for her hand and led her into the small sitting room at the front of the house. He closed the door behind them and leant his back against it to stop anybody opening it.

"Come here, Mrs soon to be Souter."

She welcomed his lips and wrapped her arms around him, enjoying their togetherness alone after all the excitement. Their kiss deepened, and for a few seconds she relished his lips demanding more. But she had to pull away, "Hey, enough of that. If Dad catches us in the house, it'll be the shortest engagement on record."

He rolled his eyes, "Don't you reckon he might be a bit more lenient with his sex rules and you not being able to stop over now we're engaged?"

"Ha ha, you wish. We're lucky we get some time together at yours. If it was up to Dad, we'd be virgins on our wedding night. Anyway, we've got tomorrow. I'll come early to the flat and we'll have all day together."

"I've got to wait until then," he groaned. She could feel his hardness against her tummy.

"Yep, I'm afraid so," she grinned wishing they could make love to seal their special night. "Come on, we better get back before someone comes looking for us."

"Okay," he sighed, "if you insist. But tomorrow we're going to spend the whole day in bed, Chris is working so we've got the flat to ourselves. I'm going to make sure you only get out of bed to eat."

"Sounds good to me," she kissed him again, loving him for wanting her. "Thank you for tonight, you've made me so happy. I love my ring," she looked into his lustful eyes, "and I love you very much."

He stroked her face, "I love you too, and you deserve a special ring. I was going to ask you in Spain, so was gutted when I couldn't come as I'd got it all planned."

If only he had come to Spain, things would have been different. But she didn't want to think about that now, she was single when that happened, now she was engaged to be married and having a fiancé changed things.

"But I'm pleased it's happened tonight," he wrapped his arms tightly around her, "it seems right somehow with everyone here, even though I was bricking myself asking you in front of them."

"You hid it well, then," she lifted her head and looked up at him, "tonight's been perfect." He kissed her brow as she pulled away from him, and moved aside so she could open the door.

"Right," he grinned closing the door behind them both, "I'm off to get some of your mum's food now I'm no longer crapping myself."

She grinned, "Funny how it didn't stop you drinking."

"Hey, if you had to go down on one knee in front of everyone and declare undying love, you'd have been drinking too." He raised his eyebrows, "You could have said no for all I knew."

"Never," she smiled lovingly.

"Have you seen, Danielle?" her mum asked when she'd returned to the kitchen.

"Not for a while, why?"

Her mum lowered her voice, "Because she's with a really good-looking chap, apparently it's someone she met at work she casually invited. She's hanging on to his every word which is not like her at all."

"Really?" Laura craned her head towards the window overlooking the garden, looking for the mysterious new man she was yet to meet. "What's he look like?"

"Tall, dark and handsome as far as I can see. Oh and smart, I noticed his shoes are shiny and polished."

"God Mum," Laura rolled her eyes, "there's only you that could be weighing a man up by his shoes."

"You can laugh," her mum shook her head, "my mother always says you can tell a lot by a man's shoes. Come on," she took her arm, "let's go outside and see if we can find them both before your father does and gives him the ninth degree."

"We'd better," Laura smiled, "we don't want him scared off if she really likes him."

They made out the door and into the garden, only to be stopped by Teddy. "I've seen Danielle kissing a man."

Their mother widened her eyes. "Have you now? You shouldn't be spying!"

"Not spying," he grunted, "Tilly crawled behind the shed and I followed her. I saw them kissing." He screwed up his face. "It was yukky. I'm not having a girlfriend if you have to do that stuff."

Her mum smiled affectionately at him. She had the patience of a saint. "You won't say that when you meet someone you like, you'll see."

"No I won't," he replied emphatically.

"Anyway, you already have a girlfriend. You've got Sadie."

"She's not my girlfriend. Haven't got one," he blushed furiously.

Laura grinned at Teddy. He was inseparable from Sadie. She too had Down's syndrome. They were at a special needs school together, and if ever the expression, 'joined at the hip' applied to anyone, it was Teddy and Sadie.

She heard her sister's voice from behind her. "Here she is, the future Mrs Souter."

Laura turned around at the same time as her mother. Danielle was balancing on her heels on the grass, clutching the arm of a much taller man.

Nothing had prepared her. The smile faded from her face.

Her blood pressure plummeted.

She felt light-headed. Fuzzy.

It took every ounce of strength to keep breathing.

Danielle smiled eagerly at them both, "This is Cohan who I told you I met at work. Cohan, this is my mum, and Laura, who's not only celebrating her twenty-first, she's just got engaged tonight too."

Her mum accepted his outstretched hand, "How lovely to meet you."

"Likewise," he replied, "Danielle's told me about you all. Thank you for letting me be part of such a special evening."

His dark eyes moved to lock with hers. Not a flicker of recognition from him.

His outstretched hand came towards her. The hand that caressed every receptive part of her naked body, the fingers that had stroked her intimately and brought her orgasm after orgasm.

"Pleased to meet you, Laura," he said through lips that had kissed her tummy and nipples only weeks earlier, "what a wonderful night for you. Congratulations."

His smile was menacing. It urged . . . *go on, I dare you*.

She didn't take his hand – she couldn't.

How long had he been in the UK? And how in God's name had he met her sister? He must have somehow engineered it.

Danielle was staring at her. "What's the matter? You've gone really white?"

She shook her head to try and shake off the fuzziness, "Too many glasses of wine I think, you'll have to excuse me." She turned abruptly and quickly made her way to the house to lock herself away from him.

"Well it has been quite a night," she heard her mother say, "the excitement must have got to her. Can I get you a drink, Cohan, and maybe something to eat?"

Laura stood in the downstairs toilet. Only a door separated her from Cohan Laity.

Keep breathing . . . in and out . . . in and out. You must.

What the hell was he doing at her party? Why wasn't he in Spain where she'd left him? How come he was in her family house in the suburbs of London at her twenty-first? It couldn't have been a coincidence, surely? She tried to remember how much of her home life she'd shared with him, but she couldn't think. The wine she'd consumed was making everything blurry.

Bloody hell . . . how had he found her, and then come on to her sister of all people?

What was she going to do?

The ramifications of owning up to Matthew about being unfaithful caused an ache deep within her. Her tummy clenched in pain. That was the last thing she wanted to do. Nobody knew anything about what had happened for that brief few days in Spain, but she couldn't have Danielle falling madly in love with a man she'd already been in a relationship with. Well, not a relationship as such, but certainly a fling involving plenty of sex.

She leant on the sink and stared at her reflection in the mirror. The bright and excited face from minutes earlier when she'd been kissing Matthew had been replaced by a dull, dark and anxious one. And as she leaned in and peered more closely at herself, staring back was poor orphan Georgie girl.

Cohan Laity had ruined her special day. The joy of her engagement had suddenly disappeared because of

him, and right now, she was in danger of losing her
future.

Chapter 8

DANIELLE

The restaurant Cohan had chosen for dinner was so high-class that she'd barely been able to stare in the window when she passed it in Reigate town centre. When she'd been about seventeen or eighteen and out with her friends, she could distinctly remember being particularly pissed one night when they'd passed it heading for a taxi office. They'd made a point of staring in the windows and pulling faces to try and disrupt the diners who would be paying more for one meal than they'd all earn in a week.

Now, years later and much more mature, she handed her coat to the waiter and followed him as he escorted her to the table. Cohan had asked if she minded making her way there on her own as he would be coming from the city after a meeting. Her dad had dropped her off which saved her a taxi fare.

Cohan stood up as she approached the table and leaned forward to kiss her cheek. She liked that, it was more sophisticated than she was used to. He smelled gorgeous. A mixture of ginger and leather, which if that didn't seduce a woman's senses, then nothing would.

The waiter pulled the chair out for her and waited until she took her seat. "Can I get you a drink, sir while you're perusing the menu?" he asked.

The menus were already on the table, Cohan must have asked for them while he was waiting for her to arrive. He smiled enquiringly at her. "Would you like a gin and tonic, and then I'll order a bottle of wine when I've studied the list."

Gin and tonic, that certainly was infinitely better than her usual midweek lagers. Cocktails were the preferred choice on Saturday nights with her mates, but only when they were flush.

"That would be lovely, thank you."

"Two Gordon's please. We'll share a tonic."

"Right away, sir."

He smiled at her, "I'm sorry you had to make your own way here, I don't usually expect dates to do that."

"It wasn't a problem, my dad dropped me off. How did your meeting go?"

"To sum it up in one word, boring. I think people have an idea an author's life is exciting, when in fact it's quite the opposite. Anyway," he pulled some tiny half-rimmed black spectacles out of his shirt pocket and put them on, "I want to find out a bit more about you tonight. Shall we decide what we're having and then we can chat?"

"Sounds good to me," she said and picked up the menu which she could see at a glance offered a comprehensive selection to tempt anyone's taste buds. A far cry from the pubs or Indian restaurants she normally frequented on dates.

"Anything you fancy?" he asked peering over the glasses which made him look sexier than ever.

She scrunched up her nose, "I'm not sure, what are you having?"

"I quite fancy the chateaubriand, but I'll need to check on the pâté."

"Don't you like it?"

"I love it, but I have a nut allergy, so I need to be careful what I eat and how food is prepared."

"Oh, what happens if you eat nuts?"

"Don't ask. I just need to make sure I don't expose myself to them. Restaurants like this are usually fine, I don't really need to worry, but I still check."

"Oh dear, I bet it restricts you on where you can eat."

"Not really. I just do my homework and choose restaurants I feel I can trust. Anyway, do you fancy the same? Do you like steak?"

"I love steak." It was true she did, but had only ever really had steak when her mother cooked it. If she ever went out for a meal, it wasn't something she would order. The price prohibited it most of the time anyway.

"How would you like it cooked?"

She preferred it cooked through, almost like charcoal really.

"Well done, I guess."

"Really? That's the quickest way to ruin a steak," he removed his glasses, "in my opinion, of course. You ought to try it medium-rare. It really does bring out the flavour, it's much more succulent. You mustn't eat with your eyes, though," he smiled, "as it can be pink and a bit runny."

The thought of it didn't thrill her, but she was keen to please.

"Okay, I'll give it a go."

"If you don't like it, I'll bring you again and you can have a well-done steak . . . deal?"

"Deal," she agreed. She'd definitely make sure she preferred it well done if it meant another meal with him.

He seemed to be fluent with the wine list and ably discussed the wines with the waiter expressing which he wanted, but what impressed her most of all was him ordering her meal for her. Nobody had ever done that for her before.

The waiter disappeared and Cohan took a sip of his drink. "I'm pleased you agreed to dinner, Danielle, I've been looking forward to seeing you since your sister's party. How is she by the way, has she come down to earth after all the excitement?"

"She seems to have done, she's certainly back to being her usual self."

"What is her usual self?" his eyebrows creased.

She didn't want to explain too much about her feelings toward Laura, he might see her as petty.

"Oh, nothing much, just the usual sibling stuff. We tend to clash a bit, we're very different."

"In what way?"

"In every way."

"Tell me, I'd like to know more about you and your family."

Should she tell him? Hell, why not?

"Laura's always been the favourite with Mum and Dad. Maybe that's because she's adopted and they somehow felt over the years she needed extra love from them." She took a sip of her gin, "You would think it would be the opposite, wouldn't you, and they'd favour their own?"

"Ah, she's adopted is she? That explains why I couldn't see any resemblance between the two of you. Physically you are very different." He gave that seductive smile of his which made her understand the old-fashioned expression, *weak at the knees.*

"Yes, we are."

"Well thankfully I'm sitting with the most attractive one out of the two of you," he smiled taking another sip of his drink.

A warm glow enveloped her. She was more attractive than Laura and he'd noticed that.

She waited until the waiter placed the French onion soup in front of them before continuing. "Mum and Dad didn't meet until they were well into their thirties. Dad was almost forty, actually. I came along straight away but they struggled to have another child. Mum began working for the church as a family liaison support worker and was an advocate to a vulnerable family . . . Laura and her parents. The father took a knife to the mother and killed her which left Laura in a pickle. Mum and Dad took her in temporarily while social services tried to place her, but because of the ordeal she'd gone through at such a young age, it was felt because she was settled at our house, it would be traumatic to move her again. So for a while Mum and Dad fostered her and eventually it was agreed they could adopt her. Mum was in her forties and well past having children when she fell for Teddy. As you saw, he's got Down's syndrome."

"That must have been hard for them."

"Yes, I'm sure it was. But they love him dearly, he's spoilt rotten though. He gets away with murder."

"I bet it was hard for you also suddenly having a new sister thrust upon you. You can't have been that old yourself."

"No, I wasn't."

She could have kissed him for his sensitivity. How come a man she'd just met understood her perfectly, yet if she ever had shown any sign of resentment or jealousy at Laura's arrival, it was stifled by her mother. *'Don't be like that Danielle, Laura needs a loving family, you are very fortunate Danielle, Laura has very little.'* On and on it went, nobody ever saw it from her point of view that she might resent having a 'new' sister.

"So," he interrupted her thoughts, "tell me about Laura and Matthew, do you think they'll have a long engagement?"

The last person she wanted to keep on discussing was Princess Perfect, she had enough at home with her.

"No idea really. Matthew lives in a flat with his brother so I guess they'll be saving up for a deposit for a house now they're engaged."

"Has she been with him long?"

"Yeah, forever. They're actually made for each other and he's okay really, but a bit dull and boring if you ask me."

"Has she had many boyfriends?"

"Only him. Nobody else would put up with her," she swallowed, "sorry, that wasn't nice. We rub along most of the time, but we have had our moments."

She really wished the conversation would move away from Laura and onto her.

"Do you think they'll stay round London when they get married?"

"I hadn't really thought about it," she dismissed, "I guess so. She likes her job but knowing her, she'll get married and have a baby before their first anniversary."

"Was she okay after the other night?" he broke off some bread, "she did dash off suddenly when you introduced us."

"Yeah she was fine. I've no idea what that was all about. She can be quite dramatic, a bit of an attention seeker if the truth be told. I can see through her even if Mum and Dad can't."

"Oh dear. Thank goodness you're not an attention seeker. I hate that sort of person. Anyway, enough about your sister, tell me, do you fancy going to the theatre one night next week if I can get tickets? There's a Rick Johnson play I'd like to see. I'd love you to come with me."

Ah, this was more like it. About time the attention switched to her.

The wine was certainly relaxing. A gorgeous bloke with plenty of money being interested in her, how lucky was she? Sod 'not interested Jed' from the wine bar, Cohan was a much bigger fish.

"I'd love to come to the theatre with you. Thank you for asking me."

"No, thank *you*. I'm looking forward to it already." His eyes darkened, indicating maybe something more was on offer than the theatre.

It was probably better to find out a bit more about him. He might be somewhat sophisticated in terms of her usual dates, but all blokes liked talking about themselves, she knew that much.

Their steaks were delivered to them by the waiter. "Bon appetite," he said and walked away.

She waited until Cohan had ground black pepper over his meal and asked, "How long have you've been writing?"

He picked up his knife and fork but waited to start, "It seems like forever, but only about five years. I wrote my first novel many years ago, but did nothing with it and left it in a drawer. Then, years later, I was working for a bank designing software, which I hated, and resurrected the story, really as a hobby. I tweaked it to make it more current and eventually got an agent who managed to sell it for me. Nobody was more surprised than me when there was a bidding war between publishers for it."

"It must have been a pretty good story for that to happen. What was it about?"

"I'll answer that in a minute. How's your steak?"

"Amazing," she answered truthfully.

"Good. I'm glad you like it. I much prefer it cooked medium-rare. Right, where were we?"

"You were telling me what your first book was about?"

"Yes, that's right. It was a thriller. I think it was the eccentric detective that resonated with the reader. He was an alcoholic loser, more or less on his final warning from his job, but he managed to solve the murders in a small town that others couldn't. The publishing deal was that I wrote two more books in the series. I had to smarten him up a bit and get him to Alcoholics Anonymous," he grinned, "so I could have a bit more mileage with him." He took a sip of his red wine and she watched his tongue wipe the remnants from his lips. *Talk about hot!*

"Is he still going strong? What's his name, by the way?"

"Hughie Crap."

"Crap? You're kidding me?"

"No I'm not. That's what I called him. He does meet a woman though and gets married. She changes the family name to Cram by deed poll."

"I think I would too," she grinned taking a sip of her wine, "Is Hughie Crap still solving murders?"

"Nah, I've put him to bed now. I tend to write other stuff."

"You must do well . . . I mean to be able to engage Juliet to publicise you?"

"I do okay. I'm very lucky, my grandfather died and left me some money, which enables me to stay for periods of time in nice places so I can write for a living."

"In England or abroad?"

Bet it's abroad. He's too suntanned for it not to be.

"Both. I do like Europe, especially Spain and Italy. It's warmer than here in the winter."

"It must be nice you can move around and have a choice. Have you been abroad recently, you've got a lovely tan?" She looked appreciatively at him, images of his white bits sending heat flooding through her.

"No, not for a while. I've been in Cornwall most recently. But I do like the outdoors so I tend to always be this colour."

"I love Cornwall, we used to have our family holidays there, usually in Truro, but we've been to Newquay too. Where were you?"

"All over the place, I do tend to get restless." He reached for the wine bottle as if he didn't want to talk about Cornwall. "Here, let me top you up."

"I seem to be having much more than you," she giggled feeling quite light-headed.

"Who cares?" he smiled seductively, pouring more into her glass. His eyes darkened. "I'm sure you've been told this many times before, but you really are quite beautiful."

She swallowed, watching his hands as he placed the bottle down. He looked directly at her eyes with his warm brown eyes, and reached over to take her hand. It felt nice.

"I'd love to take you home with me tonight, and if I'm totally honest, I'd like to take you to bed." He didn't say anymore, just held her hand waiting for her response.

God did he realise how sexy he was? Wild horses wouldn't keep her away.

"I'd love to go home with you tonight."

How charismatic was he? Blokes she normally went out with wouldn't dream of openly saying they wanted to make love to her. It would be a grope in the car after a night in the pub, or coffee at theirs with an expected shag.

He was watching her intently. She liked it. It made her feel all warm and gooey inside.

"I'm worried though," he continued with a regretful expression, "I might be rushing you. We have only just met."

Maybe she'd been too eager? Perhaps she needed to be more sophisticated? But she didn't want him to back out now. The gentle kiss he'd given her at Laura's party left her wanting so much more. How was sex going to be between the two of them? Far better than the fumbles she was used to getting that's for sure.

He tilted his head questioningly, "How about I give you time to think about it?"

"I don't need time to think about it, I am an adult."

"That's very obvious, Danielle," his eyes honed in on her cleavage which she felt confident was for her benefit, and it certainly had the desired effect.

Surely he knew how he was making her feel?

"I tell you what I'd like to do," she saw a touch of playfulness in his eyes, "save you for next time. Then I can be sure one hundred percent it's what you want too."

"If that's what you think best," she replied nonchalantly, but underneath she was totally gutted.

"I do. I've always felt foreplay starts way before you get in the bedroom, and anticipation is a great part of it. So right now I'm going to pay the bill, take you home, and eagerly await seeing you again. In fact, how about I cook you dinner on Saturday at my place? Do you fancy that?"

Did she fancy that? Was he for real?

She'd have happily gone right now, but him delaying things showed how sophisticated he was. She'd never come across anyone quite like him before. The sooner Saturday arrived the better. It would give her time to get a wax, maybe a Brazilian, and buy a new set of underwear.

She painted a sexy smile on her face and lifted her glass. "Saturday it is then."

His lips formed that oh so sexy smile of his as he clinked his glass with hers, "Yes, until Saturday."

When she returned from the ladies', he was still sitting at the table so she took her seat again opposite him.

"Before we go," he smiled, "I've got you something," he nodded towards a small, prettily wrapped box on the table.

"For me? That's lovely."

"Open it," he urged.

How thoughtful, he certainly was potential boyfriend material. She quickly discarded the wrapping to reveal a small bottle of Christian Dior *Poison* perfume. What a generous gift when he hardly knew her.

"It's a lovely present, Cohan," she smiled gratefully at him, "thank you. You shouldn't have."

"Yes, I should," his expression oozed sex appeal, and his voice turned husky, "wear it for me on Saturday night."

Her blood rushed southwards with anticipation. "I will." She'd spray it all over her body if that's what he wanted even though she actually disliked the smell.

The perfume was familiar to her . . . Laura wore it all the time.

Chapter 9

LAURA

Each weekday morning, Laura parked her car at the station and commuted from the family home in Reigate to central London. She worked as an administrative assistant in the visa and immigration annexe of the Home Office. The journey usually took about thirty-five minutes and normally she listened to music or an audio book, but today she'd done neither. Instead she'd stared out of the train window with her stomach in knots. After all the excitement of the engagement, Matthew had dropped the bombshell the antibiotics hadn't cleared the cyst on his testicle, so he had an appointment with his GP later that morning. And as if that wasn't enough to worry about, Danielle was still seeing Cohan Laity.

She was almost on auto-pilot as she made her way to her usual desk in the office. The idea of the open-plan office was to 'hot desk' each day. The rationale being that when you arrived at work, you sat in a vacant desk and loaded your laptop onto the work-station. Each desk was clear, no clutter or personal possessions were allowed. The large office was separated by pods, only senior staff had their own offices, and at the end of the corridor there were interview suites where countless meetings took place between Home Office officials and visitors wanting to extend their visas to stay in the UK.

At twenty minutes past nine, she glanced again towards her boss Ed's office which was adjacent to the main open-plan one. It had a glass window and she could see it was still empty. He was late again. How long she could continue covering for him, she didn't know. She was fond of Ed, he was a friend as well as her boss, but of late he seemed to be on a path of self-destruction. Thankfully only excessive alcohol currently, but Laura was beginning to wonder if he was taking drugs. He certainly seemed to be sniffing rather a lot, which she knew could relate to inhaling cocaine. She prayed that wasn't the case. Alcohol was one thing, but drugs made her shudder.

She reached for her phone to text Ed just as it rang. The caller identified as Jack Langton, the head of the whole department.

"Morning Jack."

"Hi, Laura. I'm trying Ed's phone but not getting any response. Do you know where he is?"

Christ, she needed to think fast. It wouldn't do for Ed, or either of them for that matter, to get on the wrong side of Jack Langton.

"He's going to be a bit late this morning, he's taking his car for a service. I'm expecting him any minute. He said it wouldn't be more than half an hour."

"Okay, er, maybe you could help then. I'm checking on the interview he did recently. I've just been contacted for some information but I can't see anything on the system."

"What's the name?"

"It's Ghandour, Tareq Ghandour TG 888121. I can see Ed saw him on the fifteenth, but for some reason the interview isn't recorded."

She waited a few seconds before answering, as if checking herself online even though she knew if Jack couldn't see it, then it wouldn't be there. It was highly likely Ed hadn't done it.

"No, I can't see anything either," she stalled, "but I do know Ed was doing some work from home last night and said he had some notes to put onto the system. I'm guessing that was one of them. I'm sure he'll give them to me to upload this morning when he gets here."

"Okay, can you prioritise it for me as I need it ASAP?"

"Yes, of course I will."

"Thanks, Laura," he cut the call.

She reached for her phone and sent Ed a text message,

> *Where are you? Jack's on the warpath.*
> *Have said you're taking your car for a service.*

A text pinged back.

> *On the tube. Be there in 15. I owe you one.*

Owe her one? He owed her much more than one. She was sick of covering for him. She wasn't paid nearly enough to be doing his work as well as her own. Sadly as the days and weeks went on, he was becoming much more forgetful and lax. It wouldn't be long before others would spot what he was up to. She'd smelt alcohol on his breath the previous day when he'd returned from a *lunch meeting,* which she knew only consisted of a lunch alone in a pub nursing a pint and no doubt a whisky chaser.

She liked her job, and she was good at it. Although she was only a junior admin assistant, her hopes were that someday someone would notice how hard she worked and promote her to a more senior role. She had the ability to do so much more than she currently did, she'd proven that by overseeing Ed's omissions, but there wasn't an opportunity for promotion. *Dead man's shoes* her dad would call it.

Ed eventually arrived and she made her way to his office to try and get the interview sorted that Jack had requested. Ed removed a thin buff folder from his filing cabinet which contained a standard interview form used to question an applicant wishing to extend his or her visa to stay in the UK. Laura glanced at the almost blank document with the name Tareq Ghandour at the top.

"You've hardly completed any of it, Ed," she chastised, "I told Jack you were working from home last night and would be uploading it. He wants it now."

"Shit, is there anything we can do?"

Funny how he used the term 'we', there was nothing in her job description that involved transcribing actual interviews. Hers was more an appointment clerk, with a checking and collating figures remit.

"Can you even remember seeing the man?" she asked frowning.

"No," he looked uncomfortable, "it was the fifteenth, our wedding anniversary, so it wasn't a good day."

What days were good? Ed seemed to be on the slippery slope to destruction.

"Do you think you could look at someone similar and poach some basic info?"

She stared at him, he couldn't be serious.

He grimaced, "You know, elaborate the interview for me, and then sort of make out we're trying to clarify some points that came up. I can tell Jack you're checking as we speak."

"But Jack'll think I haven't been doing my job properly," she glanced at her watch to check the date, "the fifteenth was two weeks ago, what if he asks why I've not done it before now?"

"I'll tell him I've given you some other work to prioritise." He screwed his face up, "Please, just make something up. Maybe ring his employer and check he still has another six months work or something vague like that and we can add it in."

"But we don't know why Jack is looking at this man, it could be one of the junior ministers asking questions. I could end up losing my job fabricating stuff."

"You're not fabricating anything, just doing it retrospectively. I promise I'll cover for you. I'll go and see Jack now while you're filling in the template and tell him I'll have the report to him before lunch and that I've asked you to check on some details. Once you've beefed it up and it's all ready, I'll upload it to the main file so the history will show I've done it, not you."

She didn't want to, but Ed was on hard times and she genuinely felt sorry for him. Much of it was his own making, but right now, she'd got stuff that she couldn't share with anyone, but if she could, she'd welcome someone helping her.

"I promise I'll make it up to you. Just do this for me and I'll get my shit together. I can't afford to get on the wrong side of Jack, I need this job."

He did need his job. She feared for him. His wife leaving him and taking their son to live in Penzance, had flawed him. He was desperately unhappy.

She sighed, "Okay. Go and see Jack now, and I'll do something. But no more, Ed, you need to sort yourself out. I can't keep bailing you out like this."

"I know, I know. I will." He moved to stand next to her and squeezed her shoulder, "I'll see you right for this, I'll pay you back I promise."

"Yeah, you will. I'll hold you to that."

She watched him head towards Jack's office to give him a load of made up waffle. *Did Jack have any idea what Ed was going through?*

She returned to her desk and clicked on the immigration interview template and waited until it came on the screen. The written notes Ed had made at the meeting with Mr Ghandour were scanty with minute detail. Having a bad day seemed an understatement from Ed when his job was of vital importance. What he'd asked her to do, wasn't right. He should know better as her manager.

Laura would never compromise herself in any way even if it meant getting him out of a fix, but she knew someone who would. Georgie girl . . . she'd do it. She'd happily lie and alter the template.

And she wouldn't give a toss, either.

After a long morning sorting out Ed's crap, Laura made her way to the staff exit of the building. It was a relief she was on a half day. She'd booked it long before Cohan Laity had come back into her life. Her intention had been to meet a friend in Oxford Street but she'd had to cancel that. Shopping and socialising was the last thing on her mind. She was heading to an internet café to find out all she could about him; he was a best-selling author so there must be stacks. She didn't want any evidence on her personal devices. The last thing she needed was anyone finding out she knew him.

As the automatic door of the office building opened, she went through and paused at the steps down to the pavement. She checked her phone again, still no message from Matthew. *Please let him be okay.*

She placed her phone in her pocket and her eyes were drawn to a man leaning on a small wall at the base of the steps.

Her tummy flipped. Only for a second though. Almost the same way it did when she first woke up as a child and hadn't realised her daddy was dead. The pain came seconds later when reality had kicked in. Just like now. Her breath caught in her throat.

Cohan Laity.

She'd been expecting him to make contact . . . he hadn't come all the way from Spain for nothing.

He was slouched against a wall with his legs crossed at the ankles playing about with his phone. He looked as cool as ever in a black leather jacket with a trendy checked scarf looped around his neck. To think she used to find his quirky attire attractive, now her skin was itching as if thousands of pimples had emerged like hives all over her body.

He looked up at her, standing at the top of the steps. "Hi," he smiled, putting his phone in his jacket pocket.

How long had he been waiting? And how the hell did he know where she worked? The normal office day didn't finish until five. Had he been opportunistically waiting for her all day to finish at that time? No. Her mother must have mentioned to Danielle she was leaving early and she'd told him. There was no other way he could know.

Right now she had to get rid of him. He was trouble.

She walked down the steps slowly and stopped directly in front of him. "What are you doing here?" she kept her voice low. The last thing she needed was to draw any attention to them both.

"Waiting for you. Can we go somewhere to talk?"

"I'm not going anywhere with you," she snapped.

"We've got unfinished business."

His voice had a threatening undertone.

"We finished our business in Spain."

"No, we didn't," his eyes seemed resolute, "I told you, I want us to be together."

"And how does Danielle fit into all this?" She paused while someone went past and mounted the steps to the office building. "I thought I'd made myself clear there isn't a future for you and I."

"You didn't mean it, though. You were scared of your feelings and ran away."

She gritted her teeth. "I didn't *run away*, I came home. To where I live, and work. And you shouldn't be here."

He gave a huge sigh which seemed to imply she was being tiresome.

His eyebrows lifted, "I did say at the time, if you wouldn't stay in Spain with me, then I'd come to you. So here I am. And I have come to see you in private; I could have spoken up at your party."

"Are you mad?" she couldn't help her voice going up an octave, "you knew I had a boyfriend and a life here, I told you that in the beginning."

"Yeah, but that was before things changed between us. I don't think either of us expected to fall in love."

"What the hell are you talking about?" she spat, "we didn't *fall in love*, we had a fling. That was it, end of. You need to understand there's no future for you and I. So extract yourself from my sister, and move on. Using her isn't fair."

"Who says I'm using her? She likes me," he shrugged, "and I like her."

"Oh yeah, I bet you do. If you don't move on, I'll tell her," she warned watching his face for a reaction but his expression remained deadpan. "I mean it, Cohan, go now, it'll be easier that way."

"Easy for you, is that what you mean?"

"Look," her voice softened, hoping to appeal to the rational side of him, "we had a nice time together, but it wasn't real, surely you must see that? You're an intelligent man. We've turned the page now, and you dating my sister isn't right."

"Well that's easily rectified. Dump Matthew, and we can say you and I met through Danielle at your party. That way we've no need to mention we met in Spain."

"I-am-not-*dumping* Matthew," she snapped. "Don't you get it? I don't want to be with you, and if I wasn't with him, I still wouldn't be with you. I don't mean to be cruel, but that's the way it is. I enjoyed our time together, but that was it. It was a holiday fling, nothing more, and I'm certainly not beginning a relationship with you here." She glared, "It's not going to happen."

He shook his head from side to side, slowly, "Then you leave me no choice than to be with Danielle until you change your mind. That way I can be close by until you come to your senses."

The man was totally mad. What didn't he get about her not being interested?

"Don't be ridiculous. You can't keep that up, any more than Danielle won't see through you." She wanted to knock the supercilious attitude right out of him so threw in, "She's fickle anyway so won't hang around you for long."

He lifted an eyebrow, "Is that right? I'm telling you, Laura, you and I are meant to be together. That's why I'm here and I'm not going anywhere until you've woken up to the fact."

She could almost hear her heart beating, he was scaring her now.

"There is no future for us," she spat, "how many times do I have to tell you?"

Her phone rang, blurting out *Perfect* by Ed Sheeran. She let it ring. It'd be Matthew telling her what the doctor had said, but there was no way she was going to answer the call in front of him.

He tilted his head, "Do you want to get that?"

"No."

"Still Ed Sheeran, then?"

What was the matter with him? Acting like it was normal to be talking about her taste in music. They'd had enough discussions in Spain about both their likes and dislikes, it was hardly appropriate now.

She tried again to reason with him. "Cohan, I can't believe the man I met in Spain would be doing all this, coming over all this way when I explained there wasn't a future for us. I never led you to believe anything different. Even on our last night when you talked about a future together, I made it clear there wasn't one."

"But you still came back and we made love."

"Yes, I know that, because it was our last time together, the end of a special few days."

Cohan stood up and stepped closer to her. He towered above her by at least a foot. His dark eyes she'd once found so charming, were intimidating now, almost hostile.

"It wasn't the end of us, Laura, it was the beginning."

How had she ever found him attractive?

She took a step back to put some distance between them. "This stops now," she put as much firmness into her voice as she could, "I don't want to see you again."

He shook his head menacingly, "We're meant to be together, but I can see you need some time to think about it. So here's what we'll do. I'll give you until Saturday to come to your senses and then I'll explain to Danielle that I want to be with you and we can take it from there."

Come to her senses, the man was deranged; she needed to get away from him, quickly. She wanted to think and couldn't do that with him stood in front of her.

"You're mad. That's never going to happen."

A dark sparkle flared in his eyes making him appear dangerous. Then just as quickly, his expression changed. A chameleon sprang to mind as he gave a brilliant smile showing his teeth.

"Until Saturday. If I don't hear from you," he widened his eyes, "well, let's just hope I do and leave it at that."

"What are you talking about?" she scowled.

"Just that a man has needs so I might be forced to move things along with your sister. I'd rather be making love to you, but if I can't, she's the next best thing."

"That's disgusting," she snarled.

"The choice is yours, Laura. I'll be waiting." He gave her an insolent wink, "You've got my number. See you soon I hope."

He walked away. If he'd have looked back, he'd have seen her watching him. It was almost as if she was in a trance staring at the back of him.

Now what the hell was she going to do? What he was suggesting was blackmail.

She felt a hand on her arm, "Laura, are you okay, you're miles away."

It was Lynda, her senior who worked in the same team as her and Ed. She'd have been heading back to the office after her lunch. "What you hanging around here for on your half day?" she asked.

Laura faked a smile, as if she hadn't a care in the world, "I was just leaving but stopped to take a phone call."

"Not bad news I hope?"

"No, nothing like that. It was my mother asking me to collect something and I was trying to work out the best way to pick it up and get to an appointment I have," she lied.

"Ah, so shopping's involved then, is it?"

"Yes, amongst other things."

"Well, make hay while the sun shines," Lynda smiled, "see you tomorrow."

"Will do," she nodded and moved away as Lynda made her way up the steps. She was going to have to walk to the next tube station, Cohan could still be around for all she knew.

A chill passed through her whole body. How had she ever got involved with him? What had possessed her? The man was unhinged. Her head began to throb mercilessly. What in God's name was she going to do? If she owned up to what she'd done, Danielle would be furious, but would quickly move on, she never stayed with one bloke for long anyway, however, her mum and dad would be terribly upset about her behaviour. Their lives were all about honesty and integrity. They'd brought all three of them up to be truthful so would be devastated to learn she'd been unfaithful to Matthew. And what about him, he'd be distraught. He'd never forgive her.

If she tried to explain, not one of them would understand it was Georgie girl. That it was her in Spain having a fling. How could they when they didn't even know she existed? Only Laura did. If she said nothing, he was going to sleep with Danielle. But worse than that, he could expose her anyway. Was it better to come clean right now rather than have him spill it all out in the future?

Nausea came in waves attacking her tummy as she walked. A familiar voice vibrated inside her head. It was Georgie girl.

Don't let him wreck your future with Matthew.

You'll end up with nothing. You have to get rid of him.

She willed herself to keep walking, one foot in front of the other, desperately wanting to get home so she could feel safe in her room. Her eyes flicked around the immediate vicinity, *was he watching her right now?*

Her phone rang again in her pocket. She lifted it out and tentatively checked the screen, half expecting it to be Cohan threatening her again.

It was Matthew.

She swiped her finger across accept. "Hi. Sorry I missed you before, how did you get on?"

Matthew's voice quivered, "I've got to go to hospital for more tests."

Chapter 10

DANIELLE

Sunday lunch was the usual family affair her mum and dad insisted on having. How many times had she heard over the years, *It's the only day we all sit down together as a family.*

Today, she didn't want to eat anything. The previous evening with Cohan had been memorable. She'd had sex before, plenty of times, but none of them had made her feel like he had. Now she knew why it was called love-making.

She checked her phone again, still nothing from him. After their mammoth night, she'd at least expected a message when she first woke up. It was now midday and yet her phone remained silent, from him anyway. Plenty of mates had texted her about their Saturday night out.

She wasn't naive enough to think Cohan hadn't been with stacks of women, but surely he must be thinking about the previous evening and how they'd made love. She did wonder about flowers from him, but wasn't aware of any florists that delivered on a Sunday.

She checked her phone again . . . just her screen saver of her with a couple of besties at the races started back at her.

Cohan had driven her home the previous evening and been so attentive in the car holding her hand, telling her how beautiful she was, and kissing her so gently outside the house before she left him. He'd whispered *speak tomorrow, gorgeous,* as she exited the car, so where was he?

Her fingers twitched to text him. The only thing stopping her was she might appear needy, and he could be working. He'd told her he kept off social media when he was writing otherwise he'd get nothing done. That was most probably the explanation, he was just busy.

She heard her mum call from the kitchen to the back garden. "Ian, Teddy, I'm dishing up," and then to her in the lounge, "Danielle, shout upstairs to Laura would you."

Phones were never allowed at the table during mealtimes, courtesy of another of her dad's old fashioned ideas, so when she went into the hall to shout Laura, she sat on the stairs and checked her phone for about the hundredth time in the last hour. Her anxiety disappeared.

Cohan's text message made her glow from the inside out.

You were beautiful last night

He'd attached a smiley face to the text. She texted straight back,

You were too. I'm smiling this morning.

He pinged a text straight back,

You always make me smile.

She'd never met anyone quite like him. The previous evening she'd been nervous, which wasn't

like her at all. Men didn't make her nervous – until him. He was so sophisticated and it almost felt like he was a league above her. It wasn't anything he specifically did that made her feel that way, quite the opposite really, it was her own perception. Almost as if she was a little girl pretending and he was a grown-up man out of her reach.

There had been no mistaking she was a woman though, with their lovemaking, she ached from it all today. Not in an uncomfortable way, but she'd been surprised how long he was able to make love for, he seemed to enjoy her every way. Thank God she had a flat stomach with some of the positions he had her in. Even when she'd gone to use the shower before he brought her home, he'd joined her for another bout.

Maybe it was the Poison perfume he'd given her that turned him on. She'd lavishly applied it just as he'd asked. He seemed to be mad for her as soon as she walked into his flat. She'd bought a new short navy dress that clung in all the right places, especially for the evening. The appreciation she'd seen in his eyes as he stared at her figure, made every penny she'd spent worth it. At that stage, he didn't know the surprises that were under it. Her underwear had cost heaps more than she normally paid, but the red and black was so sexy, she'd been turned on in the shop buying it.

His welcome kiss left her in no doubt what was going to be happening between them. It was the first time he'd kissed her properly. They just stood in the centre of his flat kissing for ages. She thought they'd adjourn to the bedroom right there and forget dinner, she'd been so ready for him. He kept breaking the kiss to inhale her and tell her how beautiful she was, and how gorgeous she smelled. She'd made a mental note to wear Poison perfume all the time if he liked it that much. Yet despite his hard-on pushing against her abdomen, he'd broken away and insisted they ate first.

He took her hand and led her away from the lounge towards the kitchen. Her tummy did a summersault watching his hands pour a glass of fizz for her. Even her scalp was tingling.

"Can I help at all?" she asked, taking the drink from him.

"No need, it's all done. Please, take a seat. I'll just add some cream to the stroganoff and we're ready."

Relief spread though her that he'd rejected her offer to help, she was useless at cooking. No need to learn as her mum did it all at home. She could manage the basics if she lived alone, but it looked very much like Cohan was talented in the kitchen as well as everything else.

The kitchen was spacious with a huge window overlooking the high street in Southwark. He'd set a small intimate table for two with tiny tea lights flickering, and the place-mats in silver and black; even the serviettes matched. There was a delicate smell coming from the tiny slim vase of freesias he'd placed in the centre of the table.

She'd been surprised at how basic the flat had been. Somehow she'd imagined he'd live more luxuriously, maybe in a penthouse flat or something. It was charming, but quite small really, not exactly what you'd expect for a best-selling author. But it was in the centre of London where space was a premium.

"The flat's lovely," she smiled relaxing as the first few mouthfuls of the drink hit the spot, "is the furniture yours?"

"No, I tend to rent furnished places," he removed some cream from the fridge, "I travel about too much to have my own furniture. Eventually I'll settle down of course, then I'll enjoy buying the sort of stuff I'd like."

How soon before he'd put down some roots?

They made small talk about cooking while he stirred in the cream to the stroganoff, and then she watched his sexy hands plate the meal. He'd certainly gone to a lot of trouble preparing for them both. If he didn't write for a living, maybe he could make a go of it as a chef.

He's so accomplished.

Over dinner, he'd told her about his mother now living in a remote part of Skye. Apparently, she'd worked as a cook most of her life so it had been easy to pick up tips from her as he was growing up.

Then they'd started to get flirty, teasing each other, touching seductively with their feet under the table, and finally feeding each other with dessert and cream. It had seemed completely natural to leave the dishes and head to the bedroom after they'd finished. Cohan took the remains of some bubbly with them and led the way. He gave her time to undress and get into bed while he went to the bathroom. She quickly removed her clothes, except the underwear.

From the minute he'd joined her naked, they'd started kissing, and he'd taken his time exploring her body and bringing her to climax with fingers and mouth. She was more than ready for him when he applied the condom and sunk deep into her. Never had she felt so aroused with a man. As he moved effortlessly inside her, and their eyes locked together, she knew categorically she was in love with him. He kissed her face, her eyes, her cheeks, her lips, and still he gave more. He penetrated deep, alternating from in and out slowly, to in and out quickly. He somehow managed to flip her over onto her tummy and keep the rhythm going. She loved feeling the weight of him on her back, biting her neck. She only needed his fingers and she was climaxing again, screaming his name as he thundered into her.

They'd cuddled together and she'd wrapped her arms around his tight chest and rested her head on him. They kissed again and again as lovers in the first throws of intimacy do. She loved being held against him and his heart beating in her ear. He made her feel happy.

"I knew you'd be like this, Danielle," he squeezed her arm.

"Like what?" she'd lifted her head from his shoulder and supported herself on her elbow watching his face as he spoke, desperate for some loving words.

"Beautiful . . . stunning . . . sexy, all of those and so much more. I'm a lucky man."

She glowed inside and out.

He was a lucky man?

It felt like she'd won the lottery.

"Is anything the matter, Danielle?" her dad asked, "you've barely touched your food and seem miles away."

He was right. She'd been moving the food around her plate but not really putting any in her mouth. Cohan was the best diet she'd ever been on.

"No, nothing's wrong, I'm just not that hungry, that's all." She put her knife and fork together indicating she'd finished. She hadn't even noticed everyone else had done so already and they'd been waiting for her.

"Can I have her Yorkshire pudding?" Teddy asked gleefully, staring at the plate of food she'd left.

"No, you can't," her mum snapped, "you don't eat off other people's plates. And you've already had two, that's quite enough."

Teddy folded his arms in a huff which was common for him. It was a typical pose if he didn't get his own way. That and pulling a mardy face.

"You aren't on one of these faddy diets again are you?" her mum nodded towards the left-over food on her plate, "I've warned you about those before."

Danielle shook her head, "I had a huge meal with Cohan last night," she saw Laura twitch, jealous to death no doubt as someone else was the centre of attention after all the fuss she'd had lately, "so I'm struggling to eat anything today, to be honest."

"Where else did you go?" her dad chipped in, "you were late getting home from a restaurant."

If he thought she'd been out with Cohan to a restaurant, then so be it. No need to give him any info to contradict that. He'd be choking on his lunch if he'd any idea what her and Cohan had really been doing.

"I went back to Cohan's for a night cap after we'd eaten."

"I see," her dad frowned. "Are you likely to be going out with him again?"

"Definitely," she answered confidently, "I'm waiting to hear from him as to whether we're out again tonight."

Dad wouldn't understand that. He was terribly old-fashioned, his belief was after a night out, you stayed in the next, and Lord forbid if you went out midweek.

"Hey, stop giving her the third degree," her mum chastised, "she is twenty-three, not fifteen you know."

"I do realise that. I'm only hoping she isn't rushing into things. Cohan's quite a bit older and, talking to him at the party, I got the impression he doesn't stay in one place for too long." He turned towards her with an apologetic expression, "I'd hate to see you fall headlong into something and end up getting hurt."

"Why should I get hurt?" she dismissed, "we've only just met. We aren't planning our wedding or anything, we're just enjoying each other's company. What's wrong with that?"

"But you do like him," her mum smiled warmly, hoping to no doubt extract more information. She was telling them nothing, not yet anyway. It was too soon, she was only just getting used to her own feelings about Cohan, she wasn't ready to share them. And it wasn't as if she had anything concrete to say. He might have been fabulous in bed, and loving towards her, but he'd not actually said anything about having any feelings for her. She was disappointed, if she was honest. Although it was far too early to be expecting undying love, it would have been nice to have something.

Please don't let him be seeing me as only a shag buddy.

Princess Perfect decided to throw a spanner in. "Dad's right. You don't really know that much about him."

"I know enough and, with respect, I don't need relationship advice from you. Not when you've only had the one boyfriend." She widened her eyes, "I hardly think that qualifies you to comment, do you?"

"Now then," her mother interjected, "there's no need for that. Laura's only making a point. Nobody is saying don't enjoy yourself, but maybe a bit of caution would be good, just in case Cohan does leave suddenly, that's all we're saying, love. Now, who's for some apple pie?"

"Meeeeeeee," Teddy grinned, "a big bit."

Danielle shook her head, "I couldn't eat anything. I might have something later if I don't go out."

"None for me, Mum, either," Laura said, standing up. "I'll help clear the dishes, then I'm off to see Matthew."

Goodie-two-shoes reached for the plates to do her, *I'll impress Mum and Dad with how useful I am,* approach. *Let her get on with it.*

Laura started piling the plates up with the crockery on the top one.

"How is Matthew?" her mum asked sympathetically.

"Worried sick."

"I bet. He should have come today. You know, to take his mind off things."

"It could be a number of things," her dad said, "it doesn't have to be cancer. He should wait and deal with things once, and if, he's told it's something ominous. Right now, nobody has said that."

"Easier said than done, though," Laura sighed, "we can all give out the advice, but when it's actually happening to you, then it's different." She left the table holding the pile of dirty plates, and headed for the kitchen.

"Are you going to help Danielle?" her dad's eyes fixed on her with a *yes you are* expression. "Your mother's done all the work preparing and cooking the meal, I think the least you could do is help with dessert."

"Can I have ice cream with my apple pie?" Teddy asked eagerly.

"Good idea, Teddy," her dad agreed, "I think I will too." He glanced lovingly at her mum, "Same for you?"

"Why not?" her mum smiled at her as she got up from the table and made her way to the kitchen, "thank you, love."

Laura was at the sink running the plates under the tap. Their mum didn't like them loading in the dishwasher with food stuck to the plates. She liked the surplus washed off so the smell didn't linger. What the point was of having a dishwasher if you did all that, Danielle never understood. Why not just load the dishwasher and put it on, for God's sake?

She hated how Laura always looked good without having to work at it. Today, even in jeans and a tee-shirt she was really attractive. She barely touched her hair some days, often scraping it back in a ponytail, yet she always looked stunning. Clothes and jewellery always suited her permanently olive skin. And unlike her who had to apply make-up daily, she didn't as her dark eyes and long lashes, were unusual and quite beautiful, negating the need for further enhancement.

Laura turned around as Danielle came into the kitchen. "I know you don't want to hear it, but I meant what I said about rushing into things with this Cohan."

For someone who had a boyfriend with a possible cancer diagnosis, why the hell was Laura concerned about her and Cohan?

Danielle reached in the cupboard above the apple pie for some plates. "What's it to you?"

"Nothing. It all seems to be happening quickly, that's all."

"So?"

"How old is he, anyway?"

"Thirty. Not that it's any of your business."

"There's no need to be like that. I don't want you to get hurt, that's all."

"Why should I get hurt? Are you jealous or something?"

"Jealous? Do me a favour. Why should I be jealous when I've got a boyfriend," she glanced down at her ring, "a fiancé actually. I'm only looking out for you. You hardly know him."

"I know enough and I'll thank you to keep your nose out. You concentrate on Matthew and leave me and Cohan alone."

"Fine," Laura started loading the wet plates into the dishwasher. She droned on, "Which restaurant did you go to last night?"

"Why?"

"Just wondered, you were late getting in."

Danielle cut the apple pie into three and gently eased each slice onto a plate. "Yeah, well I am over eighteen, Mother," she answered sarcastically.

"Bet you never even went out. What was it, a cosy night in with a bottle of wine?"

Danielle opened the freezer and took a tub of vanilla ice cream out.

Why can't she mind her own effing business?

Laura carried on. "He could have a stack of other women in tow, for all you know." She shrugged, "But if you don't want to listen, that's up to you."

"I don't," Danielle replied scooping out ice cream from the tub and putting it alongside each slice of apple pie. "Like I said, you're hardly an expert on relationships."

"I'm not saying I am. I was only warning you to be careful."

"Yeah right," she put the tub back in the freezer. "What's it with you anyway? Can't you bear the limelight to be taken off you? What you worried about, eh? That I might beat you to the altar, is that it?"

Laura let the dishwasher door go and it slammed shut. She swung round. "Altar." The colour visibly drained from her face, like the night she first met Cohan and had to run to the toilet as she'd had too much to drink.

Look well if she's pregnant. Mum and Dad'll be mortified.

"Don't tell me you'd even think about marrying him?" Laura's feeble voice made it sound like it would be the biggest catastrophe in the world.

Danielle tapped her nose, winding her up some more.

"You're mad if you're even considering anything like that when you've only just met."

"Thanks for the advice," Danielle licked some ice cream off her fingers, "excuse me if I don't take it."

Chapter 11

LAURA

Laura had taken an annual leave day off work to accompany Matthew to the hospital appointment. His GP had sent an urgent referral following his recent scan. The speed and ramifications of a sinister diagnosis halted any thoughts of telling him anything about Cohan Laity. Right now, there were far worse things to think about than her affair. Matthew needed support not more grief.

They'd been directed to a numbered area in the outpatients department and took their seats. Matthew selected a magazine from the pile that were littered around the tables adjacent to the seating area. She didn't understand how he could even flick through a magazine, she couldn't concentrate on anything. The news they were going to get was going to be life-changing, she was sure of it.

Her gaze drifted around the chairs lined up rows in the waiting areas, many of them occupied by a variety of young and old, male and female. People were munching their way through bags of crisps, chocolate bars and slurping from cans of soda courtesy of a conveniently placed vending machine at the entrance to the department. Regularly, folk waiting would stand to stretch their legs, or interrupt the various nurses that kept bobbing in and out of the rooms, to ask when it was going to be their turn.

About thirty minutes of sitting on the rock-hard seats, Matthew's name was called and they followed the nurse into the allocated room. They took the vacant seats opposite the desk with the consultant sitting upright in the obligatory white coat which indicated he was the main man.

He looked up from the paperwork, "Mr Souter?"

"Yes," Matthew nodded.

"Can you confirm your date of birth please?"

Matthew reeled it off.

They both watched the consultant intently as he stared at the medical records on the desk in front of him, almost as if by them both concentrating hard on him, he'd deliver news that wouldn't be so bad.

She reached for Matthew's hand. It felt clammy. He didn't deserve bad news. He was too young and fit to have anything wrong with him. He wasn't ever ill and had never even been in hospital.

The consultant's expression was kind, but matter-of-fact, just another day at the office for him, no doubt. "I'm not sure how much your GP has discussed with you, but I'm afraid the recent scan and blood results indicate you have a tumour on your left testicle."

Matthew's grip tightened. They'd cajoled each other that it might be nothing, maybe a benign cyst, but she'd known deep-down however much she tried to dismiss it exactly what it was from the very first moment she'd felt the pea-sized lump.

Do something bad and you will find,
Karma's lurking right behind.

Matthew cleared his throat. "Does that mean cancer?"

"Yes, it does. But first of all, let me reassure you, this type of cancer is curable. It does require invasive treatment, but I've no reason to think you won't make a full recovery."

"What is the . . . the treatment?" Matthew asked, his anxiousness evident by the tremor in his voice.

"The testicle will need to be removed surgically first of all, which we will do under a general anaesthetic. The tumour will be examined under a microscope and depending upon the type of cancer it is, we'll decide if any further treatment is necessary."

"Further treatment?" Matthew said nervously.

"Yes. Some patients require chemotherapy but other factors indicate that, such as the cancer spreading. At the moment all the tests indicate it's a localised tumour, that is to say it hasn't spread, therefore currently the treatment plan is for surgery only. After that, you'll be monitored here regularly by the hospital, but as time goes on, the appointments will become less and less. Eventually you will be discharged under the care of your GP."

"When will the surgery be?" Laura asked.

"Soon." He indicated with his head towards the nurse, "This is Diane. She'll take you next door and go over things with you in more detail. She'll be able to give you a date for the surgery. And please feel free to ask all the questions you want to. Diane is a specialist nurse and extremely experienced in this type of surgery."

He wanted rid of them. No doubt once a patient has been on the receiving end of the bad news, the consultant needed them to leave so he could see the next patient, and the next. How many other patients in a day got the same dismal news they'd had?

Diane ushered them into an adjacent room. Did either of them thank the consultant? She couldn't remember. All she could recall was her and Matthew being shown diagrams of the surgical procedure and someone bringing tea for them both.

Funny how in a crisis everyone has tea?

The rain lashed down as they sat inside the car in the hospital car park. She told Matthew to take the passenger seat, he wouldn't be in a fit state to drive. He was staring ahead like a zombie but there was nothing to see out of the windscreen as the rain was hurtling down, obscuring the view.

"I know it's a shock, but the consultant and the nurse were positive," she reassured. "You need to get this surgery over and done with first of all. Thankfully you're not going to be waiting that long."

Matthew was staring ahead but gave a slight nod of acknowledgement. Her chest hurt for him. It was such a terrible shock. And she knew he'd be scared. At any age, a cancer diagnosis would be devastating, but at twenty-seven, you certainly didn't expect it. Cancer was for old people, wasn't it?

"I've never really thought much about having kids," his voice was low, dejected, "until that nurse said about freezing sperm. Bloody hell," he scowled, "I thought I had years to think about that sort of thing."

"You will have years," she squeezed his arm reassuringly, "and you still might be able to have children naturally. The nurse said it was just a precaution, like insurance. You might not ever need to use the frozen sperm especially if you don't need the chemo."

"It's all a bit clinical though," he sighed heavily, "yesterday I was a twenty-seven-year-old bloke in the prime of his life, today I'm a twenty-seven-year-old with a cancer diagnosis and death hanging over my head."

"Don't talk like that," she dismissed, "the specialist didn't. It's a bum deal I know, but you're going to fight it, and I'll be there with you. You'll not be on your own."

"Yeah, but you didn't sign up for this when you said you'd marry me." He turned to look at her then, anxiety written all over his face, "I don't mind if you want out. In fact," his voice was no more than a whisper, "it might be for the best."

"Now listen to me," she spoke firmly to him so he knew there was no doubt, "I do not want out. I'm here now because I want to be. I love you. I'm not going anywhere. We'll tackle this together."

He hugged her then. Tightly. She swallowed the lump in her throat and pushed back the tears. Crying wasn't going to help either of them. Neither was guilt, which engulfed her like a big, black cloud. If she'd wanted to come clean, she couldn't now. Maybe later when it was all over? If she lost him, she'd have to deal with it then, but for now, he needed her support not a confession about how she'd betrayed him.

"The nurse said apart from the discomfort after the surgery, you'll be fine. I'll take some time off work and come and stay at yours so I can look after you."

"Mum will want me to go over to France to recuperate," his lack of enthusiasm spoke volumes. He often dodged going to see her in France. He wasn't keen on her husband. Or that's what he said; Laura knew a lot of it was because she'd left his father. It was his dad that had his loyalty, even though he worked in Venezuela so he didn't see a lot of him.

"You can go over there, but not initially. You'll need a few days to rest after the surgery, the nurse said, then you'll be able to go. Your mum will want to spoil you a bit, I would think."

For the first time since they'd arrived at the hospital, he smiled. "That's what worries me. I'll have a pickled liver being with her, she'll have me visiting all the wineries."

"Yeah, well, you'll have to take it steady," she warned. He was right though, she knew his mother, every hour of the day was wine o'clock. "Let's go back to yours now so you can ring her, she'll be anxious to know what they've said."

She started the engine but didn't move off straight away. She was running out of supportive platitudes. If it had been her, she'd be thinking it was all over now, just as Matthew must be thinking.

She squeezed his hand, "Come on, fasten your seatbelt."

They'd been given the worse news possible.

Now was all about dealing with it.

Chapter 12

LAURA

Matthew was sitting up in the hospital bed, the crisp white starched sheets making his fair skin look even lighter. He seemed bright enough though which was a relief following his surgery.

"Is it very sore?" Laura asked, gently stroking his arm.

"No, not really. I have to take the analgesia every four hours for the next forty-eight to keep the pain on a level and not let it build up."

"Right."

"It's not a huge cut either, I've had worse playing football."

She widened her eyes, "You've seen it?"

"Yeah, the nurse put a clean dressing on this morning so I had a look."

"Were you okay?" She knew how squeamish he was.

"Fine. That specialist nurse, Diane, came this morning as well. She showed me the false ball I can have inserted in the sac, so it'll look like I've got two."

"Oh, yes, I remember her mentioning that. Are you going to have it done?"

"I dunno," he shrugged, "what do you think?"

"It's up to you. I'm not bothered what you look like."

"No, me neither, but I was thinking about when I get showered after footie. Nobody notices your balls, but I bet they would when you've got one missing."

He had a point, blokes were twitchy about that sort of thing. "When would you have it done, did she say?"

"When they've checked everything in case I need chemo. She said they just do a tiny cut and insert the false ball."

"That doesn't sound too bad, then. Have they mentioned anything else about chemo?"

"No, but the consultant comes before I'm discharged so they reckon he'll say then. But he said before he thought I wouldn't need it, remember?"

"Yeah, that's right, he did, fingers crossed, eh," she stood up, "do you want another drink?" She reached to the locker for the bottle of cordial.

"If I must. I'd rather it was something stronger though."

She rolled her eyes playfully, "Like they're going to let you have anything like that."

He knocked the juice back she handed to him in one, pulling a distasteful face once it had all gone. "Anyway," he reached for her hand as she sat down, "it seems to be all about me right now. Are you okay?"

"Yeah, just a bit tired, work's hard at the moment."

"What, with Ed?"

She nodded. She daren't tell him the reason she was tired was because she wasn't sleeping, and it wasn't work keeping her awake.

"Are you still covering up for him? Because if you are, it needs to stop. It's ages since his wife left him, he should be picking himself up by now."

"I know, but it has hit him hard. Before all this, he was such a good boss, I learned loads from him."

"Just as well you did, that's why you're able to bail him out now. You're doing his job and your own and he's taking the piss, if you ask me."

How could she tell him what was really bothering her? How she was literally looking over her shoulder expecting Cohan to turn up any minute. He was beginning to scare her, and she had nobody to turn to.

"I'm going to see him one night after work and have a chat with him. It's hard when we're together at work to say much, he is my boss after all."

"You need to tell him you've had enough."

"Yeah, you're right," she agreed, "I thought maybe next week, when you go to France, I'll talk to him then. I'll have a quick drink after work with him and tell him how I'm feeling."

"I'd rather you met him for a drink when I'm there. Can't it wait until I get back and he can join us both in the pub? It's not as if he's shy tagging along."

"I need to say something soon, though. I might catch him in the office one night and have a chat then. I'll see. Anyway, enough about work, it's great Chris has definitely got the time off to take you to France."

"Yeah, Mum's dead pleased we're both going. I've told Chris I'm not staying for long, though. Five days max."

"What's he say to that?"

"Same as me. He reckons five days with Mum is more than enough."

She scrunched up her nose, "I feel a bit sorry for her, I bet she's been worried not being around for your op."

"Yeah, but I've been Face Timing her so she knows I'm okay."

"Still, she'll be pleased to see you in person, and Chris too. She'll love having the two of you there together."

"Yeah, she will."

Laura looked up at her mum coming into the small bay of six beds.

"Hi, Mum," she stood up, "you found us then. Come and have this comfy chair, I'll get another."

"Sorry I'm later than I intended," her mum approached the bed. "How are you doing?" She gave Matthew a warm hug, "Is everything alright?"

"Seems to be," he nodded, "I feel okay, actually. Thanks for coming to see me."

"I wouldn't have missed coming, especially with your mother not being here."

She sat down on the comfy chair while Laura pulled up a small grey visitors' chair and sat the opposite side of the bed.

"Ian and Teddy send their love," her mum continued, "Teddy's a delight as always, asking how much blood there is."

Matthew widened his eyes, "Reassure him very little, thank God!"

"I already have. That young man's imagination," she shook her head, "honestly. Oh, before I forget, I've brought you something," she reached in her bag and produced a Tupperware container, "they're homemade biscuits to keep you going."

"Aw, cheers Ann," Matthew took the container from her.

"Is it very painful?" her mum asked, watching him select a cookie.

"Not too bad," he took a bite, "the nurse says I'll probably be allowed home tomorrow now the swelling's gone down. They've put me on antibiotics to make sure there's no infection."

"Good, you'll sleep much better in your own bed. Laura says your mum wants you to go to France to recuperate?"

"Yes, all being well I'm going Monday. I wanted Laura to come with me, but she's busy at work so my brother's going to drive me. Unless you can help me persuade her?"

"I can try, but you know Laura, she'll only do what she wants."

"Err, do you two mind? I am in the room you know."

Her mum turned to her. "It would be nice for you to go with Matthew for a few days, love, why don't you?"

"I can't just randomly get time off. I have to book my annual leave way in advance, and as it's August and everyone with children wants it off, I can't see me getting a sniff somehow."

"Maybe a long weekend, then? I'm sure your boss would agree to that in the circumstances."

"That's what I keep saying," Matthew nodded, "Mum's desperate to see us since the engagement, we've only been able to Face Time and I know her and Brian want to have a bit of a celebration for us."

"Then you must go, Laura. Make it a priority. There's more to life than work, you know. You could always fly over, your dad and I could help if you're worried about the cost."

"It's not that."

"Maybe see if you can get a Monday and Tuesday off and make it a long weekend. His mum will be thrilled to see you, and you can all celebrate together."

Laura sighed, "I'll see what I can do," she looked apologetically at Matthew, "but I can't promise."

She had no intention of doing anything. It was true August was a difficult month at work, but she didn't want to be away right now anyway. Yes, it would be great to distance herself from all the Cohan business, but she needed to deal with whatever happened next. And at least Matthew would be out of the way, even if it was for a short time.

"Anyway, quickly changing the subject," her mum leant forward as if she had something of great importance to announce, "have you told Matthew about Danielle and Cohan?"

Laura's stomach tightened. She hated the way his name rolled off her mum's tongue almost in an endearing way.

"What about them?" Matthew asked.

"Well, let's just say things are moving very quickly," her expression smacked of joy, "she's head over heels about him, I can tell." Her mum turned to look at her, "It's like when I met your father, you just know when you meet the right one. We hardly knew each other but quickly realised we wanted to be together for the rest of our lives."

Jesus, she had to stop this.

"Yes, well I wouldn't put Danielle in the same league as you and Dad. She never sticks with a boyfriend, she easily gets fed up. He'll be history soon, you'll see."

"I don't think so," her mum disagreed, "not this time. Anyway, I've told Danielle to invite him round for Sunday lunch. I thought we could make a day of it." She smiled at Matthew, "You too, of course. Laura can pick you up and bring you round as I don't suppose you can drive straight away?"

Her tummy somersaulted, as if she'd gone from the top of a roller coaster to the bottom in five seconds. There was no way she was sitting around a table with Cohan Laity, especially not with her stupid sister fawning over him.

"No," Matthew shook his head, "I can't drive straight away. I've got a leaflet about do's and don'ts, and driving is definitely out as it can cause swelling."

"That's settled then. Come on Sunday and the most you'll have to do is eat and drink."

"Sounds good to me," he said chomping through his second biscuit.

"I'm not sure, Mum," Laura desperately needed an excuse to get out of it, "Matthew's probably better staying in his flat where it's quiet and he's able to rest. I'll go round and spend the day with him."

"Nonsense. A bit of company will do him good," she looked hopefully at Matthew, "you'll be okay, won't you?" Laura already knew what his answer would be before it left his lips, he was so predictable.

"Course I will. I wouldn't miss one of your Sunday roasts; you're doing Yorkshires, aren't you?"

Her mother smiled, loving all the attention about her cooking. "Absolutely. A Sunday lunch isn't Sunday lunch without Yorkshire puddings."

"Is this bloke of Danielle's definitely coming?" Laura asked. She couldn't bring herself to say his name, and hoped he hadn't confirmed.

"I expect so. I've told Danielle to ask him, so I'm sure he will."

"He might be busy, you never know," she silently prayed.

"Yes, I suppose he could be," her mum frowned, "and Danielle wasn't enthusiastic, if I'm honest."

"Probably because she knows he'll say no. It is a bit sudden to be *meeting the parents* when they've only just started dating."

"But we have already met him, at your party."

"I know, but inviting your daughter's boyfriend round for lunch may have other connotations as far as he's concerned."

Her mum considered what she'd said, and her expression changed as if the penny had finally dropped, "Yes, you could be right, I hadn't thought about that. Oh well, we shall see," she looked at Matthew, "you'll still come though, won't you?"

"Yeah, I'll definitely be there," he nodded eagerly.

"That's fine then." She picked up her bag from the floor. "I'm going to pop to see Charlie Parker, he's on B4," she looked at Laura, "you know, old Mr Parker from the back of us." Laura nodded, thinking of the old boy they'd known since they were children whose garden backed onto theirs. Her mother visited him regularly, and rather than go all the way round to the front of his house, she would climb over the small wall separating their gardens and straight to his back door.

"I've made him some biscuits too." She lowered her voice, "I don't think he's actually going to come home, apparently he's going into a care home when he leaves here. I'll just say a quick hello and drop the biscuits off for him." She stood up, "I'll meet you in the downstairs cafe, love, shall I? It'll save coming back up here." She looked at her watch, "Gosh I better dash, visiting time will be over shortly."

"Yep, that's fine, Mum. I'll stay until the end of visiting and then make my way downstairs to you."

Her mum hugged Matthew again. "Remember, we're all here for you. Laura will look after you, she won't let you down."

"I know she won't," he smiled lovingly at Laura before turning back to her mum, "and thank you again for coming, Ann. I'm looking forward to Sunday already."

That would make her mum's day. Anything to do with food, she was your woman. Coffee mornings, church gatherings or afternoon teas, she was there, generously donating her latest offerings.

Laura painted a smile on her face as her mum left the ward despite a tightness inside, like a vice crushing her chest. If Matthew and her mum knew what she'd done, there'd be no Sunday lunch with Cohan Laity.

Now she feared she was going to have to suck it up and play happy families with the twisted dickhead.

Stupid bloody Georgie girl.

She'd caused all this.

Chapter 13

DANIELLE

Danielle nestled into Cohan's arms, both of them sweating after another fabulous bout of lovemaking at his flat. Cohan had so much stamina, she'd never experienced anything quite like it before. He made all the others she'd been with seem like boys.

She savoured his smell and wrapped herself around him, putting off for a few minutes the question she wanted to ask. *What if he says no?* While she was hesitating, his breathing steadied as if he was about to fall asleep and she didn't want that before she'd said anything.

"Before I forget," she kept her head on his chest so she wasn't looking directly at him and appearing too eager, "Mum's invited you to lunch this coming Sunday, if you're free."

Silence.

Bet he won't come.

"No problems if you're busy," she quickly added, "she just mentioned inviting you as Laura's Matthew is coming after his surgery. Mum's thinking the more the merrier, I reckon it's so he isn't feeling like the centre of attention."

"I forgot about that. You did tell me about his surgery, how is he?"

"Fine as far as I know. Florence Nightingale's been on the case, so I wouldn't imagine he dare be anything but."

"Who's Florence Nightingale, your mum?"

She lifted her head and rolled her eyes at him, "I mean Laura. She's suddenly become an expert nurse on testicular cancer."

"Ah, I see. So there's no special reason for the lunch, it's nobody's birthday or anything."

"No, nothing like that," she laid back down, "it's just Mum trying to fuss Matthew up a bit. He's going to France the following day to spend a bit of time with his mother."

"Is Laura going with him?"

Who the hell cares what she's doing?

"She reckons she can't get the time off work, which will be a load of rubbish. She fancies herself as some sort of champion of the immigration crisis, solving the problem in this country single-handedly."

He yawned stroking her hair, "She'd have to be pretty special to be able to do that."

"Oh, she thinks she is, believe me."

"Is Matthew okay about her not going with him, I'd have thought he'd want her there?"

"God knows, she's definitely not going though."

"That's a bit odd, isn't it? They've just got engaged, surely they want to spend all their time together, especially with what has happened recently to him."

"Yeah, I suppose, but then again she is odd. I'd be worried if I was Matthew, I reckon that boss of hers has the hots for her. I still can't believe she invited him to her party. I mean, who invites their boss to something like that?"

"He's got nothing to worry about, though, has he? Is she the type to play away?"

"Don't think so," she shrugged, "but you know the saying, when the cat's away . . ."

"How long is he going to France for?"

"Not sure. I wish she would go with him though, six months would be good."

"You're really not keen are you?"

"In a word, no. Sorry," she lifted her head again from his shoulder, "does that make me a horrible person?"

"Not to me it doesn't," he kissed her gently, "she sounds like a jobs worth from what you've told me, and I think lunch at your parents' is a great idea. What time do you want me to be there?"

Her heart did a hop, skip and a jump, "About twelve, Dad likes a drink before lunch."

"A man after my own heart, I'm looking forward to it already." He turned and pressed himself against her, "Now, where were we . . ." he purred in her ear.

She pulled away "Done I'm afraid." She reached for her watch on the bedside table, "I'm going to have to make a move, it's after twelve."

Cohan rolled onto his back and groaned, "Can't you stay and I'll take you to work in the morning?"

"Afraid not. Dad'll have one ear on the door waiting for me to get home."

"But you're an adult, surely he knows what adults get up to?"

"Of course he does, and that's why I have to be home. He has this sort of rule that you can't stay out overnight. Not for this anyway," she grinned, "I got away with it on Saturday because I told him I was going out with my friend and staying over."

"And I liked having you with me for the whole night." He widened his eyes, "It makes no sense to me though, you can have sex with me in an evening and that's okay, just not overnight."

"I'm sure he knows that too, but they are his rules."

Cohan sat up and reached for his boxers, "What about Laura and Matthew, are they allowed *overnight* sex?"

"She doesn't stay out overnight either although she might when Matthew first comes home from hospital, but I guess Dad's logic will be they won't be having sex so soon after his surgery. I think it might change anyhow now they're engaged though, who knows. Dad can be pretty rigid." Seeing his puzzled face she added, "It's just the way they are. They're older than most parents and have their rules."

Cohan stood up and she couldn't help but admire his flat abdomen and bulging biceps. No wonder sex was good with him, his body was such a turn on.

He pulled his boxers on, "Well, I'm a bit old for all this bloody nonsense."

His tone made her feel silly and immature. "I can get a taxi, you've no need to take me home."

"It's not about that." He sat down again and the bed dipped as he leaned towards her with his hands at each side of her. "I want to wake up with you in the morning, that's why I'm pissed."

Warmth flooded through her veins, "And I like it that you're pissed. I feel the same. I want to wake up with you, too." She needed to do something, she couldn't risk losing him. Even though it had only been a short time, she was in love with him. "I'll tell them another white lie at the weekend so I can stay over with you."

He pulled a face, "I don't like the idea of you telling lies, Danielle," he moved away from her and the momentary warmth she'd felt at him wanting her to stay, disappeared. But it quickly ignited like a roaring fire with his next comment, "Don't worry about it, we'll think of something," he winked at her, "even if it's putting a ring on your finger."

He made his way towards the door having no idea whatsoever of the impact of his statement. "I'll just use the bathroom, five minutes and I'll take you home."

Her heart-rate trebled as she lay back against the pillows. Had she heard him correctly? Surely he wouldn't seriously be thinking of wanting to marry her, they'd only just met. Cohan Laity was a hot, best-selling author, and a rich one, that was his attraction, but he wouldn't know it was trying to hold onto him that kept her awake at night. She knew he could have his pick of women, so every day he chose to be with her was a bonus. She relished his company and the fabulous sex, he was the man she'd always dreamed of, but she knew she wouldn't be able to hang onto him forever. One day her bubble would burst . . . or would it?

Her eyes were drawn towards the high white ceiling as she whispered, "If there is a God up there, please make it happen."

Chapter 14

LAURA

Laura was sitting on Teddy's bed, looking at his most recent postcard he'd received showing Machu Picchu in South America. Distant cousins of her father had sent it to him, which they often did from their extensive travels. Yet despite Teddy's excitement, her mind was most definitely not on Machu Picchu when in less than two hours, Cohan Laity would be in the house.

"I want to go there," Teddy smiled gleefully, as if it was as simple as a trip to Margate.

"You and me too, it looks amazing," she agreed, staring at the picture even though she wasn't really looking closely at it; her unsightly fingernails had her attention, they were bitten down to the quicks. It was a disgusting habit she'd had since being a child, a legacy left with her from Georgie girl. But, like almost everything to do with Georgie girl, she'd managed to stop it, or at least get on top of it. She filed them down until they were almost blunt so she couldn't nibble. The only time she bit them now was when she was anxious about something. And Cohan Laity was certainly making her anxious. All night she'd been awake preparing herself mentally for sitting around a dining table with him today. How the hell was she going to get through it?

"Show me on the map where it is," Teddy asked, selecting a pin from the box so he could identify the country.

She got up from the bed and faced the wall map with him. "There look, that's South America. Machu

Picchu is in Peru," she glanced at the card still in her hand, "look for Cusco, that's actually where it is."

Teddy squinted for a second, "Is that it?" he pointed.

"Yep, that's it, well done for spotting it. Put your pin in."

His little face was a picture, bless him. How she wished all she had to worry about right now was putting a pin in a map. Her stomach had been churning all morning thinking about the day ahead. If only she could get out of it. It was awful of her, but she'd even willed Matthew to have a bit of a relapse so she had an excuse to get out of lunch. The idea of Cohan Laity in the house frightened her.

Teddy reached under his bed for his scrapbook to file the postcard. She watched his tongue come out as he concentrated on putting some glue on the back and pressing it down on the page.

"That's it. Are you going to add it to the contents page?" she reached for a pen from his desk and wrote Machu Picchu on a scrap piece of paper as she knew he wouldn't be able to spell it.

He took it from her and carefully started writing it down, "Can we look at some train pictures next?" he asked eagerly.

"Not today, we've got guests coming for lunch."

"I'd rather look at the trains with you."

She sighed, "Yeah, me too, but we can't." She glanced at her watch, "I've got to go and get Matthew shortly anyway."

"Is he better now?"

"Much, thank you. He's going with his brother tomorrow to see their mum in France."

"On an aeroplane?"

"No, they're driving and going through the channel tunnel."

Teddy's eyes lit up, "I want to go through the channel tunnel."

"Mum and Dad might take you one day, if you ask."

"Will you come with us?"

"I'm not sure. I'll be going on holiday with Matthew from now on."

"Is that 'cause you're getting married?"

"Yes, sort of."

"Is Danielle getting married?"

Once again her stomach turned, "No, nothing like that," she dismissed quickly, "Mum's just invited her boyfriend to lunch, that's all." The same fear she'd had when Danielle had joked about marriage, caused a shudder to rush through her. Danielle didn't know the real reason Cohan was here, or that he was hardly likely to be marrying her.

"I think she is getting married," Teddy insisted, "I saw some magazines on her bed with ladies in white bride dresses."

Typical Danielle, she probably was dreaming about marrying him and having some sort of celebrity wedding. She'd see Cohan as a really good catch. Good-looking, plenty of money, and good sex. What was there not to like? If she only knew.

"She'll only be looking. That's what ladies do. It doesn't mean there will be a wedding. It's the same as going to town and browsing around the shops. You don't buy everything you see. Danielle will only be flicking through the magazines."

"Yeah, but I heard Mum telling Dad, she thought . . . " he hesitated as if trying to remember the right words, "she thought it was serious."

"That doesn't mean it is, though," Laura said, taking her phone out of her pocket. She couldn't possibly contemplate anything like that between Cohan and Danielle. It didn't bear thinking about.

"Anyway, I'll text Matthew now and tell him I'm on my way to pick him up. Do you want to come with me?"

"Yeah."

Laura's stomach was churning, over and over, as she sat in the lounge waiting for the nightmare to begin. She'd taken her time collecting Matthew, and must have been a bit spaced out on the drive back to her house as he'd asked if fourth gear was for when third wore out.

She sat clutching a Diet Coke, silently cursing having to drive him home later as she could really do with a glass of wine to steady her nerves. She'd have the customary one glass while eating her lunch with Cohan sat at the table, though she'd have to stop at one, tempting that it would be to have a whole bottle.

Any minute now, he'd be arriving. He was going to be in the same room as her. She felt sick at the thought. *But what could she do?*

Her mother had been busy the previous day and all morning, making sure everything she served would out do a Michelin star restaurant. Every surface in the house gleamed. Her dad had complained the house smelled like a *tart's boudoir* with the lilac and mandarin reed diffuser strategically placed on a table in the lounge, and the plug-in white linen air freshener next to the sofa.

She'd contemplated faking sickness and staying in her room which was still an option, but she'd remembered her father's wise words as she'd struggled with an older lady at the office when she'd first started work. Veronica Edge had worked in the department for many years as a senior administrator, and Laura had overheard numerous people complain about her. She'd heard her described as 'old school' and 'set in her ways'. Apparently, she found IT a particular challenge despite being sent on numerous courses. She preferred to do things by pen, which would be alright in a small office, but not suitable in a busy department.

If Veronica Edge's intention was to make things difficult for Laura, she certainly succeeded in that. Just small things, such as filing she'd efficiently done would be criticised, an urgent letter she'd been charged with addressing and posting hadn't got to the recipient. There were insignificant things which weren't her fault, but Veronica Edge inferred that any 'little slips' were down to her. Laura was puzzled as to why this woman appeared to have it in for her.

When she'd complained to her dad about her making things difficult at work, he'd told her to think it through before she tackled the woman, "Watch and observe her," he'd said, "find out if there's a particular pattern before challenging." He was only trying to be fair to Veronica Edge, implying she might have her own problems, and then maybe Laura could offer some help.

That was sensible advice for Laura, but not Georgie girl . . . she was having none of it. She observed her alright, then at the first opportunity, went to Jack Langton, the head of department, and spun him a yarn about feeling Veronica Edge was biased against her because of the colour of her skin. Laura was by no means black, but there must have been some black blood in her family way back as she certainly was dark.

Jack Langton had refuted Veronica would even contemplate anything racist. He went on to discuss the work place being multi-cultural, that staff embraced diversity, and none were prejudiced in any way. He said he could categorically swear Veronica Edge didn't have a racist bone in her body.

Laura had worked hard at appearing anxious and upset, even managing to shed a few tears. When she left Jack's office, he'd promised her he would speak to Veronica Edge informally to find out if she was aware of the impact of her behaviour. Laura nodded her gratitude and added that she felt uncomfortable being in her company, it was making her dread coming to work, so if it was at all possible, she'd like to move if an opportunity arose elsewhere in the building. Jack has assured her it wouldn't come to that.

Whatever had happened next, she wasn't privy to. Veronica Edge went on long-term sick leave and eventually took early retirement. That meant greater responsibilities for her which she was more than happy to take on. She was bright and a fast worker so quickly ingratiated herself favourably with the senior staff. A week or so later, her dad had asked how things were going with the woman that she was having problems with.

"She's gone off sick and I'm not sure if she's actually coming back," she told him.

"Oh dear, I was right then, she obviously had some health issues. Good job you didn't tackle her."

I didn't tackle her, it was Georgie girl.

She would never put up with anyone's shit – she was the daughter of a murderer, after all.

She'd tossed and turned all night and concluded that rather than faking sickness and disappearing into her room, as hard as it was likely to be, she was going to watch and observe Cohan as her dad had suggested with Veronica Edge, even though she was anxious to the point of throwing up.

How he was going to play it?

There was a tiny part of her that wanted him to announce they'd been lovers in Spain, then it would all be out on the open and he'd have no hold over her, but that urge lasted only a second. If he did that, she'd have to face her mother and father's disappointment, and that would be unbearable. And then there was Matthew, he'd be absolutely devastated.

Funny how her mum and dad's disapproval came before her fiancé's – why was that?

The minutes ticked by as she sat in the lounge waiting for the man himself to arrive, she glanced across at Danielle who was sitting on the sofa flicking through a copy of the latest celebrity magazine. No doubt she'd be imagining herself as one of the famous floozies wearing half a dress with their hair extensions strategically positioned around their shoulders for a glossy, *look at my life which you can never have,* photo.

Danielle looked stunning in a black mohair jumper and short black and white checked skirt. She must have spent ages straightening her blonde hair as it looked like she'd just stepped out of a salon. Her make-up was a bit overpowering for the daytime, but that was Danielle. She thought she was some sort of super-star and had to have a full face of slap on all the time.

Her expensively manicured nail extensions were coloured burgundy. All for what, though? No doubt she was having great sex with him, Laura could vouch for that, Cohan had shown her stuff she'd never do with Matthew. But if Danielle knew the truth about Cohan Laity, she'd run a mile.

Matthew was flicking through the sport in the Sunday paper. He'd done so well with his surgery and she felt a warm glow inside as she glanced at her engagement ring. If only Cohan would disappear, then they could concentrate on their future.

"Another beer, Matthew?" her dad asked.

"Cheers," Matthew nodded handing him his glass.

"Don't be giving him too many, Ian," her mother warned, "he has had surgery."

"Beer won't do him any harm," her dad dismissed raising an eyebrow, "it's all that wine in France he'll have to watch."

Matthew smiled with affection at her mum and dad. He told her often enough how much he liked her parents. His mum had been living in France for five years with Brian, a younger chap she'd left his dad for. Understandably, Matthew wasn't that keen on his mother's husband, but he was fond of his mother even though he struggled with her for leaving his dad. They'd both visited her together a couple of times but not for long, Matthew would only stay a few days before he was itching to be back.

Right now, she was pleased he was going to visit her for a few days. He was easily getting over the physical aspects of his surgery, he was young and strong, but he did need some emotional support and currently she wasn't in the best place to offer that. She was too busy trying to circumvent Cohan's next move.

The doorbell rang, piercing her ear and giving her a start. It was almost as if the decibels had increased now he'd got closer to her. Danielle jumped up and brushed the creases out of her skirt so she looked perfect for him. She rushed to the front door to let him in.

Laura's heart felt as if it was coming up through her chest and into her throat. Any minute now she'd be face-to-face with him.

Please don't say anything about Spain.

The sitting room door opened at the same time her mum came out of the kitchen minus her apron, which she must have discreetly tucked away in a drawer.

And there her nemesis stood, tainting their cosy family lounge.

He was clutching a bottle of red and a small bouquet of flowers, wearing a casual jumper and trousers that had designer written all over them. His eyes flicked to hers, only for a second though. It was so quick, nobody else would have seen it. The fake smile that showed off his teeth, followed.

"Hello," he said cheerily, and handed the flowers to her mum. "These are for you, Mrs Foley, thank you so much for kindly inviting me."

"Oh, please, it's Ann, and you really shouldn't have."

"It's the least I can do. I'm looking forward to a roast. Danielle tells me your Sunday lunches are legendary."

Jesus, her mother's *you wait and see* expression said it all. Her dad reached out his hand and Cohan shook it and offered him the bottle of wine he'd brought. The Wolf Blass Shiraz was a particular favourite of Cohan's. They'd shared a bottle in Spain with a delicious lunch he'd cooked at his apartment and he'd told her how much he loved it. After lunch, he'd led her from the dining room to the sofa, and gently undressed her, kissing and caressing every part of her, and the anticipation was incredibly arousing. He'd encouraged her to straddle him while he sat on the settee. The whole experience was intense and fulfilling. Afterwards, he'd grabbed a blanket and they'd slept entwined on the sofa, and taken a shower together before going out for the evening.

He's brought that wine on purpose.

Bastard.

"I wasn't sure what meat, *Ann*," he emphasised her mum's name acknowledging the permission he'd been given to use it, "was cooking, so I've gone for red. You don't have to use it for this meal though. You can save it if, you want to, Mr Foley."

"Not at all," her dad smiled, examining the label, "we'll enjoy this. We're having beef, so it's perfect. And I'm happy with Ian."

"Great, Ian it is, then," Cohan smiled.

Danielle was clinging onto his arm, "You've met my sister Laura briefly, haven't you, although she wasn't that well at the time if I remember rightly."

"That's right," he smiled as if recalling how she'd ran to the bathroom when he turned up at her twenty-first. Nobody would have any idea he'd met her since that night outside her work place.

She nodded to him. Only a slight tilt of her head to acknowledge him, no way was she going to raise a smile or extend a hand to him.

"And this is her fiancé Matthew who you met that night also. Cohan reached out his hand and Matthew took it.

"Hello again. Danielle tells me you've had surgery recently, how are you doing?"

"I'm good, thank you. I'm heading for France tomorrow so I must be on the mend."

"Lucky you, I love France, I spent some time there myself researching one of my books. What part are you going to?"

"Bordeaux."

"Oh yes, I know it well. There's a fabulous vineyard there, well there are a few," he smiled, "but Saint-Emilion is my favourite."

"Yes, I've been there before, it is a great place. My mother's lived over there a while so I'm fortunate when I go over, she takes me to the best places."

Her dad interrupted. "What can I get you to drink, Cohan?"

Cohan moved his gaze from Matthew to her dad, making a point of clocking their beers, "A beer would be nice, whatever you're both having is fine with me."

"Have a seat then and I'll fetch you one. Is Boddington's okay?"

"Fine thanks, Ian."

Ian?

For God's sake.

He sat down on the sofa and Danielle hoisted herself next to him with a gleeful expression as if to say, he's all mine. As if anyone would want him . . . he made her skin crawl.

Laura headed for the kitchen, anything to not be in the same room as him. How she was going to eat anything, she didn't know. Being near him was the worst nightmare imaginable. She had to suppress the urge to scream out loud to tell everyone what was really going on.

"Can I help with anything, Mum?"

"You're alright, love, I can manage if you want to stay and chat with the others."

"No, I'm not bothered. Dad's doing enough chatting for all of us."

"Oh he will be. I think he's quite impressed with this chap. He seems nice, don't you think?"

"I'm not sure," she kept her voice low, "he seems a bit old for her, if you ask me."

"Only the same age difference as your dad and I."

She shrugged, "I wouldn't get too attached to him if I was you. You know Danielle, he'll be history before you know it."

"I don't think so," her mum said, opening the oven door to check on the meat, "I've seen a real change in her since she met him. I have a feeling she could go all the way with this one."

Please don't say that, Mum.

She'd endured lunch by making sure Danielle and Cohan were at the opposite end of the table to her. There had to be a degree of interaction between everyone, but Teddy was a great distraction next to her. He loved being the centre of attention, so she concentrated on him, shamelessly encouraging him to show off, which meant Mum having to gently reprimand him several times. Laura wasn't bothered. Anything so she didn't have to pay Cohan any attention.

Cohan kept them all entertained about his travels in his usual charming way, but Laura barely looked at him, purposely keeping her eyes averted. Mum and Dad were their customary selves, providing a meal fit for any top-class restaurant, and Matthew listened patiently to everyone, not really joining in much. And Danielle was Danielle, pouting, fluttering her eyelash extensions, and flicking her hair around, gazing at Cohan as if all her Christmases had come at once.

Fortunately, Matthew flagged after he'd eaten lunch which could have been more the effect of the beer and wine rather than his surgery, but Laura didn't care. It gave her the opportunity to get away and take him home. She'd successfully managed not say a single word to Cohan, confident nobody spotted anything. But in the car on the way back to his flat, Matthew surprised her, "You don't like Cohan, do you?"

"What makes you think that?" she asked, concentrating on the road ahead.

"I could tell. You hardly said a word to him, in fact, you didn't."

"Didn't I?" she needed to cover herself, "to be honest, I'm not struck on him. I think he's a bit full of himself."

"Full of himself? He seems okay to me. It sounds as if he's done well from his writing."

"I'm not saying he hasn't, but he's been left some money by a relative so if his books aren't a success, it doesn't matter that much. He's not going to starve."

"I never heard him say that. I thought he made plenty from his writing?"

Bloody hell, he didn't say it. She knew that from him telling her in Spain. "Danielle told me. Don't say anything though as it might not be common knowledge."

"I won't say anything, he'll probably tell us the next time we see him anyway. He seems an open enough bloke to me."

"Next time we see him? I doubt there'll be a next time. You know what she's like, she'll have another bloke by next weekend."

"Nah, she won't, she's mad for him, anyone could see that."

"Do you reckon?" Laura replied nonchalantly, her insides churning, "Even if she is though, it doesn't mean he feels the same way about her. She's not the sharpest tool in the box."

"Meow, meow," Matthew made a claw hand, "I bet you he does feel the same about her. He was really touchy feely, as if he couldn't keep his hands off her."

"I never saw that," she said.

"You were in the kitchen. Didn't you see him reach and kiss her hand at the table after lunch?"

"No."

She had and wanted to scream . . . you bloody fraud.

"I'm telling you," Matthew continued smugly as if he had inside information, "they'll end up together, I bet you."

God, not Matthew as well as Mum.

If only they really knew.

Chapter 15

LAURA

They'd called into the Barley Mow pub; Ed had almost begged her to go for a drink with him after work. It meant missing her palates class, but right now supporting him was more important. He was a good boss and she was fearful he could end up losing his job if he didn't pull himself together.

She took a large a gulp of her red wine even though she didn't need Dutch courage to tackle Ed, she was well able to do that, the alcohol was more to calm her frayed nerves. Since Cohan Laity had come on the scene, she was constantly twitchy and looking over her shoulder, she ached with tension and seemed to have a permanent pressure headache. But right now, she needed to push Cohan to the back of her mind. She looked directly into Ed's sad eyes and spoke firmly, "You need to get some help, Ed. You can't carry on like this, or you'll end up losing more than you already have."

"I am trying," he grimaced, "it's been a nightmare since Emma left. She might as well live abroad than where she is, I hardly see Ben now."

"I'm not saying it isn't hard, but you've got to get a grip. It's not going to do you any good if you lose your job. What then? Where will the money come from to go and visit Ben, or to do nice stuff with him when you have him in the school holidays?"

He scratched his forehead, "I know you're right, I'm just pissed off all the time and the evenings seem bloody endless. I see them both in every room of the house, Emma in the kitchen cooking dinner, Ben in front of the TV, I just don't know how the hell it's got to this. I could seriously kill that fucking moron she's gone off with."

"Well, that wouldn't do much good. A prison sentence and coming out when Ben's eighteen would be a bit of a waste."

"Yeah, but who says anything about getting caught," he replied cynically, taking a sip of his pint.

"What, you think the answer is to murder someone?" She widened her eyes, "Not sure that's a good approach for a senior manager working at the Home Office."

"Who cares? If you hate someone that much and you don't want them to exist anymore, then yeah, it crosses my mind daily."

"But even if he was out of the way, that doesn't mean Emma would come back to you."

"I'm not saying she would, but there's a part of me that wants him gone. Get rid totally, because of what he's done to my family."

He looked uncomfortable. Maybe he thought it was shock registering on her face, but it wasn't that, it was more . . . empathy. Yes, empathy was the right word. She recalled someone in class at college answering the teacher when she'd asked the difference between sympathy and empathy. One of the students had said, *'If someone stood in a puddle of cold water, you'd be sympathetic knowing how uncomfortable they'd be, but to be empathetic, you'd be in the puddle with them.'* The teacher had laughed and remarked it was a simple, but good example.

Well, right now, she most definitely was in the puddle with Ed in terms of wishing someone dead. Did that make her evil? Maybe there was something genetic inside her making her feel as she did, her father had killed after all.

Ed carried on, "You're much younger than me and I'm sure you don't have any evil thoughts like I have, and I hope you never do. I've lost my way a bit, and the drink isn't helping. This time last year, I was a family man, happy, in love with my wife and had a great kid. Life was good, but Richard Bastard Thomas has taken all that away from me. That's why I want rid of him."

The loud crash of a glass breaking made her visibly jump, and she turned her head automatically towards the bar. Those closest cheered as if a barmaid smashing a glass was to be applauded. A sliver of ice slid down her spine, and her stomach plummeted yet again. Perched on one of the high stools in the corner of the bar, was her nightmare, Cohan Laity. He must have followed her from work. It was getting totally out of hand now; she was going to have to do something. But what? She berated herself daily for not telling the truth in the first place. If she had, he wouldn't have any hold on her. Was it too late now? An image of Matthew sprung to mind in France with his brother and mum. How could she do that to him? He'd been through the worst thing imaginable. For her to come out now and tell him she'd been unfaithful would break his heart.

"Laura." Ed touched her arm, "Are you listening?"

"Sorry," she said, focussing on him, even though she could see Cohan out of the corner of her eye with *his* eyes fixed directly on her, "what were you saying?"

"I was trying to thank you for being there for me. These last few months have been crap and the only stable thing in my life right now is you."

Should she go over and tell Cohan to do one? This couldn't continue, it was creepy and freaking her out.

"It's fine, Ed, you'd do the same for me, I'm sure."

"Course I would, but still, I reckon I'd have been sacked without you. You've covered for me with Jack and I am grateful. More than you'll ever know."

She'd have to get a taxi home, no way was she going on the tube with Cohan around. How soon before he became violent? She'd watched a programme about stalkers and their victims, and remembered a girl being shot dead in a Harvey Nichols store by an ex-boyfriend. The way Cohan was acting, that could easily happen to her. A chill ran through her and the fine hairs on her arms stood on end. She rubbed them up and down.

"So, what's the plan?" she asked, pulling back her shoulders, desperately hoping to appear normal so Cohan wouldn't see she was fazed by him, "Are you going to try and cut back on the booze?" Bit of a daft question really when he was knocking his pint back with a whisky chaser.

"I start each day with the intention of doing so," he sighed, "but by the time I'm finished at work, I'm dying for one. It blots out the pain." He took a gulp of his pint as if to make the point he needed it.

"Yeah, but does it? When I'm upset about anything, alcohol makes it worse. I get even more maudlin. Have you thought about joining an AA group?"

"I'm not a sodding alcoholic . . ."

"I'm not saying you are," she interrupted, "but they might be able to help you. I'm sure it's open to anyone drinking more than they should. Attending a class each week might help you. It's not as if you're doing anything else. It sounds to me as if you're going home each night and just sitting and drinking, at least in a group you'd be talking it through with others in a similar situation."

She could feel Cohan's eyes boring into her, willing her to look at him, but she wouldn't give him the satisfaction. "Just think about it, Ed, that's all I'm saying. I could look up some classes for you, if you want."

He shrugged, gulping down more of his pint. At least it wasn't a definite, *no*. She would research some groups and let him have the details, what he did after that was up to him. Right now, she needed to get away from Cohan. "I really should be making a move."

"So soon? Can't I tempt you to have another?"

"No, not tonight. Remember, I've got to drive home when I get to Reigate, and you should be making a move too."

"I know," he agreed, hopefully understanding *making a move* translated into he'd had enough.

"And please try Ed to get yourself back on track. You're a great bloke and a fantastic boss, don't throw all that away. I understand you're grieving; anyone would be the same, but you've got to keep going for Ben. He looks up to you."

"You're right," his expression was pained, "and I promise I'll try and do better. Anyway, before we go, how's Matthew doing, you said earlier he's in France?"

"Yes, he's visiting his mother for a few days, he's doing well, thank goodness. She's persuaded him to stay for the weekend."

"That's good to hear. He knows you're meeting with me, right?"

"Yeah, course. Why?"

"Erm . . . I don't know really," he shrugged, "I wouldn't want him to think I was coming onto you or anything while he was away."

"Don't be daft, Matthew wouldn't think that."

"No, course he wouldn't, sorry. He knows you'd never be unfaithful."

You're right, Laura wouldn't, it's Georgie girl who's the problem.

He reached for her hand, "Thanks for tonight, you're a good mate looking out for me."

She left his hand where it was, hoping Cohan was still watching. What did she care if he thought she was being unfaithful to Matthew? Maybe if he suspected she might have another bloke in tow, he'd back off.

"Can I ask you a favour?" she smiled.

"Course, anything?"

"Before you get the train, will you wait with me while I get a taxi?"

"Sure, but why, you always get the train? You're not late for something, are you?"

"No, it's not that."

"What then?"

Should she say something? Since Cohan had come to the UK, she was becoming more and more anxious. She'd turned dizzy in the shower that morning which she was certain was down to stress. It might help to offload.

"I seem to have a bloke following me around and I'm scared he gets on the train."

Ed frowned, "What, like a stalker?"

"Not really, more a man who seems to turn up everywhere I go." She glanced at her watch, "It's getting a bit late so I reckon it's best to get a taxi back to Reigate station and pick up my car. It's daft, I know, when there are still loads of people around, but he really makes me . . ." she left the sentence unfinished.

Ed's eyes were full of concern. "Do you know who he is? Is it someone you've met before?"

"No," she lied, regretting straight away mentioning it, Ed wasn't the type to let it drop. "It's just some nutcase, I'm sure," she side tracked, "I've only seen him a few times, but he unnerves me." She daren't say he was sitting just a few metres from them right now, Ed might decide to confront him.

"You need to tell the police," he said firmly, "they'll sort it. You can't have someone making you scared to go about your business."

"I know, but I could have misread the situation."

"How often have you seen him, for God's sake?"

"Only a couple of times." Best to play it down and hope he'll forget all about it after tonight. If he asked again, she'd say it had stopped.

Ed's frown deepened, "Define a couple of times; you'd hardly be worried about a bloke you've seen *a couple of times.*"

"Perhaps three or four times then, I can't remember. Anyway," she reached for her bag from the back of her chair, "maybe we ought to be making a move?"

"Yeah, okay." As Ed knocked back the last mouthful of his whisky chaser, she stood up and covertly glanced towards the bar. The stool was empty, Cohan had gone. Was he worried she'd told Ed and feared he might be challenged? He was confident she wouldn't tell Matthew, but he wouldn't know about Ed. *Good. Let's hope another bloke had unnerved him and he's cleared off.*

She was still going to take a taxi, though; he could be somewhere around the corner waiting for her.

Ed picked up her jacket and held it for her to slip her arms into. "Seriously, Laura, you need to speak to the police."

"I'll see how it goes," she dismissed, "he might just get fed up and move on."

"You hope. These weirdos get fixated, you have to be careful."

"I will, I promise," she said buttoning up her jacket.

"I mean it. I could come with you to the police with Matthew being away, if you like?"

"I'm not sure. I'm hoping it's something and nothing, and by the time Matthew gets back, he'll have disappeared."

"You've told him though, haven't you?"

"No," she screwed up her nose, "he'd only be worried over there."

"Yeah, but he'd want to know, Laura, I know I would."

She flung her bag over her shoulder. "Let's wait and see. He might just disappear as quickly as he came."

"Yeah, and then again he might not."

Ed was absolutely right. As far as she could see, Cohan Laity was going nowhere.

Chapter 16

DANIELLE

Danielle sat in the lounge and checked her phone again, still nothing from Cohan. He had said he'd text when he came in from his meal out. He was meeting with his agent and joked that a couple of hours with him and he'd be well ready for home.

She fiddled about on Facebook while Laura was watching some stupid police documentary on TV. Why she liked those, Danielle never understood, *must be due to that jailbird real father of hers.* Their dad was just as bad, he loved anything to do with police procedures and catching criminals. He was always bringing books home from the library about murders, both solved and unsolved. Dad and Laura both seemed to thrive on discussing notorious cases, they most probably could commit the perfect murder between them and get away with it.

She glanced at What'sApp again, still nothing. The lounge door opened, and Teddy came in from the youth club. Their mum and dad had dropped him off on their way to a church meeting, and one of the other dad's had brought him home.

Princess Perfect looked up from the TV, "Hi, Teddy, have you had a good time?"

"Yeah," he grinned raising his fist in glory, "we won at five-a-side football."

"What was the score?" Danielle asked.

"Five two. I nearly scored but the goalie saved it."

"Damn him," Danielle cursed, "remind me to break his legs next time I see him."

Teddy looked uncertain. He was so literal he'd think she meant it. "I'm only joking," she reassured, "don't worry. Anyway, you go and get ready for bed, I'm just going to make a coffee so I'll get you a glass of milk and a biscuit."

"Can I have coffee?"

"Not at night, you won't sleep."

"Will, I promise."

"Go on, get ready for bed, Mum'll be home shortly."

Teddy stomped out of the room as the credits were coming on signalling the end of the TV programme Laura had been watching. "Do you want a coffee?" Danielle asked.

"Not for me, but before you go, I wanted to tell you something."

"What?"

"About Cohan."

"What about Cohan?"

"He's not what you think he is."

She sighed heavily, hoping to convey she wasn't really interested in anything she had to say. Cohan had tentatively mentioned he felt Laura had seemed a bit strange around him the day he came for lunch. It would be jealousy . . . there was nothing else it could be.

"Why is he, *not what I think he is?*"

Laura hesitated, as if she wasn't sure how much to say. "He made me feel uncomfortable the day he came for lunch. He kept staring at me. I don't think you should trust him."

"Staring at you? In your dreams." Danielle pulled the most disapproving face she could, "You aren't his type at all."

"How do you know his type, you hardly know him," Laura snapped.

"I know enough and you're lying. He said you didn't like him."

"He's right, I don't. You could do much better."

"Who the hell do you think you are?" Danielle's voice became louder, "What business is it of yours? Why don't you stick to your cosy life with Matthew and stay out of mine?"

She reached for her phone off the coffee table and put it in her jeans pocket. She needed to get away from Princess Perfect's accusations, she was spoiling her happiness with Cohan. As if he'd be remotely interested in her. He'd told her often enough *she* was the most attractive out of the two of them.

Bitch.

In the kitchen she filled the kettle with water and took some milk out of the fridge to busy herself. Laura followed her in. "Honestly, I'm not trying to cause trouble, I'm looking out for you. I reckon he's a problem and you'd be better off without him."

"Have you heard yourself?" she said, "who do you think you are, criticising my boyfriend? I don't say anything about your choice of dull predicable Matthew."

"Look, I'm sorry if I've upset you," Laura scrunched up her face as if she regretted saying anything, "I'm only trying in my own way to warn you not to get too serious when you don't really know much about him."

"And I'm telling you I'm not interested in anything you've got to say, so keep out of my business. You're just jealous; he told me you could barely look at him when he came for lunch. Why? He hasn't done anything to you. The way I see it, he's been nothing but nice to all our family. So what is it? You getting your nose pushed out, is that it?"

"Don't be daft," Laura dismissed, "I don't trust him, that's all."

"Well tough, because I do. End of."

She felt her phone vibrate in her pocket and reached for it. There was a text from Cohan.

Sorry I'm late, just having a shower and I'll ring you.

She breathed a sigh of relief, the message calmed her. Thank God she had him. Princess Perfect was trying to cause trouble. *Well, she could get knotted.*

Teddy appeared in the doorway and made his way towards the stool at the breakfast bar. He hoisted himself up and reached for his glass of milk. "Are all these biscuits for me?"

"Yeah," Danielle said, "but eat them quickly or I'll get told off for giving you too many."

They heard the front door open, "Is it Mum and Dad?" Teddy asked grabbing a couple of the biscuits and shoving them in his dressing gown pocket.

"It will be."

The kitchen door opened and their mum came in, "Alright," she smiled at them, "has the kettle just boiled, love?"

"Yeah, do you want a coffee?" Danielle asked.

"I'd love one, and make your dad one too, would you. He's putting the car in the garage." She turned to Teddy, "How was youth club?"

"We won at football."

"Did you, sweetheart?" she ruffled his hair, "well done."

"I'm just on my way up," Laura said, "I've got an early start in the morning."

Danielle envied Laura being able to work flexitime, she'd love to be able to go into work either really early, or mid-morning and stay later, but there wasn't an opportunity at the advertising office. Her hours were boring nine to five.

She busied herself making the coffee's so she didn't have to say anything more to Laura, she was furious with her for slagging Cohan off. *Bet she's miffed I haven't given any credence to her jealous remarks.*

Her mum replied to Laura, "I'll be up first thing with you, love." And she would. Their mother would never let anyone leave the house without breakfast inside them and a hearty packed lunch.

Laura moved towards Teddy and gave him a hug, which he loved. He thrived on affection. She rarely hugged Teddy, she couldn't bear him slobbering anywhere near her.

"Night, night, sleep tight," Laura said to him, "make sure the bed bugs don't bite," she hugged her mum, "see you in the morning."

As she walked past, she nodded to her, "See you tomorrow."

Danielle gave a bright smile back so their mum didn't cotton on anything had gone on between them. "See ya."

Spiteful little madam trying to cause trouble.

She was going to tell Cohan what she said about him.

As if he'd fancy her.

In the privacy of her room, Danielle waited for Cohan to call. She picked up straight away when her phone rang, "Hi, gorgeous, sorry I couldn't see you tonight, I missed you."

"That's alright," she glowed from the inside out that he'd missed her, "you've got to work. How did your dinner go?"

"Okay. My agent and I have been discussing plots and sub plots. He wants me to do a series of books, which I wasn't keen on initially, but I'm coming around to the idea."

She prayed the plot was set in the UK. He'd already mentioned in passing that he was considering doing some research once he'd decided where. A knot gripped her insides, she couldn't bear him leaving.

"Did you decide where you are going to set the stories?"

"No, not really. We both threw a few ideas into the mix, I can make that decision later. Which reminds me, I want to go to Chatsworth House in Derbyshire, how are you fixed with your dad's overnight rule," he paused, "can you escape and come with me?"

"I'm sure I can," her heart leapt, "don't worry about my dad, I'll sort something, Mum's a great ally. When are you thinking of going?"

"This weekend, if you fancy it. I know a fabulous little hotel and I thought we could go on Saturday and have a mooch around, enjoy dinner in the hotel and visit Chatsworth the following day. How does that sound?"

"Sounds perfect to me, thank you."

"No need to thank me, I want you to come. The hotel is lovely, but the bed will be cold on my own if you can't come."

He wanted her with him; she could hardly contain her happiness. Nevertheless, the little niggle was still there about Laura's spiteful remarks, even though she knew she was making it up.

"I'm looking forward to it already."

"Me too. How was your evening, did Laura stay in with you?"

"Yeah, and she'd been a real bitch tonight. She's implied that you're interested in her. Says the day you came for lunch you were watching her all the time and it made her feel uncomfortable."

"Watching her all the time?" he repeated. "I told you she was a bit weird that day. Why would I be watching her when I'm with you? You didn't feel that way, did you?"

"No, I didn't notice anything like that. I thought you were very sociable talking to everyone around the table. From what I can remember, Teddy was being a pain and she was messing with him. And then Matthew flagged so she took him home."

"Yes, I remember. Teddy looks like he can be quite a handful."

"That's an understatement."

"Does Laura know how things are between us?"

How are things, you never say anything about the two of us?

"In what way?"

"That we're together, a couple. I'm puzzled as to why she would think I'd be looking at her when I'm with you. You're beautiful, intelligent and very sexy, all any man could want. Why the hell would she think I'd be interested in her?"

That was all she needed to know. It was her he wanted to be with. She wanted to blurt out she was in love with him, but the last thing she wanted was to come across as needy and scare him off. Not when things were going so well between them.

He didn't wait for her to answer. "All I can think is she's feeling a bit vulnerable with Matthew being away and all he's been through. I'll make sure I'm careful around her, the last thing I'd want is for her getting the wrong idea about me just because I'm a friendly person Or for you to be worried in any way."

"I'm not. I wish I hadn't said anything now."

"No, I'm glad you have. She's clearly insecure. Didn't you tell me that she's from a broken family?"

"Yes, and her dad murdered her mother when she was a child."

"That's right. I would imagine that sort of thing would make anyone screwed up. She'll perhaps be better when Matthew's back, maybe. It's soon, isn't it, did he only go for five days?"

"Yeah, but he's staying for the weekend apparently."

"I see." He yawned, "Anyway, enough about those two, I think I'm about ready to hit the hay."

"With your glass of milk?" she joked. He'd told her that every night after his shower he had a glass of milk. It amused her as Teddy did the same.

"You can laugh, but I'll still be here at ninety with strong bones and all my own teeth, you'll see."

She'd love *to see* and be around with him when he was ninety, which would imply they had a future together. "We're still on for tomorrow night, aren't we?" she asked, mentally making a note to take a change of clothes to work.

"Definitely. Hey, is it tomorrow you're starting your first project?"

He remembered. He really was the best.

"Yes. I'm going to be supervised, but it'll be the first time I'm working directly with a client and planning an advertising campaign."

"Good for you. Break a leg, as they say. You can tell me all about it tomorrow."

"Will do, if there's anything to tell, that is. It's only an initial meeting to get the client's first thoughts, and then according to Juliet, the hard work begins."

"Yeah, but you're bright so you'll make a success of whatever you do, I know you will. Right, I'll say good night and look forward to seeing you tomorrow."

She was loathe to let him go, she could talk all night whereas he was always brief on the phone as if he had something else on. "Brilliant," she answered brightly, "see you then. Night night."

"Night, gorgeous." He cut the call.

Warmth spread though her whole body. It was her he wanted. He'd proven that by asking her to go away with him to Derbyshire. Laura was just a jealous cow trying to cause trouble.

As if he'd be remotely interested in her.

Chapter 17

LAURA

Laura approached the house breathless from her morning run. Exercise was normally a weekend routine which she loved, but at the moment it didn't bring her any enjoyment. Pounding the pavements and pushing herself further used to be pleasurable, but not today. Her mind was in turmoil and she couldn't switch off, no matter how hard she tried.

She stopped at the gate to allow her breathing to steady. The 1960's semi-detached house she'd lived in most of her life almost gleamed in the sunshine. The windows and paint work sparkled, and her dad's hanging baskets full of colourful pansies made the house look homely and welcoming, a far cry from the two up, two down chaotic terraced house where Georgie girl had lived.

Her mum and dad had bought the house when they'd first got married. Before he retired, Dad worked in a bank from leaving school, and in those days, managed to secure a mortgage with a low interest rate. He always said that if he hadn't been able to do that, he could never have afforded such a huge house on the outskirts of London.

She closed the wrought iron gate behind her and walked towards the front door. Matthew was coming home from France the following day, which she should have been pleased about, but it only added to her anxiety. There was part of her that wished he was staying longer because if he was out of the way, Cohan Laity had less power over her.

Her intention once she'd let herself in the house was to head upstairs for a quick shower, but her mother called, "Is that you, Laura?"

"Yep," she said, poking her head around the kitchen door, "What's up?"

Her mum was sat at the kitchen table and looked up from her iPad, "Matthew's texted me to ask where you were, says he's called you a few times. I told him you'd gone out for a run and were going straight to the hairdressers."

Laura reached on the kitchen unit for her phone she'd put on charge before she'd left. She had two missed calls from him.

"Did he say it was urgent?"

"No, nothing like that."

"Okay, I'll ring him back after my shower."

"Before you dash off, have you seen those?" Her mum's eyes moved towards the draining board to a huge bouquet of red roses, "They were delivered just after you went out."

She widened her eyes, "They're nice. Who are they for, Danielle?"

Cohan must have sent her them. Bloody creep.

"No, silly, they're for you."

"Me?" she walked towards them, doubting they could possibly be for her, until she saw in bold handwriting on the front of the tiny envelope, *Laura Foley*.

"I thought Matthew had sent them and said in the text they'd arrived, but he sent one back saying he hadn't sent any flowers. I wonder who they're from?" her mum asked eagerly.

Unease spiralled through Laura's body.

"Open the card, love," her mother urged with an expectant look on her face.

Laura took the small envelope from the spear in the middle of the bouquet. She knew who they were from, even before she opened it. She stared at the card. There was nothing written on it, only a smiley face.

Bastard.

She had to think quickly, "They're from Ed at work," she conjured up, putting the card back in the tiny envelope so her mum couldn't see it.

"Ed?" her mum frowned, "Why would he be sending flowers?"

"As a thank you. I encouraged him to join an AA meeting and found one local to him." That was partly true, but he hadn't agreed to go yet. "He's been to two meetings and feels things are really improving and moving in the right direction," she lied.

"That is good news, and how thoughtful of him sending flowers," her mum's expression became puzzled, "but roses seem a bit much as a thank you. I would have thought an assortment of carnations and freesias would be more appropriate."

"Yeah, maybe you're right," Laura agreed, hating herself for telling more lies, "Ed's pretty clueless though, he'll have just asked for some flowers and given an amount he wanted to spend. I bet the florist assumed they were for a girlfriend or something."

"You'd have thought the florist would ask though. I always think roses are really more from a loved one, like a husband or a fiancé, which reminds me, you better ring Matthew quickly, the lad will be worried sick wondering who's sent his fiancée flowers."

Laura slipped the card in her pocket. "I will do. I'll go and ring him now."

"Shall I put them in the lounge? I think the conservatory might be a bit hot for them."

"Yeah, whatever you think," Laura replied cheerfully. They could go in the bin as far as she was concerned.

Her mum scooped them up and headed towards the lounge, "Don't forget to thank Ed after you've spoken to Matthew. Roses are expensive so this little lot must have cost a pretty penny."

"Will do," she said, trying her best to smile. If only her mum hadn't told Matthew, now she was going to have to tell more lies.

She tried to call Matthew but got his answer phone. France was only an hour's time difference but maybe he'd gone to a winery and there wasn't a signal? Hopefully passing the flowers off from Ed would appease him, but for how long? And now she was going to have to ask Ed to say he'd sent them if Matthew asked him. The situation was getting worse by the day. Her head began to throb. Danielle must have told Cohan what she'd said about him staring at her over Sunday lunch, which she'd only done to try and put her off him. That's why he'd sent the flowers, they were a punishment for implying things about him, she was certain. He'd be gleefully wondering how she was going to explain them.

Laura hurried along the high street towards her hairdressers. She'd had to leave her Mini in a car park a few streets away from the salon and then walk as there was no parking any nearer. She'd been going to the same salon for the last few years every fourth Saturday and the owner, Heidi, had become more of a friend than just her hairdresser. She was running late which she hated, the arrival of the flowers had delayed her.

The air was damp and it had started to drizzle so she quickened her pace looking forward to a nice warm coffee at the salon. As she progressed along the street, she felt a familiar unease creep through her. Her instincts told her she was being followed. Just lately, it seemed Cohan Laity was loitering around every corner. Her health was starting to suffer because of him. She was losing weight which she knew without the stark reality of seeing it on the scales. The belt she was wearing, she now had to fasten three more notches in, as well as tightening her bra straps and she could ill afford to lose any weight there.

A whistle caused her to look again nervously over her shoulder, which was stupid. As if Cohan would be making a noise to attract her, he'd be more covert, hiding in a doorway, or something like that. The street was full of the usual Saturday morning bustle, shoppers weighed down by heavily laden bags, and families sat in the cafés drinking the latest fancy latte or creamy hot chocolate. Her eyes darted around the street, but she couldn't see him. That didn't convince her he wasn't there, though.

As she finally reached the salon and was about to open the door, Ruby the young apprentice barged out. Laura stood back to let her pass and held the door for her, "Where you dashing off to in a rush?"

"Oh, hi, Laura, I'm just off to get some throat sweets, I reckon I've got a cold coming on."

Laura pulled her head back, "Keep your distance then, a cold's the last thing I need."

"Me too, I've got a hen night tonight and I don't want to miss that."

"Go get your lozenges then and let's hope they help."

"Will do." She was about to walk away but stopped, "Hey, has that boyfriend of yours got a brother going spare?"

"Matthew?" Laura frowned, "why do you ask that?"

"He rang earlier. Oh God," she put her hand over her mouth, "I shouldn't have said anything. I've put my foot in it now."

"Why, what did he want?"

"Err . . ." she pulled a face, "I'd rather not say."

"Tell me. You've half said it anyway."

"He wanted to know when your next appointments were, said he was planning a surprise trip for you one weekend."

Matthew planning a weekend away . . . that was most unlikely. Matthew proposing was the only time she'd ever known him to be spontaneous. He ran everything by her, even at Christmas and birthdays, she didn't get a surprise present. He was very generous but liked her to choose what she wanted.

Her skin prickled and once again her heart was racing, there was no way Matthew would ring the salon. There was only one person it could be. "Really," she played along, "how exciting, a trip away. Don't worry, I won't say anything. Did you give him the times I would be coming in?"

"Yes. I told him you come every fourth Saturday but he said he knew that, just wasn't sure when you were next in."

"You told him today, did you?"

"Yes. Was that all right?"

She felt the colour drain from her face, "Course," she reassured, "I told him earlier in the week I was at the salon this morning, typical bloke, he never listens."

The unease that had crept in was now spreading through her whole body. *Was he watching her right now?*

"Anyway," Ruby said, "grab a coffee from the machine and I'll be back to wash your hair in a second. I'm only popping next door to the newsagents."

Coffee? She couldn't stomach coffee, she needed to get out of there.

She walked into the salon and spotted Heidi spraying a customer's hair. Heidi raised her hand to indicate five minutes and she'd be with her.

Laura reached in her bag for her phone, pretending she'd just received a message and made her way towards Heidi. "I'm really sorry, I'm going to have to go. A bit of an emergency, I'm afraid."

"Oh dear," Heidi paused, waiting for an explanation.

"Nothing serious," Laura shook her head, "but I'm going to have to go home. I'll ring you later and explain." She wouldn't ring, she'd just text an excuse once she'd thought of one.

"Okay, no probs. You sort whatever you have to. Take care driving home."

"I will," she said, dashing out of the salon.

She made her way from the high street as quickly as her legs would take her towards the car park she'd left her Mini in. She wrapped her jacket around her tightly, as if it would protect her. Her eyes flicked from one side of the road to the other, clocking every man she saw, quickly eliminating they weren't Cohan. But she was certain he was out there, watching.

She turned into the small one-way street as it was a quicker route to her car, but realised her mistake when she sensed before she saw it, a car coming from behind and slowly moving alongside her. The car's electric window came down.

Cohan leaned out with a surprised expression on his face, as if he'd naturally stumbled across her. "Hi, Laura, can I give you a lift?"

"Get lost," she spat, and continued walking. She was minutes away from her car.

"That's not nice, I've missed you."

He continued crawling alongside her. She quickened her pace. "I'm warning you, I'm going to the police if this carries on."

Should she turn back to the salon, she'd be safe there? But she was almost at her car, if she could just get to it, she could drive straight home and get far away from him.

"And what are you going to tell the police, eh? That we met in Spain and you were an insatiable slut?"

"I'll tell them everything, so I can get rid of you, you nutcase."

"Now, now, there's no need to be so hostile. Do you want to grab a coffee somewhere so we can talk?"

She stopped walking. Rage overcame her fear. She turned towards the car, her heart hammering so much, she could hear it in her ears.

"What a bloody saddo you are," she spat, "following a woman around that has no interest in you whatsoever. When are you going to get it into that thick skull of yours, I have no intention of ever being with you, end of? So, why don't you do us all a favour and clear off."

"I can't do that. What about your dear sister, she'd be devastated?"

"Not so much as when I tell her why you're really here."

"But you're not going to do that are you? You daren't," he smirked.

Oh, how she wished she could knock that supercilious look off his face. "You just watch me," she snarled.

"I wish you would, I really do. Then, once it's all out in the open, we can be together, just you and me, Laura."

She tapped her forehead with her index finger, "You've got a tile off, we'll never be together. Now I'm warning you, get lost before I call the police."

"Okay," he gave an exaggerated nod of his head, "I can see you're not going to talk nicely. I'll get off, but I'll be seeing you around, no doubt at your mother's. Say hi to Matthew for me, won't you."

"Piss off!"

"Tut, tut, tut," the window closed and he pulled away.

Her legs were shaking so much, she could barely walk. He'd gone in the direction of the car park where she'd parked her car so she didn't want to go that way. She cut down an alley way to an adjacent street, and almost fell into a shabby coffee shop on the corner. Scared he might ditch the car and come and find her, she made her way to a table at the back where she couldn't be seen from the window. Sweat was beginning to trickle down her back. She tried to gather herself by taking some deep breaths in and out to slow down her thumping heart.

The waitress hovered and took her order for a latte she didn't really want.

How the hell had he found out which hairdresser she used? She could only assume Danielle told him. Surely though, she'd be suspicious of her boyfriend asking about her sister's hairdresser? But then again, it was Cohan Laity. He'd charm it out of her, probably complimenting her on her hairstyle and asking if she had it done locally or in the city. Danielle would be so eager to please, she wouldn't notice if he slipped a question in about whether they used the same salon. She would have said no, and most probably inadvertently told him which salon she did use.

Laura inwardly sighed. If Matthew started asking random questions about women's hair salons, she'd think it odd, but Danielle was superficial so wouldn't click on. She'd just be thrilled he'd complimented her on her hairstyle.

The waitress returned with her coffee despite it being the last thing she needed when her blood pressure must be sky high. *What the hell was she going to do?*

She didn't normally take sugar, but she stirred in two cubes from the bowl on the table to give herself some energy. Perhaps it was time to involve the police? They might warn Cohan she was going to press charges if he didn't keep away. As Ed had said, there were laws about stalking. Matthew needn't know, the police had a duty to work confidentially. She didn't have to tell them she'd had an affair with him in Spain, either. She could make out it had all started once she'd been introduced to him by her sister. Okay it was a lie, but did it matter? Georgie girl was a good liar, she could pull it off.

She took a mouthful of the sweet coffee. Never had she hated anyone so much as she did him. If only her real dad was alive, he'd protect Georgie girl, she was absolutely certain of that. Cohan Laity wouldn't be smiling then. He'd be where he deserved to be – in the ground pushing up daisies.

Now there's a thought.

Chapter 18

LAURA

Laura was at the filing cabinet cursing the lateness of Ed again. He knew the importance of today, where on earth was he? The pep talk she'd given him had scarcely made a difference. For a couple of days he seemed to improve, especially getting into work on time, and he did appear to be much brighter, but his son's birthday had thrown him into turmoil as he wasn't able to visit him. Seemingly his ex-wife and her new partner had taken him to Disneyland, Paris.

She'd patiently listened to him rant and rave about that, then becoming more morose about the empty house again, and finally he'd admitted he wasn't sleeping. She'd tentatively suggested a trip to his GP to get some anti-depressants and possibly sleeping pills, and he'd made the right noises to let her think he was considering it, but she wasn't convinced he would go.

Jack, their boss, came into the main office and approached her with a thunderous scowl on his face. He nodded toward Ed's vacant office. "No sign of him yet?" he asked raising an eyebrow.

"Er . . . no, I'm sure he won't be long though."

"I'm glad you're sure, Laura, because I'm not." He glanced at his watch, "Can you try his mobile again and while you're doing that, I'll go and see if I can get Lynda to cover for him this morning. I need someone to represent *his* department, the meeting's in less than an hour."

"Will do," she replied, and tried to inject a level of optimism in her voice, "he'll probably walk through the door any minute now."

Jack's head shake was a confident prediction he wouldn't. "Let me know when you've located him, would you?"

"Sure," she smiled as if she was going to do just that, while deep down she knew Ed had gone AWOL despite knowing only too well what today was all about. The Government minister was expecting presentations from each department, so Ed knew it was an important day for Jack. All Heads of Departments knew, they'd been told categorically they needed to be there.

She pressed Ed's number on her phone again. Frustration kicked in while she waited for the recorded message to end. "Ed, where the hell are you?" she hissed, "the meeting's in less than an hour. Jack's been in three times already this morning, you've to get here ASAP." She considered for a second he might have been in an accident, so softened her voice, "Can you at least call me back, I'm worried about you."

She walked into Ed's office and spotted the untouched letters she'd left there on the previous Friday for him to sign so she could mail them. He'd disappeared mid-afternoon and she hadn't been able to trace him. Even if she sent them out first class now, they were much later than they should be. The letters had to give adequate time for people to give notice to their employers if they'd been called in for an interview, and likewise if their application to extend their visa had been turned down, they had to be given sufficient notice about making preparations to leave the country. There was a stringent algorithm they had to adhere to and they were unlikely to be within it if they didn't go off today. They weren't the standard template letters which had an electronic signature either, these had to be read by Ed and checked against each individual file, even though she'd already done that. Six months ago, Ed would have stayed late if necessary, verified them and added his signature.

The unsigned letters irritated her and prompted an overwhelming urge to forge Ed's signature. She knew there weren't any errors in them as she'd filled in the personal details of the recipients and checked the outcomes against each applicant's file, just as Ed had taught her to do. Who would know? He was hardly likely to sack her; he'd be grateful she'd saved his bacon . . . again.

She eased herself into the thick leather chair at his desk. Her dad's voice echoed in her head about the importance of having a strong work ethic. How when she first started work after college he gave her the talk about integrity, and *doing the right thing when nobody was looking.* Maybe she shouldn't sign them? It wouldn't be her fault if the letters arrived late. But it would make things easier if she just got them done. One less black mark against Ed, who, after today, would most likely be looking at a severe reprimand from Jack, supported by HR. The one thing she'd tried so hard to avoid.

She selected a random file from the cabinet to look closely at a letter with Ed's signature on it and reached for a pen. Examining the lines and loops carefully, she stared to scribble on a piece of paper until she was able to do it accurately. Once she was satisfied that it was a true likeness, she quickly forged his signature on each of the letters before taking them across to her own desk. It was unnecessary to change desks but as the admin part was her job, she did it away from Ed's office.

Once they were all complete and in envelopes, she put them in the basket ready to be collected and taken to the post-room. She blew out a breath and eased herself back into her chair. Had she really forged Ed's signature? No, obviously *she* hadn't. It was Georgie girl, *she'd* done it.

Thirty minutes later, Jack appeared at her desk looking slightly dishevelled. "Anything?" he snapped.

She shook her head. "I'm sorry, no. I'm starting to worry about him to be honest."

"Well don't," Jack spat, "we've got bigger things to worry about than him. Have you got access to his presentation?"

"Yes."

Of course she had, she'd prepared it and put it on PowerPoint. Ed's head wasn't in the right place to plan any sort of presentation. She'd extracted all the necessary figures and put them onto each slide with salient points about how they'd improved on last year's data, and their further trajectories. It was all there ready . . . just a pity Ed wasn't.

"I've asked Lynda if she'll stand in for Ed," Jack continued, "she's full of cold and not at her best, but she's agreed to do it."

Bloody Lynda. Pity she hadn't been off sick, that way she might have been given an opportunity to do the presentation. There wouldn't have been anyone else, there was no way the others in the team would have the balls to stand up in front of anyone. And while she was only a junior member of staff as opposed to Ed and Lynda, she could easily deliver the presentation given half a chance. And she'd do it well. She gave Jack a relieved smile, "Oh, that's great. Does she need any help at all, or is she happy to wing it?"

"Wing it?" he scowled, "I hope you're joking. You don't *wing it* with a minister."

"Sorry, I didn't mean that quite as it sounded. I just meant does she want me to go over anything with her?"

She knew Lynda, competent as she was at her job, she'd be bricking herself doing any sort of public speaking.

"I've no idea," he scratched his head, "maybe go and ask her, we can't afford to mess this up."

"Okay, I'll go now. Don't worry, Lynda won't let you down, she's really competent."

"Let's hope you're right," he sighed, "go and help her any way you can. And as soon as Ed turns up, tell him I want to see him." As he started to walk away, he threw in, "Do not let him leave without seeing me today."

"Will do."

Poor Ed, by the look of Jack's face, he'd be lucky to hang onto his job.

She headed for the coffee machine and pressed for a latte, she knew Lynda was partial to a frothy coffee and a biscuit or three, but she didn't have any of those. While she waited, she glanced at Lynda sitting at her desk in the corner, it was evident she wasn't well at all from the pile of tissues in front of her. She was blowing her nose, and her eyes looked red and puffy.

Laura approached Lynda's desk clutching the paper cup, and injected some sympathy into her voice, "Jack asked me to come over and see if you needed any help. You poor thing, you look awful. Here, I've brought you a coffee." She placed the hot coffee on the desk blotter.

"Bless you, Laura, you're a life saver, it's not one of my best days, that's for sure. I could kill Ed for this, have you heard from him yet?"

She shook her head, "Afraid not. I'm getting a bit worried about him. I've left messages, but he hasn't responded."

"Probably hung over and sleeping it off somewhere."

So Lynda had an idea how Ed was drinking. She didn't respond to her comment about him, she wasn't sure how many knew Ed was a friend out of work, and on occasions joined Matthew and her for a drink. She'd been surprised he'd actually attended her twenty-first party, she wouldn't have invited him, but Matthew had.

"Anyway, have you had chance to look at the presentation?" she asked Lynda.

"Yes, it's excellent, at least Ed's done a good job there. I'm just going to have to read from it, parrot fashion. And he's put some bullet points at the bottom of each slide to refer to which will be helpful."

"That's good then," Laura smiled. *Thanks for that, Lynda, but Ed didn't do a good job, I did.* And, the prompts were for Ed. Normally he wouldn't have needed anything like that, but since his wife had left him, she wasn't confident about his ability.

Lynda blew her nose, "Jack's going to explain I'm standing in for Ed, that way I hope I'm not questioned too much," she tossed the tissue in the bin, "I hate anything like this, and I can't even stop my nose from running." She started to cough, "I actually feel quite sick, and can't really be bothered with this today of all days."

"No, I'm sure you can't," Laura sympathised, "you shouldn't actually be here. Have you taken anything?"

"Yeah, stacks, but I still feel crap. I'm going to have to apply a bit more make-up before I go to the boardroom, anything to hide my bright red nose." She reached down at the side of her chair and started rummaging in her handbag.

The opportunity was too good to miss. In fact, it didn't even take any thinking about, at least not on Laura's part. A second later and the coffee cup went over hard and fast, spilling in a wave over the blotter and over the edge of the desk.

"Shit!" Lynda squealed, jumping up from the chair as the latte soaked down the front of her cream blouse and onto her taupe-coloured skirt.

Bingo!

"Oh God, are you alright?" Laura reached for the coffee cup and stood it up, while Lynda pulled her blouse away from her chest and grabbed a tissue from the box. "What the hell happened?" Lynda cried out.

"I think you caught the blotter as you reached for your bag."

Lynda rubbed frantically at her blouse but was only making the stain worse."

"It hasn't scalded you, has it?" Laura asked.

"No, thank God, the latte's from the machine are never that hot," she glanced down at herself, "what a bloody mess. I can't do a presentation looking like this." She shook her head, "I don't know what the hell to do now, they're expecting me in ten minutes."

"Shall we go to the ladies' and take your blouse off? I could try rinsing it and putting it under the dryer."

"There isn't enough time for that," Lynda dismissed, "I don't want to do the wretched presentation anyway, maybe this is a sign."

"I'd lend you my top but I think it might be a bit tight."

"Bit tight? You're too kind, the last time I wore a top like that, I was about fifteen. It'd never fit me."

"What are you going to do, then?" she asked expectantly.

Lynda scowled, "I really don't know," and just as she said that, her face changed, as if she'd had a light-bulb moment, "it's a big ask, I know, but how would you feel about doing the presentation?"

Clever Georgie girl.

Laura had to hold back the grin. "Me?" Her voice didn't sound like hers; it was purposely much higher.

"I'm sorry to have to ask, but I'm desperate."

"You must be to be asking me." Laura's brows creased, "I've never delivered a presentation before. What if I'm asked questions about the department, I'm not privy to management discussions?"

"Jack would answer those and steer them away from you. In fact, he'd introduce you just the same as he would have done me. He's was going to tell them I'm stepping in for Ed as he's currently in A&E, so I'm sure he'd say that for you."

Laura portrayed an anxious face, but inwardly her pulse was thumping, *whoopee*. "Have I any time to think about it?" she asked cautiously.

"Not really. Please Laura," Lynda pleaded, "I'll make sure you are compensated in some way, I promise. You're a confident young woman, I think you can do it. And remember, it'll put you in good stead for promotion in the future. It's great experience as only senior staff ever get to engage with the minister."

"Okay," she nodded feebly, "if you're sure and Jack'll be okay about it."

"I am, absolutely, you leave him to me. I'll go and find him right now and tell him I'm going to have to go home. My head's not in the right place at all. You do a quick run through of the presentation and then follow me down to the boardroom. Is that okay?" Laura nodded keeping the uneasy expression on her face. "And don't look so worried, Jack will be fine, I promise you. We've had discussions about you before and all think you show great promise. The figures have all been verified haven't they?" They had, she'd seen to it. All figures by each department had to be confirmed centrally before a minister received them.

"Yes, everything's done."

"Okay." Lynda stood up, "Don't worry about anything, just give it your best shot."

Laura gave a half-hearted smile and quickly made her way to the ladies. She didn't need to run through the presentation, she knew it backwards. The most important thing now was looking the part.

Inside the ladies' toilet, she looked at herself in the huge vanity mirror. Georgie girl stared back with a smug look on her face, *Go girl.* She reached in her handbag for her bronzer compact, quickly applying some to her face, and rubbed some pink Vaseline to her lips. She looked smart enough in her navy pin stripe jacket, and despite knowing the presentation off-by-heart, butterflies whirled around her tummy. But she knew adrenaline would see her through. All she needed to do was deliver a slick presentation.

This was her opportunity to shine.

Chapter 19

DANIELLE

"Morning, Danielle," Juliet floated past the main office in the latest Christian Dior pale blue suit. "You okay?" she asked pausing at the door. There had been a real shift in how Danielle was perceived at the office since dating Cohan. She wondered if that was the reason she'd been given the opportunity to work with a client, albeit a relatively unknown one.

Danielle smiled back, "Morning. I'm fine thank you." Best to ask how she was, she was still her boss, after all, even though she couldn't stand her, "You?"

"Yes, busy, you know how it is, no rest for the wicked. But that's good, bills to pay etcetera." With that she was gone, no doubt harassing some other member of staff now she wasn't on her case quite so much.

Danielle switched her computer on and waited for it to boot up. Juliet had done the press releases about Cohan's new book, and was in the process of facilitating a *meet the author* session in Soho. Cohan had explained the public pay a specific fee for the evening. Those attending are given nibbles and an alcoholic beverage when they first arrived, and, after about forty minutes, he comes in and takes a seat with the facilitator, and she asks him about his writing career. He'd joked that he liked to see the questions beforehand to try and think up some witty anecdotes. Seemingly, the audience are given an opportunity to participate in a question and answer session, and the evening culminates in a book signing. She was hoping

Cohan would ask her to come and had dropped several hints she would like to, but as yet, he hadn't invited her. If he did, she had her eye on a vivid blue dress from Karen Millen which enhanced the colour of her eyes. She'd tried it on and really liked it, but the only thing stopping her buying it was a recent letter from the bank about her overdraft which was escalating. No surprises there, she was spending more lately on clothes and accessories because Cohan Laity was not your average boyfriend; he was somebody, so as his girlfriend, she needed to look good at all times. She just wished he would take her to some swanky places such as the Shard for drinks, dinner at the Ivy, or afternoon tea at the Ritz, where she could be seen, instead of the second-rate wine bars and pubs he seemed to favour. The nights in his flat were cosy, but there was more to life than great sex.

The positives at work made a difference though, at least they were all more respectful now her and Cohan were an item. But were they an item? She wasn't sure where she stood with him, which frustrated her. He'd begun working on the outline for his new novel and mentioned going to Belgium to do some research and that had sent her into a turmoil. She couldn't bear the thought of their relationship ending. He always seemed attentive and caring, and the sex was amazing between them, but he never indicated they had a future together. Except when he'd joked about putting a ring on her finger, but that was ages ago and he'd never mentioned it since.

He occupied her thoughts all of her waking time, and days when she wasn't with him consisted of daydreaming about him. How one day they'd be married in the local St Michael's church and have a honeymoon somewhere hot like Barbados. Because Cohan had money, their wedding would be spectacular.

No sit down buffet and disco in the evening for them. They could have their reception at Manley Grange. She'd seen photographs of it in a magazine and it looked incredible. They'd have champagne and canapés, followed by a five-course meal, and they'd dance to a professional band. Their first dance would be to Adele's *Make You Feel My Love.* She'd have her friend Hannah as bridesmaid, but she'd be forced to have Princess Perfect as well, Mum and Dad wouldn't have it any other way. Laura would be reluctant though, she'd want to be the bride and the centre of attention, not taking on a bit part of being a bridesmaid.

The daydream continued. She'd eventually get pregnant, so she could give up work. They'd have a boy first, and then a girl. The children would go to private schools and enjoy creative activities like ballet, sport and horse riding.

"Morning, Danielle," her colleague Maria interrupted her fantasy as she entered the open plan office.

"Hi, Maria, you look happy."

"I am," Maria grinned taking her jacket off and hanging it on the coat stand. "You know Mr *Drop Dead Gorgeous* who I see on the train each morning," she paused waiting for a nod, "well, can you believe he actually winked at me today when I got off. I told you he keeps watching me. I reckon I'm in there."

Danielle raised her brows, "You be careful, don't be rushing into anything with a random bloke you don't know."

Maria rolled her eyes, "What, like you did with Cohan?"

"That's different. I did go out to lunch with him first and others were there. And he has got a contract with this office, so I'd say he was safe. You haven't any idea about *Drop Dead Gorgeous*, he could be a serial killer for all you know."

"God, when did you get so sensible?" Maria scowled, as she took her seat. "Okay, I'll go for coffee the first time I meet with him, if that makes you happy. But after that . . . who knows," she grinned.

Danielle sniggered, "Yeah, who knows."

Maria booted her computer up, "Anyway, how's things going with Cohan, still good?"

"Yeah, very good," she smiled, "I'm mad for him."

"I think we've all guessed that."

The pinging of her phone interrupted them. Danielle reached in her bag and a grin formed on her lips. She couldn't help it, anything to do with Cohan made her happy. His usual good morning message caused her tummy to flutter.

Morning beautiful. Missed you. Enjoy your day

His sweet smiley face at the end of the text made her feel warm inside. It was personal and exclusive to her. How did she get so lucky to have him? She sent him a quick text back.

You too. I've missed you. Looking forward to seeing you tonight

"Anyway," Maria carried on, "how is *moving things along* with Cohan going, any more thoughts on that?" The ringing of the desk phone interrupted them, "Tell me when I've answered this."

The previous week, Maria had suggested she didn't take the pill and let nature take its course. Danielle had to admit she was tempted. But if Cohan didn't want a child, he might dump her and she didn't want to be left with a baby at her age. Children were much further down the line and she would have to be married otherwise Mum and Dad would have a fit. But, what started off as a jokey remark, was gaining momentum in the recesses of her mind. The last couple of days while Cohan had been in Skye visiting his mother, she'd been considering faking a pregnancy to move things along a bit. If he went ballistic and didn't want to know, she could have an instant miscarriage, maybe going down the route of already starting to bleed. That had happened to her hairdresser, so she knew it most probably was common in early pregnancy. If Cohan seemed okay with her being pregnant, she could then play-act and string it out for a bit. Eventually she'd have to fake a miscarriage, but by then he could well have suggested they move in together. Or perhaps even marriage. She certainly wouldn't turn him down if he asked that. That really would be a dream come true.

Cohan had been really sweet to her before he went away, almost apologising for having to visit his mother for a few days. Her hopes had soared when he'd said next time he went, he would take her with him. Surely that meant something if he wanted to introduce her to his mother?

With a light heart, she reached for a pen. On the blotter she wrote, Danielle Laity, and underneath, Mrs Cohan Laity. Both had quite a ring to them.

It had been a long drawn out day at work, but finally Danielle arrived at Cohan's flat, taking a taxi as he'd suggested so he could have a meal ready for her. *He really was so thoughtful.*

She knocked and opened his front door. "It's me, can I come in?"

"I'm in the kitchen," he called back.

Her heart raced with anticipation and excitement, he'd only been away three days, but it felt like forever. He looked up from stirring some creation on the stove as she walked through the door, "Hello, you," he smiled, causing her tummy to flutter. She rushed forward to his open arms and savoured his smell as he clasped her to him. She fitted perfectly against his wide chest and clung to him. She truly was the luckiest girl in the world to have him as her boyfriend.

He pulled away from the hug and cupped her face with his hands. His eyes searched hers, as if he was looking into her very soul. He kissed her lovingly, taking his time and leaving her in no doubt how much he'd missed her.

She stroked the side of his face with the back of her hand, "I'm so pleased you're back," she purred, "I missed you so much."

"Me too, and after we've eaten, I'll show you how much," he grinned sexily, before taking her hand and pulling her along to the open plan seating area separated by a kitchen island. "Here, sit," he smiled, "you've been working all day, make yourself comfortable while I pour us a drink. Dinner will be a while yet, do you fancy a glass of red, I've got a fruity merlot open?" He made his way back towards the cooker and reached for a glass from the cupboard.

"No wine for me, can I just have water?"

"Water?" he scowled, "fish urinate in water you know."

"You don't say," she smiled, "maybe I'll risk it, just this once."

"Okay, don't say I didn't warn you," he joked, "one glass of water coming right up."

His warm welcome gave her the nudge she needed to fake the pregnancy, and that meant she couldn't be drinking alcohol, not for a while at least if her plan was to succeed. But he could well dump her. What then? A pulse pounded in her temple in anticipation of what she was about to do, but that wasn't going to stop her. She couldn't afford to lose him . . . she just couldn't.

He handed her a glass of water with ice and a slice of lemon and perched himself on the sofa clutching his glass of wine. "You mentioned you'd been off work while I was away, what was wrong?"

"Sort of a tummy upset."

"What, you ate something off?" he asked, taking a sip of his wine.

"I'm not sure."

His expression was full of concern, "But you're okay now?"

"Still a bit queasy, but I'm much better."

"Are you sure? You look a bit pale, have you been to the doctor?"

She was looking pale on purpose. Normally after work when she was seeing him, she applied more make-up, but not tonight. And less was obviously good if it brought out the caring side of him. She liked it. He looked genuinely worried, and deep within her chest, tenderness gripped her which gave her momentum to carry on.

She took an exaggerated deep breath in which she hoped would imply the gravity of the news she was about to give him. "No need, I know what's wrong with me."

"You do?" he stared, waiting for her to explain.

She took a gulp of water and put the best tortured expression on her face she could.

"What is it?" he urged, "You're starting to worry me?"

"I'm sorry, it's nothing serious, it's more, erm . . . life-changing . . . for me that is, not necessarily for you."

"What are you talking about? For God's sake, tell me what's wrong," he urged.

She looked directly into his eyes. "I'm pregnant."

He screwed his face up, "Pregnant?" He stared at her intensely for a couple of seconds, and then eased himself back slowly onto the sofa, resting against the cushion behind him. "Are you sure?"

"I've done a test," she said, nervously gnawing the inside of her cheek.

He still seemed to need further clarification, "You're on the pill though, aren't you?"

"Yes, but it isn't one hundred percent effective."

"Obviously not." He took a large gulp of his wine and rested the glass down.

"I'm sorry, it's a bit of a shock I know. I've had a day or so to get used to the idea."

"Bit of a shock? That's an understatement," he blew out a breath, "it's one hell of a shock. I can't quite believe it to be honest."

"No, me neither. I'm far too young for anything like this."

"Yeah me too, and I'm much older than you." He shook his head, as if to say it wasn't happening, "Have you told anyone?"

"No. I wanted to tell you first," she quickly added, "but I'm not having an abortion, that's not what I want."

"Hey, steady on. Who said anything about an abortion? I'm not denying it's a bit of a jolt, I just need a minute or two to get used to it." He reached for her hand, "Are you okay?"

"I think so," she put on a pained expression, "I'm dreading telling Mum and Dad though, they're going to be disappointed in me."

She stared at his face intensely, trying to judge how he was taking the news. At least he was still seated and relatively calm. That was a good sign. It had been a massive gamble; he could well have gone ballistic. If he had though, she had a plan B to miscarry pretty quickly.

He cleared his throat, "I'd better be there when you tell them."

"There's no need," she dismissed, "really. It might be better on my own."

This is going much better than I hoped.

"No, I want to be with you," he insisted, "you need my support. We're in this together, after all."

His eyes were puzzling her, she couldn't quite read them. He was saying all the right things, but his anguished expression indicated all was not well in his mind. She almost wanted to blurt out she'd made it all up, and she wasn't really pregnant, but she'd started the lie now, so needed to see it through. And the fake miscarriage was an option anytime. She waited, and he must have realised she was worried about what he was thinking as his expression abruptly changed, and his face became much more relaxed. She'd noticed previously his mood and persona could change literally within seconds.

"I know, why don't I take your parents out for a meal and we can tell them together?" Before she had time to answer, he added, "With Laura and Teddy, oh, and Matthew of course, I know a lovely little bistro we could all go to."

She shook her head, "I don't think a meal in a restaurant is the right place to tell them about the pregnancy to be honest, they're going to be pretty shocked, and we certainly don't need to invite Laura and Matthew." No way did she want Princess Perfect out with them for a meal.

He frowned, "I'd like them all to be there when we announce things though, they are your family after all.

Maybe I can come on Sunday at lunchtime like before," he suggested, "then we can tell your mum and dad together with the rest of the family at the same time."

She'd rather break things to her mum and dad on their own, just her and Cohan without Laura and Teddy being there. Even though it was made up, they wouldn't know and they were likely initially to be shocked. But it does take two to make a baby, after all, so it would be odd if she shut him out.

"Of course you can come for Sunday lunch, there's an open invitation for anyone to attend. I'm still wondering if it would be better if we tell Mum and Dad on our own though? Teddy will be there on a Sunday and you've seen what he can be like."

"All the more reason to tell them together, he's your brother, so needs to know." He reached for his glass of wine, "Will Laura be there this coming Sunday . . . Laura and Matthew?"

"She might be," *who gives a stuff about Laura?* "most of the time she is, and Matthew has an open invitation. Mum fusses him because his own mother lives in France." She pulled a face, "I still think it's best if we see Mum and Dad on our own to tell them. I can let Laura and Teddy know later."

"No," he was adamant, "let's tell them all together, I'm sure Laura will be thrilled to be an aunty," he smiled. "I tell you what, don't mention anything beforehand; that way it'll be quite a surprise for everyone. We can all enjoy a celebration then."

She frowned, "You're taking this very well . . . much better than I expected."

And he was. It almost seemed too easy.

"What exactly did you expect?" he didn't wait for her to answer, "I'm not an ogre."

"I know that," she smiled lovingly at him, "I guess I was worried you'd be furious. I even thought you might not want anything more to do with me."

"Don't ever think that. Granted it's a bit of a shock, but I've always wanted children, much further down the line, though. But right now, it's sinking in. I'm a great believer in fate and things happening for a reason. If I'd waited until the right time, it might never have happened." He took her hand, "And," he brought her hand to his lips and kissed it, "I can't think of anyone more beautiful than you to have my child."

Her heart rate soared. She'd expected far more resistance.

"I'm still dreading telling Dad, he'll be terribly upset with me."

Cohan shook his head, "I don't think so. Once he gets over the shock, he'll be thrilled to be having a grandson."

"Who says it's going to be a boy?" she asked indignantly.

"Me. I bet it is, you see. Look, the timing's rubbish, and I've never even considered this before, but I think when we do tell your family, we need to say we're going to get married."

Her tummy leapt like she was coming down from a fast slide. It was all going amazingly well.

"Married!? That's a massive step. We hardly know each other."

"Yep, I know that, but thinking about it, it's exactly what I want. I want my son to have my name."

Play along, you've just won first prize in how to bag a rich husband.

"He or she would have your name anyway," she reassured, "I'd make sure of it."

"Yes, but I want it all to be legal," he said. She loved his concerned look. Almost like he was worried she'd turn him down. As if.

"You want that, don't you? Please don't tell me you feel differently to how I feel about you?"

He hadn't mentioned love, but that would come later, surely? For now, everything was going brilliantly.

"Of course I feel the same," she squeezed his hand, "it's just that we haven't known each other long. I don't want to be in a position where you feel pressurised into something you might regret later."

"Don't be silly. We've got to make some decisions. We're having a child and the most sensible thing is to be married. Who cares how long we've known each other? It's what we feel inside that counts. Okay, maybe it's come much quicker than we thought, but we can make this work. There are no guarantees in life, but I promise I'll do my best to make you happy." He leant forward and kissed her, then carried on, "You leave your mum and dad to me, I'll use the Laity charm to talk them round," he winked, "do you think you could get Laura and Matthew there on Sunday? I like the idea of the surprise element."

"I'd like that too," she smiled, even though she didn't, "I'm sure I can get them there. But what about your family, I don't really know much about them, when can I meet them?"

"I can't believe I've only just left Mum's. I'll give her a ring later and tell her, she'll be thrilled to bits. She's desperate for me to settle down and have kids. We'll have a little trip to see her, if you want?"

"That'd be nice."

"Right, so we're sorted then. You'll keep schtum until Sunday and get everyone there for our announcement?"

"Of course I will."

"And after that, we'll need to make some arrangements. I'm not suggesting we get married right away, but I'd prefer to before the baby's born."

No way could she afford to wait otherwise she'd have to resort to a cushion up her jumper. The quicker the better as far as she was concerned, then once she was married and faked the miscarriage, she could say she wanted to wait a while before they tried for another baby.

It had been the right decision to move things along. She still had to face her dad's wrath though, he wouldn't be very happy. And all of this was going to take the limelight away from Princess Perfect. Her wedding plans were going to have to take second place now she was in pole position. *That'll knock the smile off her face.*

Cohan's concern and support confirmed her instincts had been right, he clearly was a good man, and seemed keen to include the whole family in the announcement, which was sweet and she loved him for it. Nobody was going to have any idea she was faking it. She smiled inwardly, *it had all been so worth it.*

"Right, that's all sorted then," he kissed her gently again. "You sit there while I go and dish dinner and I can tell you about my news, which now seems almost like fate."

"Aw, don't leave it like that," she groaned, "tell me now."

He smiled tenderly at her. "Well, you know I've been looking for a bolt-hole somewhere so I can make a start on my next book?"

"Yes. You're setting it in Belgium aren't you?" The tummy rollercoaster had landed and flat-lined. He wouldn't be going now, surely?

"I was thinking of travelling abroad, but that might have meant leaving you which I didn't particularly want to do. So I thought about staying here for a while, this was of course before I knew about the baby," he smiled, "now I'm definitely staying here. Anyway, this morning, on the way back from Mum's, I went and viewed a property which is round the corner from your parents' house. I've noticed it a few times when I've dropped you off. I'm not sure if you know it, it's a tall imposing house, down Gravel Pit Lane."

"Yes, I know it. It's old Mr Parker's house, he went into a home a few weeks ago. It's got a huge garden which actually backs right onto ours. Mum used to nip across the small back wall and keep a check on him when he was there."

"Yes, that sounds like the one. I was thinking about renting it for twelve months so I can write my next book. It's got a lovely sitting room overlooking the garden which I thought I could use for an office. Do you want to come and have a look at it with me to see if you like it?"

Bugger! That sort of house wasn't at all what she had in mind. Her dreams were much more of a flashy apartment, maybe near water of some sort with a balcony so they could sit outside. But she'd got more than she could ever dream of so any house would be a start, and after a while she could start hunting for a nice flat somewhere they could buy rather than rent.

"Sounds lovely, I like old places," she pretended, *old places were the pits*.

"It'll be handy being close to your mother when the baby arrives."

For a minute she'd forgotten there was supposed to be a baby. "Oh yes, that will definitely help, I'm sure. I don't know the first thing about babies, do you?"

He pulled a face, "Absolutely not, I'm an only child so you won't be able to rely on me." He grinned so sweetly at her, "We'll just have to make it up as we go along."

How apt. That's exactly what she was going to be doing for the foreseeable future.

A wave of pleasure rushed through her. How lucky was she? And the best thing about it all was, she was going to push Laura's wedding into second place. Princess Perfect was going to have to wait until after she became Mrs Cohan Laity.

Chapter 20

LAURA

The Barley Mow pub was round the corner from work where she always met Matthew midweek for a drink. He would travel from Coryton where he worked as a chemical engineer, and they'd spend a couple of hours together before making their way back to their respective homes.

They cosied up together in their usual corner seat with their regular beer and a wine, and still on a high about her day, she explained how she'd had to stand in for Ed and do the presentation in front of the Home Office minister.

Matthew was munching on some crisps, "Sounds like you did brilliantly, I'm really proud of you. Ed better watch himself, he may well be out of a job soon, and with a bit of luck, you might be in the running."

"Doubt it," she dismissed, "I haven't got the experience, but one day maybe." She'd delivered a slick presentation, and she could tell from Jack's face before he'd spoken to her afterwards, that he'd been impressed. Ed had eventually arrived in work looking sheepish and dishevelled, and Jack had sent him straight home and told him to return in the morning at a specific time for an appointment with HR.

Matthew tipped the crisp bag into his mouth to get the last bits, "We'll have to go out for a meal to celebrate, you doing great at work, and me not needing chemo. Thank God it's definite and the tumour was localised."

She reached for his hand, "I'm so relieved for you, I dread to think of the implications if it had spread."

"Me too," he lifted his pint and she clinked it with her glass of wine, "here's to both of our good news. And thank you by the way, nurse Foley for the *Beating Cancer* book you gave me. I'm now on a mission to increase my vegetables, drink less alcohol, and the consultant says I can go back to the gym now, so that's good because the book stresses the importance of exercise for physical and mental health."

"You're not unhealthy, though," she dismissed, "but the book does have some good ideas, and I liked the bit about positivity and not allowing anything negative or stressful in your life. That's good for us all, I reckon."

"You're right, and you've been a rock, Laura," he stroked the side of her face, "I don't know what I'd have done without you."

"You'd have done the same for me."

"I know I would, I'd do anything for you." He leant forward and gave her a gentle kiss, "You know how much I love you, don't you?"

"All the time," she smiled lovingly at him, "and I love you too, very much."

And she meant every single word. Matthew was easy to love, he'd never let her down, unlike her who'd let him down big time. It was pointless dwelling on that though, what was done was done. She needed to move on. He didn't need that sort of stress, not after all he'd been through.

"Anyway, swiftly moving forward," he said, "I talked a lot to Mum while I was over in France. Because of what's happened, I don't want to waste any time now, I want us to get a date set for the wedding."

His eyes were eager, and she was about to agree it was exactly what she wanted too, but her eyes were drawn towards the bar, as if subconsciously checking.

The last time she'd been there with Ed, Cohan had been there too, watching her. And just the same as before, he was there again, stood at the bar talking to a bloke. He caught her gaze with his penetrating eyes and she quickly looked away. She couldn't believe the audacity of him.

Shit. She was going to have to stop using the pub after work. It was the regular for local workers to nip for a drink before commuting home, but for now, she was going to have to change her movements. She'd already made up her mind she was going to the police about him, as Ed had suggested, but Matthew coming home had delayed her. She should have gone while he was in France.

"You want that too, don't you?" Matthew asked bringing her back to the moment.

"Sorry, what did you say?"

"I said you want to set a date for the wedding too, don't you?"

"Yes, course I do," she took a sip of her drink, "how soon though, it'll take some organising?"

"What, even if we have a small wedding?" he asked with an enquiring expression.

In her peripheral vision she saw Cohan raising his glass, as if toasting her. *The bloody nerve of him.*

His presence made her feel guilty, which would be the very reason why he was there. She'd not come next week, she'd have to make up some excuse. There was no way she was having him anywhere near her. He'd got away with following her to the pub twice now, there wouldn't be a third time.

"I'm not sure Mum and Dad will be happy with that. You know what they're like, first daughter married and all that."

"Mmmmm," he paused, "so there's no point in asking if you fancy dashing off to Gretna Green on our own or anything like that?"

She faked a laugh, "No point at all."

A wave of queasiness passed through her. Even though she wasn't looking directly at Cohan, she felt his eyes boring into her. "I'll speak to Mum and see if she'll suss out the church for any possible dates when she's next there."

Matthew looked uncomfortable. "Does it have to be a church, couldn't we go for a hotel, or even a registry . . ."

"No," she interrupted, "I'd never be forgiven. You know Mum's close links with the church."

"Yeah, well, it's not your mum's wedding, it's ours. We can get married where we want."

The last thing she wanted was to be having this particular conversation, not right now with Cohan's eyes boring into them both. Fortunately, Matthew had his back to him, but he'd be going to the bar soon and sure to see him.

Her tummy tensed as she realised if Matthew spotted him, he would invite him over to join them. She couldn't face that. She needed to get out of there quickly. But they took different trains home. What if Cohan followed her?

She glanced down at her watch. "Shall we make a move? Do you fancy me coming back to yours and we can talk about it some more," she gave him a sexy look, "amongst other things."

"What, tonight?" he frowned, "Chris'll most probably be around midweek."

He knew she was less responsive when his brother was in the flat. She hated going to his room with him. It smacked of them having sex.

"I know," she smiled eagerly, anything to get them out of the pub, "but it'll be nice to spend a bit more time with you tonight."

His face said it all as he reached to finish his pint. They hadn't had sex since his op, and although neither of them had actually planned anything that evening, she needed to get out of the pub quickly before he spotted Cohan, so sex was a good incentive. She'd get a taxi from Matthew's. It'd be costly, but that was the least of her worries.

She reached down for her bag but it had worked its way under the table. As she bent further to retrieve it, a familiar voice made her blood turn to ice.

"I thought it was you two."

Oh, God no.

There he was, Cohan Laity, large as life, stood at their table.

Matthew reached out his hand, "Now then, mate, fancy seeing you here."

"Yeah, fancy. I'm just out for a pint with a mate of mine; he uses this pub regularly as he only works around the corner."

You bloody liar, you've followed me here.

"He's got good taste then," Matthew said, "it's a great pub, we come most Wednesdays after work, don't we?" He looked at her, his eyes urging her to join in. She didn't speak, and could barely manage a nod. Clutching her handbag was enough evidence as far as she was concerned that they were leaving.

"We were just going, actually," she said firmly.

"That's a shame," Cohan smiled that sickly smile of his which might fool everyone else, but not her. "Are you sure I can't get you both another drink?" His penetrating eyes moved from her to Matthew. And Matthew would have most certainly agreed to another pint normally, but the promise of sex must have been the decider.

"Another time maybe, we were just leaving."

"Sure, next time, then."

She stood up and Matthew did too.

"Oh, before I forget," Cohan said, his eyes focussed directly on her, "I'm coming for lunch on Sunday, Danielle and I have got a bit of an announcement, I hope you'll both be there?"

"We're not sure what we're doing yet," she glared.

Matthew gave a puzzled frown, "We'll make an effort though," he said, more for her benefit as they had nothing planned, "for a special announcement." He gave Cohan a playful nudge, "It's not got anything to do with a ball and chain by any chance, has it?"

Cohan raised his perfectly groomed eyebrows, "All will be revealed on Sunday. What I will say is," he smiled smugly at Laura, "we're all going to be seeing much more of each other, but," he paused as if giving her time to digest the bomb he'd just dropped, "anything more than that, my lips are sealed."

She wanted to puke at the enormity of his words.

Matthew laughed, "Oh right, we get it. You do right, keep schtum, that way you won't get into any bother."

"Too right," Cohan agreed smirking, "anyway, if you'll excuse me, I'd better get back to my friend, it's my round I think."

"See you Sunday then, mate," Matthew nodded.

Laura didn't even acknowledge him. She turned and walked away, not caring if Matthew was behind her. She squeezed past the punters standing near the bar drinking, trying to put as much distance as she could between her and Cohan. *Seeing more of each other? Not if she could help it.*

Matthew followed her out of the pub and they began walking in the direction of the train station. He took her hand, "Nothing like making it obvious you don't like him."

"I'm not bothered, I don't."

"What's he done to you? I think he's okay."

"Yeah, well, I don't."

"You better get used to him if he's going to be your brother-in-law."

"Don't say that, please."

"What else could it be? Bet you they'll announce they're getting engaged."

"I doubt it. They've only just met."

"What does that matter? He strikes me as the type to go after what he wants. How old do you reckon he is anyhow?"

"Who cares. I wish you hadn't said we'd be there on Sunday. Whatever they have to say, they can tell Mum and Dad. We don't need to be there."

"Yeah, but we've been invited now. It'll be nice to celebrate with them if it is their engagement. Hey, I bet he gets her a great big rock with all his money, your Danielle will be beside herself."

Please no. It couldn't be happening.

They crossed the road heading for the station. The irony of Matthew saying Cohan *was the type to go after what he wants*, added to the anxiety she was already experiencing. She knew that only too well. And right now, all she wanted to do was get to the safety of home. But she'd told Matthew she'd go back with him and he was expecting it. She'd only done it because she'd spotted Cohan and needed to get away before Matthew saw him too. Her mum had mentioned that Cohan was coming for lunch again on Sunday, and she'd already devised a cunning plan to get out of it. She wasn't going to tell Matthew about the family lunch, she was going to suggest them spending all day together, maybe a walk and a lunch out on their own, and then back to his flat to bed for the afternoon. The idea had been to tell her mum Matthew had booked a lunch out for them both to celebrate getting over the surgery.

He put his arm around her, "Can't wait to get you to bed," he breathed in her ear.

She'd have to go now, there was no getting out of it. Or Sunday lunch by the sound of things. Christ, surely Cohan and Danielle weren't getting engaged? What a fool Danielle was not seeing through him. But then again, could she really blame her? Cohan was a master at deception . . . she had no idea when she met him in Spain, he was a psychopath.

She reached in her bag for her phone, "I'll just text Mum and tell her I'll be late."

He rolled his eyes, "God alive, she knows who you're with. I don't see why you've got to text her to say you're coming back to mine. We are engaged for Christ's sake."

"Yeah, but you know what they're like. I'd rather this than them not caring.

How the hell was she going to cosy up to Matthew and have sex? She couldn't think of anything worse right now. But he was a bloke, and was worried sick about things not being right in the sex department even though she'd reassured him it would be just the same between them as it was before the operation. She loved him and had meant exactly that when she's said it. And she always enjoyed making love with him. It was nothing like the frantic mind-blowing sex she had with Cohan, but that had been pure lust, and there hadn't been any feelings attached to it. Not on her part anyway. Whereas since their engagement and commitment to each other, sex between her and Matthew had meant so much more, and had only halted because of his surgery. She had wanted to make sure things were perfect between them, but Cohan had thrown her completely. Tension radiated out of every pore, but she couldn't back out now. He'd be wondering what on earth was wrong after it had been her suggestion.

She finished the text and pressed send.

"How late did you tell her you were going to be?" he asked.

"I didn't. Just said I'd be late and not to wait up."

"Good," he whispered huskily, "'cause the way I'm feeling right now, you're gonna be very late."

Chapter 21

LAURA

"This is bloody stupid, Laura," Matthew said, "sat in a coffee shop in town when we should be at your house. It looks bad us just turning up in time for lunch, you know your dad likes me to have a drink with him before we eat."

"I know, and we'll go in a bit. I just can't face waiting around for the great Cohan Laity to arrive. I don't want to be in his company any more than I have to."

"Why?" he frowned, "I don't get it, he seems a decent enough bloke to me. And if they are going to get married, we'll all be related so we need to get on."

The thought of being in the same room as Cohan made her feel physically sick, but she needed to be careful and not draw any suspicion on herself.

"I'm just not keen, that's all. He seems a bit slick to me, and what do we know about him . . . nothing? They haven't known each other long, so I reckon it's all a bit quick."

Matthew took a gulp of his coffee, "Yeah, but money's obviously not a problem, they don't have to save up like us for somewhere to live. Anyway, they might not be getting married, for all we know they could just announce they're going to live together, that's all. Like you say, they hardly know each other."

"I doubt that very much," she pulled a face, "Dad wouldn't go for that, you know what he's like."

"Don't I just," he rolled his eyes, "but he might have to mellow. Be nice if he did, it'd make it easier for us. Maybe we could spend some nights together instead of all this having to be home at your age. It is pretty ridiculous, especially now we're engaged."

"I know. It's just the way he is," she sighed, "anyway, you're probably right, we perhaps should make a move," she gulped the last of her coffee, "I'd best make an effort so I don't upset Mum."

He leant forward to kiss her. "Do you know, your eyes go much darker when you're not happy? If you never spoke a word, I could tell by the colour of your eyes if you're mad or not."

"Really," she smiled, "be warned then when we're married, I won't bother raising my voice when I'm cross, I'll just glare and you'll know something's wrong."

"Yeah, you do that. A dumb wife – it's everyman's dream."

She laughed, "Come on, let's go and hear this announcement, eat our lunch and then we're out of there. I'll tell them we have to meet your friends for a drink early doors, so don't let me down whatever you do. We'll go to yours and leave them two with Mum and Dad, billing and cooing about whatever this announcement is."

"Fine by me. Chris isn't back until tomorrow so we've got the flat to ourselves."

By the time they arrived at the house, Cohan was sat with her dad having a beer. Tiny hairs on the back of her neck stood on end as they walked in the lounge and he stood up and shook Matthew's hand. She kept well back in case he tried to give her a friendly kiss on the cheek; she was having none of that. He was menacing enough across the room without being up close.

She didn't even acknowledge him. "I'll just go see if Mum wants any help," she said looking at her dad before making her way to the kitchen. Her mother was her usual busy self, mixing the breadcrumbs and sausage meat together for the stuffing, while Danielle was stood propping up the sink unit. She wouldn't get her hands dirty, that's for sure, too worried she might chip one of her acrylic nails.

"You made it then," Danielle said, the sarcasm evident.

"I didn't think I had a choice."

"Now then," her mum interrupted, "that's enough. Danielle, why don't you get Laura a drink, lunch won't be for about an hour."

Danielle glared at her, "Do you want a glass of wine?"

"Yeah, why not." Although something much stronger than wine would have been better. Anything to dull the experience of spending time in the psychopath's company.

"Where's Teddy?" she asked her mum.

"In the shed. Be a love and go and get him, would you? It's about time he came in and cleaned himself up. I honestly don't know why he's hidden away in there; he usually loves it when we have company."

"I'll go and see what he's up to and drag him in."

"You do that, he might come in for you."

Laura made her way down to the shed at the bottom of their huge garden and Teddy was peeping at her out of the tiny window. He opened the door and gave her his beautiful toothy smile.

"Mum wants you to come in now and get ready for lunch."

He screwed his face up, "Do I have to, can't I stay here?"

"No. You have to come and eat lunch. You're hungry, aren't you?" Teddy was always hungry. He was quite tubby despite Mum monitoring what he ate, but part of that was related to the genetic chromosomes of Down's syndrome.

"I want to stop here."

"Yeah, you and me too, but we can't."

"Why?"

"Because it isn't polite."

"I don't want to be polite."

She sighed, "If it's any consolation, I don't want to be polite either, but we have to."

"Why?"

"Because Mum and Dad expect us to. I think there's going to be some sort of announcement, so we have to be there for it."

"What announcement?"

"I really don't know, Teddy, we'll have to wait and see. Come on."

He closed the door behind him. "I'm going to eat my dinner and then come back."

"That's okay, I'm going out afterwards too."

"Do you like him?" Teddy asked as they walked towards the house.

He was referring to Cohan, it couldn't be anyone else, he loved Matthew. She didn't want to say anything negative as he was most likely to blurt it out over lunch. "I don't really know him. Danielle likes him though."

Teddy didn't answer.

"What have you got against him?" she asked as they approached the kitchen door. She held onto the handle before going in.

He shrugged his shoulders, "Dunno."

There was no point in pressing him right now, but she would do later. It was completely out of character for him to dislike anyone. Something was wrong. She needed to find out exactly what was bothering him.

"Come on, the quicker we have lunch, the quicker you can go back to the shed."

They all sat in the lounge having their pre-lunch drinks. Danielle was clutching Cohan's hand, almost as if she let go, he might escape, and Laura gripped the stem of her wine glass so tightly, she was surprised it hadn't snapped. Could Cohan feel from across the room how much she loathed him? She hoped so.

"Before we enjoy one of your lovely lunches, Ann," Cohan smiled at her mum, "I've got an announcement to make, if that's okay?" He gave Danielle a sickly smile and she was lapping it up with her perfectly coated pink lips. Her teeth appeared whiter, she must have had some sort of bleaching done to them, they'd certainly changed colour.

Her mum looked like she was visualising the colour of her wedding outfit already, and her dad was smiling encouragingly, no doubt thinking his daughter had done good with best-selling author Cohan Laity.

Cohan cleared his throat. "I've asked Danielle to marry me, and she's agreed."

No, no, no. Please no.

"How wonderful," her mother squealed and beamed at Danielle, "I'm thrilled for you, darling."

"Just a minute," Cohan interrupted, "there's more." He turned and gave Danielle a pathetic lapdog look, "Do you want to tell them, Danielle?"

She saw her sister visibly swallow and put on a feeble voice, "I'm going to have a baby."

Oh my God!

Someone, please wake her up.

Their dad's expression altered, as if he was in pain. He'd be hugely disappointed and Danielle would know that. He'd told them often enough growing up, courtship, engagement, marriage, children. He liked things done in a respectable order.

"I know it's come as a total surprise," Cohan interjected, "Danielle and I are just getting used to it ourselves to be honest, but I want you both to know," he looked confidently at her dad, "with your permission, of course, we're going to be married as soon as possible."

This isn't happening.

It can't be real.

She must be dreaming . . . surely? She stifled an urge to scream out loud and tell them all to stop; she'd heard enough.

Her mum eagerly rose from her chair and Danielle and Cohan stood at the same time. She watched her mum fling her arms around Danielle first, and then Cohan.

"A baby? I can't quite believe it. Are you happy, darling?" she asked Danielle.

"Of course, Mum, we both are. It's taking some getting used to though."

They turned to look at her dad whose grim expression said everything. He cleared his throat. "It's quite a shock, I must say. I had hoped you'd both," he looked at her also to show he meant both of his daughters, "be married before having a child."

"I do understand, Ian," Cohan continued, "neither of us have planned this, but now it's happened," he looked at Danielle, "we are actually happy. But we want you and Ann to be happy to."

Slick git. Laura could happily puke on his shoes.

Her dad took an obvious deep breath which seemed to convey his acceptance, albeit grudgingly. He pushed himself up from the chair, it was evident he wasn't overjoyed. Danielle's expression was hopeful; she loved their dad as much as she did. She wouldn't want to upset him in any way. But Ian Foley was a gentleman. He leant forward and reached for Danielle. It brought tears to Laura's eyes. She knew it was a big thing for her dad to congratulate them when he'd be so disappointed in Danielle.

"I can't pretend I'm delighted about the way you've gone about things, but a child is a gift from God and you have been blessed," he nodded at Cohan, "both of you." He took Cohan's hand and warmly shook it, "I can see you make Danielle happy and that's all any parent ever wants for their children."

"Thanks, Dad," Danielle smiled, "it means everything to have your blessing."

"You have that, darling, and I hope you are prepared for this, children change your lives completely." He smiled warmly at Cohan and repeated the words he'd said to Matthew only weeks earlier, "Welcome to the family. This calls for something special so we can celebrate."

Danielle, pregnant with Cohan Laity's child, she couldn't be. What a bloody fool.

Deep breaths, in and out, in and out.

Matthew jumped up and extended his hand to Cohan. "Great news, mate, congratulations," he hugged Danielle, "really pleased for you both. Sounds like you're going to be beating us to the altar."

Danielle gave a smug smile, as if she hadn't thought about that at all when she'd known very well. "Yes, I suppose it does."

Oh, she'll love that.

Laura knew it was expected that she congratulated them both. But she couldn't move. Her bottom was fixed to the chair. Would her legs even hold her up?

Please, God, make this go away.

Teddy wasn't moving either.

"Laura," her mother's voice broke her trance. She knew she was giving her a gentle nudge to congratulate them, but how could she?

With every fibre of her being, she willed herself to stand and make her way towards Danielle. Her legs felt like jelly as she hugged her, "My God, you a mum, I can't believe it."

Danielle laughed, "No, me neither. You'll have to be on hand for babysitting duties, that's for sure, Aunty Laura."

She tentatively reached out her hand to Cohan, it was all she could manage. But he was having none of it. "Come here," he pulled her towards his chest in a tight embrace, "we're going to be family now."

A threat if ever she heard one. Nobody in the room would be any the wiser, but she knew exactly what he meant. It was precisely what he'd set out to do, ingratiate himself into her family, and what a way to do it. It was one almighty tsunami.

His breath was nauseating, his powerful aftershave repulsive. She quickly pulled away. A second in his embrace was one second too long. Teddy still hadn't moved. For a fleeting moment, Laura wished she'd been him. He'd be excused for not jumping about with excitement.

"Teddy," her mum urged, "have you got anything to say to Danielle and Cohan?"

She couldn't stand it a minute longer. She had to get away. Her mum coaxing Teddy to offer his congratulations was the last straw.

"Excuse me a moment," she interrupted and made her way out of the lounge. She didn't care what it looked like, she could barely breathe.

Her sister having Cohan Laity's baby . . . it was the

stuff nightmares were made of.

He'd be inextricably linked to the family forever.

Chapter 22

LAURA

Laura was sitting with Matthew in his hospital room, waiting for his procedure to insert the ball prosthesis into his sac where they'd removed his testicle. They'd both been surprised he'd received a letter to attend the small private hospital in central London to have the procedure done. Matthew had telephoned thinking there'd been a mistake inviting him there for the procedure as he wasn't in a position to pay privately, or in a scheme, either. He's been reassured that the hospital undertook NHS work as well as private work, and he was indeed an NHS patient.

Days after he'd been given a date for his surgery, Laura had received a letter to say her eye surgery to remove a tiny cyst was going to be carried out at the same hospital. She'd completely forgotten even seeing a specialist earlier in the year with everything that had happened since Spain. The cyst was minute, but it irritated her when she applied her eye make-up and the consultant she'd seen had said it was a simple procedure and would be done under a local anaesthetic as an outpatient.

The private room the receptionist had escorted her and Matthew to was a far cry from an NHS ward with its contemporary design. Her eyes travelled around the room admiring its cream fabric wallpaper, aqua and cream stripy curtains, and modern-day art adorning the walls. The bed was adjacent to a full-length panoramic window overlooking a pretty garden with manicured lawns and a stunning water fountain in the centre. She thought how nice it would have been if Matthew had undergone his initial surgery there to remove the testicle, rather than the clinical NHS hospital where he had other patients either side of him, one of them quite poorly which meant he hadn't got much rest.

While he was admitted by the nurse taking his details and doing his observations, Laura went and sat in a waiting area and people-watched, giving it half an hour before returning to his room. He grinned as she walked back in. He was sat in the armchair in his patterned hospital gown tied up at the back.

"What do you think?" he laughed, easing the gown up to show her a glimpse of his paper knickers.

"Charming," she giggled, "don't be taking them home with you to wear around the flat."

"Spoilsport," he teased, and reached for a green paper hat, "and look what completes the outfit, I just need to put this on when they come for me, and I'm good to go."

She pulled up a chair next to him. "Shouldn't you be in the bed?" she asked thinking that was expected.

"The nurse said I didn't have to. She reckons they'll take me down in a wheelchair but I'll come back on a trolley."

"Oh, right. Did she say how long you'd be?"

"She didn't give a time, just said it wouldn't take long. They're going to do some sort of block she said, so I'm not going off to sleep."

"That's better then." She stared at the abstract picture above the bed, and the ample fitted wardrobe filling the full length of the wall behind the door, "One thing's for sure, I won't get a comfy room when I come in for my eye, the letter said I'm being done in the outpatients department."

"Are you really that bothered about having it done?" he frowned.

"Course I am. I want it removed."

"But I can't even see it."

"That's 'cause you're blind," she grinned, "I know it's there and it irritates my eye and makes it run. The consultant said it needed to be done, and it's only a five-minute job."

Matthew pulled a pained face, "Yeah, but I don't think you should be messing around with your eyes, what if his hand slipped?"

"Don't be ridiculous," she laughed, "honestly, what are you like?"

"Rather you than me, that's all I can say. I wouldn't let anyone near my eyes. Anyway, before I forget, when I go to theatre, in my bag," he nodded towards the sports holdall near the wardrobe, "there's a present for you."

"A present?" she reeled back, totally surprised. Matthew wasn't one bit spontaneous.

"Yeah, I wanted you to have something, sort of to signify all this was over, and to thank you for being there for me."

"You dafty," she put her head to one side, "I don't need a gift, of course I'm going to be there for you."

"I know, but I wanted you to have something. Open it when I'm in theatre."

"I will do." She leant forward and kissed him. "Matthew Souter, do you know how much I love you?"

"No," he joked, "you never tell me."

"Well I'm telling you now, I love you very much. Always."

The door opening interrupted them; it was the nurse with a porter. "They're ready for you, Mr Souter. I'm just going to check your details on your wristband, and then we'll take you down." The nurse turned to her,

"There's a coffee area if you wanted to go there and wait, or you're welcome to stay here in the room, he's not going to be that long."

"Thank you. I'll probably have a walk in the garden and then come back and wait if that's alright?"

"Course it is," the nurse reassured.

She stood and gave Matthew a gentle peck, "See you shortly."

"Yep. Don't forget what's in my bag," he looked slightly embarrassed in front of people. How he'd ever proposed at her twenty-first, she didn't know. He wasn't one bit showy.

"I won't. See you in a bit."

She left them to it and went for a walk around the grounds. Bless him buying her a gift, he was such a good man. It was a relief after all the cancer upset, they were finally concluding on that. He had to have regular check-ups, but the consultant had reassured them they would become less and less until eventually he'd be discharged.

After a walk in the fresh air, she bought a coffee and took it back to Matthew's room. She fished in his holdall and removed a tiny gift bag. It was evident it was jewellery with a designer's name on it, and the grey box inside. She carefully opened it, and wrapped around a small velvet cushion, was a silver bangle with an inscription engraved on the outside. Her heart constricted as she read the message, *Linchpin, I love you.* Her eyes filled with tears at the beautiful message and its sentiment. She'd endeavoured to be his linchpin, trying hard to support him and hold everything together after the devastating cancer diagnosis. If he only knew what else she'd been battling against as she strived to do that.

Thankfully, since Danielle had announced her pregnancy, it had been relatively quiet on the Cohan front, which she wasn't entirely sure was down to her cunning, as she suspected, or he'd lost interest in her, which she hoped. She'd mixed up the evenings she met Matthew after work at the pub, despite his protests that a Wednesday suited him best, and she had changed her hairdressers so Cohan didn't know where she went to. She kept conversations with Danielle to a minimum in terms of her life, and became vague with her mother about what she was up to, that way she was confident neither of them could inadvertently let something slip.

Danielle and her mother were immersed in wedding plans. They'd somehow managed to get a modest wedding organised in a local hotel and her mum and dad were footing most of the bill. Dad had insisted. According to Danielle, they were going to organise a church blessing of some sort after the baby was born and combine it with a christening. By all accounts this was going to be the main event.

Laura couldn't care less. She'd run out of ideas about stopping the wedding now there was a baby in the mix. And despite her initial horror at the thought of it, she secretly hoped life would be easier for her with Danielle living with Cohan. Okay, so they'd be at the back of her in old Mr Parker's house they were renting, but at least he wouldn't know her movements via Danielle. And with a wife and baby, he wasn't going to find it easy to keep following her about.

She bitterly regretted her actions with Cohan and berated herself daily for not confessing all in the first place. The nightmare was never going to go away now, she'd just have to learn to live with it. But she had a long-term plan she hadn't discussed with anyone. She was going to marry Matthew as soon as she realistically could after Danielle's wedding, she'd even got a provisional date booked for March the following year. Her mum had told her about a cancelled wedding at the church and she'd jumped in and booked the slot. She still had all the other stuff to sort out, but at least she had a date. Until then, she was going to do everything in her power to persuade Matthew to move to one of the refineries abroad. He was always on about it, the fabulous life they would have if they lived in France. Not near his mother, though, he wasn't keen on that but he did like the lifestyle France offered. She'd always resisted the discussions, worrying about being too far away from her mum and dad, but now, because Cohan was going to be part of the family, she was determined to move there. Matthew was a chemical engineer, he was bright, and keen to move on to a senior role so could easily get a job in France. And Matthew wouldn't stop there, he'd said often enough it was the role he was interested in, he wasn't bothered where it was. His aim was to eventually be a refinery manager, and he'd do it. Her mum and dad would be able to visit often, but she'd never invite Danielle and Cohan with their baby. She was going to put as much distance as she could between them. So, the plan was there in her mind, and she was determined to pursue it. It wasn't going to happen immediately, but by the time her and Matthew were married, she'd have engineered it so they'd be ready to go.

On the work front, things were improving since giving the presentation to the minister. Jack had been almost gushing with his praise and said he wanted her to complete a training course so she could become a recognised civil servant, which was a huge step-up from an admin role. That would mean extra responsibilities, but with that came extra pay. He'd instructed Ed, at her next development review, that was the plan going forward. She knew she could do more than she was currently doing, so the challenges ahead excited her and drove her on.

Ed had received a written warning about his conduct since the presentation debacle, and had not had an alcoholic drink since. The shock of Jack spelling things out to him about the likelihood of him losing his job appeared to have done the trick. He was like the old Ed, functioning diligently, and work was once again easier than the previous few months had been.

So, life was by no means perfect, she was still looking over her shoulder, and had the wretched wedding to get through, but Cohan following her seemed to have stopped. She'd been roped into being a bridesmaid alongside Danielle's friend, and there was no way she could get out of it without arousing suspicion. Quite how she was going to get through it though, was a different matter. It certainly was going to be a significant challenge. Part of her still wanted to stop the wedding, but how could she? The baby had changed everything. That didn't stop her rebuking herself daily about what she'd done to Matthew, and allowed Cohan Laity to cause havoc within the family. He didn't care for Danielle, she was certain of that.

She put Matthew's gift on her wrist, loving him for it. It was a beautiful thoughtful gift she was going to cherish. A flashback of Cohan giving her a bracelet in Spain momentarily interrupted her joy. How naive she'd been to think Spain had been her secret and nobody would find out about it. She'd left Spain with fond memories of her time with Cohan and had worn the bracelet he'd bought her. And when it caught Danielle's eye, she'd lied and said she'd bought it for herself as it was so pretty.

An impulsive idea crept up, and rapidly gained momentum.

Something old, something new.

She could give the bracelet to Danielle to wear on her wedding day. She was marrying the loathsome man, she could have his loathsome jewellery. Hopefully that would hammer home to him how she'd totally discarded him, and his emotionally binding gift had ultimately proven to be worthless.

Chapter 23

DANIELLE

Today was her wedding day. She leisurely languished in a warm bath at the small boutique hotel. Tonight she'd be moving to the honeymoon suite with Cohan. She was a little curious by his insistence of a low-key affair at the modest hotel. He had explained her father wanted to pay the lion's share, despite him offering to help, and he felt they should respect that. But he had promised her a holiday later on in the year to somewhere exotic and said he'd prefer to spend the money on a luxurious six-star hotel where they could indulge themselves and be spoiled. He was going to try really hard after their short break in Cornwall to get a little further with his current work in progress, and then he'd focus on their proper honeymoon. He'd said he would get something sorted before she was too far advanced into the pregnancy so there weren't any risks.

That had focussed her mind. It was still early days therefore her so-called pregnancy wasn't showing. She planned to have the fake miscarriage on the last day of their break. Cohan had been determined to go to Cornwall, apparently he'd had family holidays there as a child when his father was alive, and they'd explored all the tiny coves together, so couldn't wait to show her the isolated beaches that the tourists didn't know about. She couldn't think of anything worse. She wasn't a strong swimmer, and avoided water at all costs. All that salt would play havoc with her high-lights.

She thought about her stunning cream wedding dress hanging up next door. How she'd loved choosing it. She'd rejected her mother's offerings off the rack in the shop. She knew exactly what she wanted and it wasn't a blancmange wedding dress. She wanted something fitted and sophisticated. And she wanted to look hot on her wedding day so Cohan couldn't take his eyes off her. She'd eventually found the perfect one in a bridal magazine and was able to locate it at an exclusive shop in central London. The bridesmaid dresses were charcoal grey, which wasn't the most flattering of colours but that's why she'd purposely chosen it. The last thing she needed was Princess Perfect with her thick dark hair and perfect skin tone looking sensational in a bold bright colour and stealing the show. Her other bridesmaid was big on quirkiness and personality rather than having much going on in the looks department, so she wasn't such a worry.

Danielle inhaled the lemon zest bath bomb which had created all the girlie bubbles, and rubbed some up and down her arms. The engagement ring Cohan had given her caught her eye. She disliked it intensely. Since being a little girl she'd wanted a solitaire diamond and even hinted as such to Cohan. Yet one night, completely out of the blue after they'd eaten dinner, he produced a small box which she knew contained a ring. What puzzled her though was the condition of the box, it looked old as if he'd picked it up in a second hand shop. His face had been eager as she opened it and stared at the red ruby ring.

"It's a family heirloom," he'd smiled enthusiastically, "do you like it?" He didn't wait for her reply, and what could she say exactly? She didn't.

"Put it on," he urged, "it was my grandmother's."

She'd slipped it onto her engagement finger, hating everything about it.

"Don't you like it?" he asked, his face looking decidedly icy.

"It's nice," she replied. Should she be truthful, she'd be expected to wear it for a long time?

"I thought if you had this, I could get you a diamond eternity ring when we go on our exotic holiday? I'm sure a ring with diamonds around it would show off the ruby. Would you like that?"

Would she like it? She'd love it! "That would be lovely; it's always been a dream of mine to have a diamond. It's not that this isn't nice, and it's a lovely idea," she quickly added, "but I'd really like to choose my own, with you, of course."

"And you shall. When we go to the Caribbean, I can get you something special. We'll get so much more for our money as it'll be tax free. Places like St Maarten or Aruba are tax havens and they have endless shops full of diamonds. I'll get you something special, I promise." He smiled lovingly at her, "But for now, I'd love you to wear my grandmother's ring. Her and my grandfather loved each other so much, and I hope it brings us both luck in our marriage."

She couldn't argue with that. And the ring really wasn't that bad, it just wasn't to her taste.

A tap on the door interrupted her thoughts.

"How you doing, love?" her mum asked, "its half past and the hairdresser's here."

"Okay, I won't be long."

She stepped out of the warm bath and wrapped a luxurious bath towel around herself. She smiled at her reflection in the mirror. Today was going to be her day, the day Cohan put the gold wedding band on her finger and she became Mrs Laity. At least the wedding band she'd chosen had been new. It was only plain, Cohan had urged her to go for a similar ring to his. She was proud he wanted to wear a ring, so many men didn't these days. So she'd gone for the plain gold bands, seemingly he didn't want anything ornate, he just liked plain thin gold so hers was a replica of his.

She removed the towel and vigorously rubbed her skin dry. She stared at herself naked in the mirror. Her figure was lovely, which it needed to be so she could look good in the fitted dress she'd chosen. Her mum had been dubious about it, hinting in the shop about possible weight gain and it might not fit when the wedding day came. The sales lady had indicated it could be let out slightly if that happened, but added that, in her experience, brides were usually more prone to losing a few kilograms before a wedding. Danielle knew categorically she wouldn't be gaining any weight before the wedding and insisted it was the dress she wanted. She couldn't wait for Cohan to see her in it. It had been costly, but her mum had given in when she knew how desperately she wanted it.

Sullen Laura was far from the dutiful sister in all of the preparations. When she was first asked to be her bridesmaid, the ungrateful little madam had said no, until their mum had made her change her mind. Laura would be jealous that the focus of Mum and Dad's attention would be on the eldest daughter for a change, typical Princess Perfect, just 'cause it wasn't about her. Even when they'd had girlie days shopping for the bridesmaid outfits, Laura had been distracted. Her mum said it was understandable that Laura was a bit peeved as her and Matthew had announced their engagement first, but she'd reassured she would come round when she got to know Cohan a little better, and of course when the baby was born.

She recalled a conversation she'd had with Cohan. He'd asked what Laura thought about them getting married. He remarked she'd been cool when they announced the wedding and baby. He'd soon learn exactly what Princess Perfect was like, he was going to be joining the family after all.

"That's Laura," she explained, "she's like that. Always wants to be the centre of attention with Mum and Dad. She's just jealous that it's me getting all the interest for once."

"Do you think that's it?" he frowned disbelievingly, "I wondered maybe if she didn't like me or something? She never has much to say. Matthew's fine, but she always seems so distant. I've hardly had as much as a conversation with her, so I'm unsure what the problem is. Has she said anything?"

"No, nothing," she dismissed and kissed him, "who could possibly not like you? I really wouldn't worry, she's like that with me. Remember, we've pushed her nose out of joint with having our wedding before hers. She's got to wait now until next year."

"I see. Do you think she'll set a date after we're married?"

"She already has done."

"Really? Not wasted any time then. When is it?"

"March sometime, I think. Mum did say but I can't remember the exact date."

"After the baby's born, then?"

"Yeah," she lied.

"So you'll be able to be her bridesmaid?"

"If she asks me, I suppose so. Who knows with her? She'll probably get married in a tepee or something weird like that and not have any bridesmaids."

"Oh, I'm sure she'd want you. You're her sister, after all."

"Yeah, but I've told you, she's not my genetic sister so we aren't close. She's more interested in Teddy than me."

"But he's not her genetic brother either, is he?"

"No, I know, but she loves him. It's always been the two of them. I've been made to feel the odd one out. I'll be glad to be out of that house to be honest."

"So are you marrying me because you love me," he teased, "or more because you want different digs?"

She tapped him playfully, "I love you silly. I wouldn't be marrying you if didn't."

Although he smiled affectionately at her, he didn't reply. Sadly, he'd never said he loved her. Even after great sex, he never said those words. Yes, he told her she was beautiful, gorgeous, incredible, but not once had he uttered those three little words which would have meant so much. Maybe it was just him, hadn't he shown her he loved her by wanting to marry her? Of course he had. She was being silly. And there would be years ahead for them to be expressing how much they loved each other.

Wrapped in the complimentary fluffy white robe, she opened the bathroom door. Her mum and the hairdresser were stood waiting for her. "Here you are, Danielle," her bridesmaid thrust half a glass of bubbly at her. She hesitated, recognising the wave of displeasure that passed over her mum's face. If only she knew there wasn't a pregnancy. But right now, she needed to keep up the pretence.

"It's just a small glass, Ann," Hannah reassured, "one won't hurt, today of all days, we are celebrating after all."

Danielle took the glass from her friend's outstretched hand, "Thanks, Hannah, that's sweet of you. Cheers."

As they clinked glasses she noticed Princess Perfect was stood looking out of the huge window minus a glass of bubbly in her hand. Typical. She'd be just like her mum thinking half a glass of alcohol and the so-called baby would be born with spina bifida at the very least. For God's sake, she could have one glass. The time wasn't right today, but she really needed telling, causing Cohan to be concerned about her not liking him. Who the hell did she think she was? She would tackle her about it . . . when she was married, though. She'd tell her to be nice to her husband, or else. But not right now, today was her day. Hers and Cohan's.

Laura could do one.

Jealous little cow.

Chapter 24

LAURA

Laura stared out of the huge window overlooking the beautiful hotel garden with the birch trees swaying in the breeze, and the water trickling down the ornate fountain. Today was the day of nightmares. Since the announcement of Danielle marrying Cohan and them having a baby, she prayed for a miracle to stop it. But nothing had. She checked her watch. In less than three hours, Danielle was going to become Mrs Cohan Laity. How the hell had it all happened?

She'd travelled down in the car the previous day to the hotel with Matthew, and they'd chatted about their own wedding. She'd made noises, but her mind wasn't on their future and Matthew had sensed it. "What's the matter?" he asked, "I can see Laura Foley's in the car with me, but it's like talking to a statue."

"Sorry," she squeezed his knee, "I'm just not looking forward to this at all."

He lifted her hand up in front of him, "Have you been biting your nails again?"

She quickly pulled it away. "I know, it's disgusting, I'm trying to stop."

"Look," he sighed, "I know you don't like Cohan that much, but you can't let them getting married affect you. You're just going to have to suck it up."

Don't like him that much? If you only knew.

"I know. I'll be glad when it's all over, though."

"You'll be glad when it's all over? What about me? Sharing a room with your brother is not my idea of a riotous stay in a hotel."

She smiled, "I don't particularly want to spend the night with my auntie either, but I've got that straw."

"I don't get why you aren't with Danielle, you're her sister, surely you should be together in a room?"

That was the last thing Laura wanted. She might have ended up blurting everything out. Danielle was still cool with her since she'd implied Cohan had been looking at her oddly, so if they'd got in a discussion without their mum to referee, she could so easily have exposed him.

"She's got her school friend with her, and she is the other bridesmaid. Auntie Kath is finding it hard doing stuff since her husband died, so Mum wanted her to have someone with her. I don't mind sharing with her really, she is lovely."

"Well, keeping us apart and this whole bloody sex curfew is stupid as far as I'm concerned, and like I said yesterday, I'm going to speak to your dad about all of it. Chris going to Amsterdam has changed things. If he decides to stay there after his two year contract, you never know, we might be able to buy the flat from him. I'm sure my dad will help us with the deposit."

It did make sense. Matthew's brother being offered a contract in Amsterdam would give them a great opportunity to start their married life together, and the flat was lovely. But she couldn't concentrate on anything but Danielle's wedding.

He carried on. "I can't afford the mortgage on my own so it makes sense for you to move in with me until our wedding. And I'm going to be firm with your dad, he has to move into the twenty-first century."

"He won't be pleased; I'm telling you now. You know what he's like."

"Don't I just. We should be in a hotel room together for this wedding. He knows what we are doing, for God's sake, he's a bloke. I bet he didn't wait until his wedding night to have sex with your mum."

"Oh, don't, please. I can't think of those two doing stuff like that."

"What, you reckon they laid in bed reading their bible on their wedding night?"

She rolled her eyes, "That's a better image than them having sex."

He shook his head, "I'm going to speak to him, Laura. Since Danielle got pregnant, he must have mellowed. That's life, adults in relationships have sex. I'm going to spell it out to him that I can't afford to stay in the flat without you, and I'm going to lay it on about us buying the flat from Chris. You know your dad, he's all for securing property."

"Well, good luck with that, that's all I can say. He'll be really twitchy."

"Let him. I'm going to get your mum on our side. She can talk him round. You do want us to live in the flat together, don't you?"

If she was totally honest, she wasn't entirely sure. Part of her was looking forward to Danielle leaving, and there just being her mum and dad, and Teddy, even though she felt guilty for feeling that way. But the wedding was niggling away at her, as if she had a duty to at least try and stop it. A shudder ran down her spine every time she thought about Cohan Laity living at the back of them in Charlie Parker's house. Moving in with Matthew would definitely put some distance between them. The idea that Cohan Laity could drop by their house opportunistically with Danielle, or even on his own, was too frightening to even contemplate.

"Of course I want to live with you; I'm just not sure it's going to be as easy as you think."

"Just you leave it with me. Let's get this wedding over with, and then we can concentrate on us. Okay?"

"Okay," she sighed. Should she let everything take its course, or was it worth one last attempt to stop the wedding?

"And I hope you've told Teddy I'm not sitting up half the night telling him any more World War Two stories. That's okay when I'm sober, but not when I've had a skinful. I'll just want to get my head down when I get to the room."

Laura knew Teddy wouldn't leave Matthew alone. He was really excited to be sharing a room with him and had brought a book about the D-Day landings.

"Good luck with that as well," she grinned, and Matthew pulled a knowing face back.

Laura continued to stare out of the hotel window and listened to her mother fussing round Danielle. Even though she'd resigned herself to not getting involved, now it had come round to the actual day, she had an overwhelming urge to try to stop the wedding. Her hair and make-up was all done, all she needed to do was slip on the hideous dress Danielle had chosen.

She'd forced herself to text Cohan,

We need to meet

As soon as she pressed send, she instantly regretted it and willed him to have changed his number so he didn't get it. She played a mind game with herself, if he didn't answer, then it wasn't meant to be. She'd tried, and that would satisfy her conscience.

She almost jumped out of her skin when her phone beeped. With her hands shaking, she opened the message.

I'm in the bar. Would love to see you

The stupid smiley face emoji aggravated her; it wasn't a request to socialise. Her temple started to throb. If only she could knock the smile of his supercilious face.

"I think I'll just nip for a walk around the gardens, I've got a bit of a headache," she said rubbing her forehead.

"Oh, dear," her mum looked concerned, "I've got some aspirin in my bag, I'll get you a couple."

"I'm okay, a walk in the fresh air might do the trick." She headed for the door.

"Don't be long, then," Danielle cut in, "the last thing we need is to be searching the hotel, looking for you. You need to be here on time."

"I know, and I won't be long. I'll be back in ten minutes, I promise."

As she closed the door to leave, she gave a sigh of relief to be out of the way. She could hear Danielle moaning at the hairdresser, "No, I don't want it tight like that, you'll have to soften the curls."

Laura walked swiftly along the hotel corridor and down the stairs to the bar. Thank God he'd suggested meeting in public, it was much safer than his room. She was too scared to be alone with him and, if they were seen together in public, it wouldn't look amiss. It could be perceived as some last-minute detail because tradition dictated Danielle couldn't see him the day of the wedding. Matthew and her dad had taken Teddy out, so there wasn't any likelihood of them spotting her in the bar.

She decided to attempt reasoning, even though nothing about the man was reasonable. Although she knew in her heart he wouldn't take any notice, it was the least she could do considering she'd been the one that had allowed him in.

He was sat at an isolated table beside the window, casually flicking through his phone. A dull weight of dread thumped hard in her chest. Being in his company was marginally easier when others were around, but on her own, he scared her. Thankfully the table was far enough away from anyone to overhear what she was about to say.

Had she really spent almost a week in Spain making love with him? It seemed incredible now that it had actually happened. How did she get it so wrong? He was extremely attractive though; only he could make the casual attire of shorts and a tee-shirt he was wearing, look good. Even after all that had happened, she could appreciate why Danielle was in love with him. He oozed charm; he had that in bucket loads.

Sweat began to trickle down her spine, and her skin prickled as if a hundred tiny mites were crawling all over. She apprehensively approached him, determined to say what she had to, and then get away as quickly as she could.

"Hi, Laura," he gave her a welcoming smile as if everything was normal and he was about to become her regular brother-in-law, "please, have a seat." He nodded to the chair next to him, but she took the one opposite.

"Can I get you a drink?" he asked lifting his half-full glass which looked to contain a spirit of some sort. As if she'd be drinking with him.

"No," she shook her head, "I'm not here to socialise."

"I see." He tilted his head, "So you're not here because you've finally accepted you and I are meant to be together."

The blatant arrogance on his face had her insides raging with fury. Was that how her father had felt when he plunged a knife into her mother? She kept her voice low, "You have to stop this," and continued with a firmness she didn't actually feel, "you can't marry Danielle, she deserves better. *Much* better.

"I quite agree. I do too, but I can't get better. I've tried, but you keep refusing to accept us together."

"There is no us, and there never will be. Please, I'm begging you, call it off now. Leave us . . . my family, alone. Danielle shouldn't have to pay for my mistake."

"Pay?" he exaggerated the shake of his head from side to side, "I don't actually see it quite like that. A marriage is the beginning of two people's lives together," he raised an eyebrow, "or three as in mine and Danielle's case. I'd much rather it was you marrying me today, Laura, and even now if you'd just stop fighting how we both feel, we could be together. I know there would initially be a lot of flack, but we could go away and come back when the dust has settled."

"You can't be serious," she dismissed with contempt, "why would you ever think I'd marry you? You're out of your mind. I'm marrying Matthew, that isn't ever going to change."

He fiddled with his index finger, as if he was getting dirt out of the nail, and gave a wry smile, "But if Matthew was to find out you'd been unfaithful to him, what do you think would happen then?"

The palms of her hands felt sticky, and the knot in her tummy tightened. It would ruin everything for her and he knew it.

"He'd call our engagement off," she told him bluntly, "but you're not going to tell him, are you, because if you were, you'd have done it by now. Anyway, that's not your style, is it? You get your kicks from stalking and causing upset, and despite me telling you time and time again that I'm not interested, you still persist." She snapped despairingly, "What is it going to take for you to realise, I. Am. Not. Interested? And even if there wasn't Matthew, I'm never going to be with you . . . ever."

He was trying to appear nonchalant, but his eyes let him down. They were dark and full of fury. "Then you leave me no option than to marry Danielle," he shrugged, "that way I can be part of your life. I've told you we're meant to be together. You know deep-down I can make you happy, like I did in Spain. Matthew won't ever do that."

She rose to her feet, a little too quickly as blood whooshed through her ears. Speaking to him had been a complete waste of time. "Marry her for all I care, but I'll tell you this, I will do everything I can to make sure Matthew and I move as far away from London as we can get. And you will not be invited as *part of the family* to visit. So all of this wanting to be close to me, is a complete waste. I'm not allowing you in my life. It's not going to happen."

His stare was menacing. "We'll see, shall we?"

Her body felt like it was trapped in a vice and the screws were turning. The room began to tilt and sway.

He glanced at his watch, "Well, much as I've enjoyed our little chat, perhaps we ought to be making a move," his expression became smarmy, "You look beautiful by the way, I can't wait to see you in your dress."

She turned on her heel to flee, but he had one last jibe. "I'll be holding my breath when the question comes up if there's a reason why Danielle and I shouldn't be married. Do feel free to speak up, won't you?"

The man was deranged. If she had access to a knife right now, she could quite easily use it to pay him back for the havoc he'd caused. The relief to have him out of their lives might be worth the consequences.

She made her way back to the security of the hotel room as fast as her legs would carry her. It had been a mistake trying to reason with him. She swallowed a lump down which was threatening to choke her. To think her stupid sister was going to have his child. If only she'd had the courage to say something at the very beginning. Now she was going to have to witness the Cohan Laity charade, where he was going to bind himself to Danielle in a legal ceremony. He'd fooled the whole family, but the biggest loser in it all was Danielle. And when he got tired of all the stupid games, he'd callously dump her. Sadly, she'd have a constant reminder of him for the rest of her life. And it was all because she'd been irresponsible and had an affair with a madman.

If she could think of a way of getting rid of him and not getting caught, right now, Georgie girl would do it. Anything to be free of the monstrous psychopath who'd managed to drive a coach and horses straight through her secure family unit.

Chapter 25

DANIELLE

It was the third day of their honeymoon and she was sitting opposite Cohan enjoying their breakfast in the hotel. She spread a slither of butter on a slice of toast and smiled at her gorgeous new husband as he buttered his liberally.

"You like a bit of bread with your butter do you?" she grinned, "I swear you put more on each day."

"That's the idea. I'm enjoying it while I can as I don't have it at home."

"I know you don't, why is that?"

"It's full of fat."

"Er, yes, tell me something I don't know, that's why I hardly eat it."

"Well you should. You're eating for two now so you'll be putting on weight anyway."

Thanks for that. Another reason for not wanting to really be pregnant.

"I might get used to it, that's why. Anyway, I'm not bothered, what you don't have, you don't tend to miss."

He took a mouthful of his toast and she watched his angular jaw chewing. Delight was written all over his face. "I do love it," his sexy tongue licked the butter off his lips, "it reminds me of being a child. But I know it isn't healthy, that's why I only indulge on holiday or if I'm out for a meal. Anyway, quickly changing the subject, I'm taking you to Kynance Cove today, and as it's expected to reach 22 degrees," he tilted his head, "I'm hoping you'll come for a swim with me."

She sighed, "I've told you, I'm not the strongest swimmer, I'd sooner sit with my Kindle or watch you. I could download one of your books and see what a fabulous writer you are," she quickly added trying for a reprieve.

He waved his index finger from side to side, "Tut, tut, tut, you're not getting out of it that easily, I have my books at home in the study, you can read one of those when we get back. Today, I want my beautiful new wife to come and swim with me. I'll look after you. I know every inch of the waters around here; you'll be perfectly safe with me."

"We'll see," she smiled hoping by the time she got to the beach, she'd have thought up another excuse, "have you finished? I just need to go up and grab my bag and use the loo. You coming?"

"No, I'll meet you down here. I'm going to ask at the desk what's on in the evenings. I want to take you somewhere nice tonight to celebrate being married for three whole days. I can show everyone it is possible that an average bloke can snare a gorgeous young woman."

She wiped her napkin on her lips. "Flatterer. I know you're only trying to get me in the water."

He winked. "I only ever tell the truth."

As she tossed the napkin on her plate, her sister's delicate bracelet she was wearing got hooked underneath the sleeve of her blouse. She gently freed it with her fingers. It was pretty, so needed to be on show.

Cohan's brows creased and his jaw became tight. Something flashed beneath the surface of his hardened expression. It was disturbing how his mood seemed to reflect in his eyes. Agitation was written all over his face, which was an immediate transformation from seconds earlier when he was joking with her.

"Where've you got that from?" he snapped, glaring at the bracelet.

She looked down at it, "Laura gave it me."

"It looks rather expensive to be giving away. Did she say where she got it?"

"In Spain. Said she thought it was really eye-catching when she first got it, but then realised it was one of those cheap impulse buys and hated it now. Reckoned it was tacky. She gave me it to wear for the wedding, you know, *something old, something new,* but it didn't quite look right with my dress, but I do like it. I don't think it's tacky, do you?" She twisted her wrist around watching the bracelet sparkle, "I think it's quite pretty."

His face was full of fury. Why was he cross, she didn't get it? He stood up quickly and almost kicked his chair out of the way.

"What's the matter?" she asked. What the hell had changed his mood from light-hearted, to thunderous in seconds?

"Nothing," he snapped, "hurry up, and don't forget my swimming trunks." She stood and followed him and they made their way out of the breakfast room.

"See you in a bit," she smiled lovingly. He didn't answer as he turned and made his way to reception.

She headed for the lift and pondered over his mood change. Quite why he'd flipped over the bracelet she had no idea. Maybe he'd thought it was from another bloke and he was jealous? That thought made a warm glow spread through her. She wanted him to be jealous; maybe she shouldn't have been quite so honest about Laura giving her it? It was a bit strange of Laura anyway, normally she wouldn't have given her a cold, so it was odd she wanted her to have the bracelet. But it was rather beautiful so she was pleased to have it. She liked the silver and gold combination, and would keep it on as it wouldn't tarnish if she did decide to paddle around in the water later. She wasn't going to have much jewellery on for swimming but she needed a bit. A chain and bracelet would really compliment her new swimsuit.

After using the bathroom, she walked back into the bedroom. As she reached for the beach-bag from the wardrobe, she thought about their lovemaking. It had been amazing, and she loved their intimate dinners each evening together. Cohan was so entertaining and seemed genuinely interested in her family, although that did irritate her slightly. Who cared about Laura and Matthew's wedding and when it would be, or if she or Matthew had ever been abroad together? Wasn't the honeymoon supposed to be about them both, not her family?

She thought about their wedding ceremony. It hadn't been exactly what she wanted, she'd have preferred a much more lavish affair, but Cohan had promised she would have a special party and be able to invite who she liked later. That would be better as he'd hardly invited any of his family and she'd barely spoken to his mother. But apart from the speed of the wedding, everything was perfect between them, just the slight blip at breakfast about Laura's bracelet; she wasn't going to dwell on that, though. If he was jealous then let him be, she had much more to think about. Her focus needed to be on faking the miscarriage but not spoiling their time together. If she announced an early miscarriage now, the sex part of their honeymoon would have to stop for a couple of days. He might even suggest she saw a health professional. She couldn't go down that road. Far better if she was at home and she could pretend to visit her GP once the supposed bleeding started and make out he'd sent her for a scan. That would be much more plausible.

She stared at the messy bed, fresh from their lovemaking. How lucky was she? What was it her dad used to say, *you're not just a pretty face, Danielle.* Okay, maybe he meant it in relation to her schoolwork, but it also applied to her life right now. She'd managed to snare the wonderfully talented Cohan Laity, and best of all, she was in love with him. Things didn't get much better than that.

She removed her new, expensive navy and white bikini from the drawer. It was skimpy and showed her figure off to perfection. She grabbed his trunks and some sun cream, and put them in the bag with the towels provided by the hotel.

Mrs Danielle Laity, she smirked as she made her way to the lift. She'd done it all herself . . . married a hot-looking rich bloke, although she wasn't yet sure how rich, and she'd got one over on Princess Perfect too, whose face had looked like she was chewing a wasp the day of the wedding. She probably fancied him herself. And who wouldn't if they were stuck with dull as dishwater Matthew. Laura had shown no interest whatsoever about the wedding. Everything had been a chore. Mum was always making excuses for her, *she's probably a little bit jealous as you've sort of pipped her to the post, you concentrate on your day, don't worry about her.* And precious Laura had even had the audacity to try and sabotage their relationship by suggesting Cohan was looking at her in an inappropriate way and making her feel uncomfortable.

As if.

Chapter 26

DANIELLE

The sun was blistering down and apart from a few couples walking, they had the beach to themselves. Cohan had explained Kynance Cove had a network of interconnected caves making it a favourite for smugglers in the past. It certainly was beautiful with its aquamarine water and soft white sand. Apparently, it had been a particular favourite beach of his dad's and he'd been there stacks of times. Seemingly, his dad had liked the isolation, away from the popular beaches that holiday makers favoured.

Danielle passed Cohan a sandwich courtesy of the hotel who'd kindly packed them a generous picnic.

"Thanks." He opened the bread to see what was inside despite the reassurance from the chef they catered for all allergies and there wouldn't be any traces of nuts in the hamper they'd prepared. He must have been satisfied as he took a bite which meant he almost consumed the crust less sandwich in one bite.

"They've looked after us almost too well each day," she smiled, loving being with him at his favourite place, and knowing she looked fabulous in her new bikini, "we've hardly touched anything today."

"Yeah, well, swimming and food have never mixed as far as I'm concerned. I don't want all this really as we're eating a lot at night. The cooked breakfast fills me for most of the day."

"Yeah, me too," she added munching on another sandwich, "but I don't want to take any food back."

"We'll leave it for the seagulls like yesterday. Good job we're heading home tomorrow, I'm getting quite stowed with all this food."

"I know what you mean but make the most of it as I've told you, I'm a rubbish cook."

"And I've told you to stop worrying about that. I'm used to cooking for myself. You'll be out at work every day, well at least until the baby's born, so I'll make sure you have a decent meal when you come in. Be nice to me in a morning," he raised his eyebrows and gave her a sexy grin, "and I might even do you some pack up."

She was relieved his moodiness from breakfast had disappeared. She was going to ask him what had brought it on and reassure him again that the bracelet hadn't come from a previous boyfriend and it really was from Laura, but he seemed much brighter, so she left it. No point in spoiling his jovial mood now. She smiled lovingly at him. If a bracelet upset him, it was a good job he didn't know about the fake pregnancy. She sighed inwardly. As if she'd be giving up work to have a baby at her age . . . no way. Maybe in a few years when they'd travelled a bit together and bought a swanky house, then she'd think about it. Old Mr Parker's house which backed onto her parents' was okay for now, but she wanted to choose one with him for them both, their own home, where they would raise kids eventually, when she was ready. Not right now though.

"Come on," he stood up and reached out his hand, "it's now or never, Mrs Laity. Either you come in the sea with me, or I'm going to have to accept that you don't like water so a relaxing two weeks in a six-star hotel in the Caribbean will be a complete waste of money."

She grinned and took both of his hands, letting him pull her up. She brushed the sand off her bottom. "Never let it be said I won't do anything for a free holiday."

The water was initially cold when she first got in and a bit of a shock to the system, but once her whole body became immersed, it wasn't quite so bad. She swam alongside Cohan marvelling at his physique and power in the water. She pottered around doing a bit of breaststroke which she'd learned with her mum and dad as a child, and finally admitted defeat about trying to keep her hair dry when she lost the clip securing it on top of her head.

Unease crept in about how far out they'd swum when she turned around and noticed the beach was getting further away. "Shall we head back now?" she asked treading water as best she could, "I think we've come out far enough."

"In a minute, let's just go round this corner, I want to show you something."

"Round which corner? I don't want to go behind those rocks," she said anxiously.

"It's only for a minute. I want to show you where my dad used to take me."

"But I'm getting out of breath; I'm scared I'll not make it back."

"Sure you will. Come on, hoist yourself on my back, I'll pull you the rest of the way."

She took a deep breath and managed to climb on his back. He swam along effortlessly as if he was pulling a pussy cat, not a fully-grown woman. As she glanced over her shoulder, she could no longer see the beach where they'd been sitting earlier. "I don't want to go this far, Cohan, please can we turn around."

"We're here, look, I'm just heading over there," he pointed to some rocks and a cave which she could see were getting splattered by waves.

"There's a place on the rocks we can rest on before we head back."

She continued to allow him to move towards the rocks. No point in arguing really, she wasn't sure she could make it back without him.

Minutes later, he eased her up to an area where she could sit on a tiny shelf of a rock which only just managed to accommodate her. She was glad to be out of the water, even though water surrounded her and was the only way back. He hoisted himself up beside her, a little higher on a rock, brushing the water off his face and rubbing his eyes. "Isn't it just beautiful here? Look ahead, all you can see is water."

She followed his gaze. To her, there was no beauty. It was water, and more water lapping up and around them as they perched on the rocks.

"Yes, it's lovely." She turned her head toward the cave but all she could see was a huge black hole.

"I wonder if anyone has ever been in there?"

"Aye, smugglers of olde," he said in a pirates voice. "Do you want to go and have a look?" he teased.

"No thank you. Actually I'm getting quite cold. Can we head back?"

"In a minute. I haven't said why I've brought you here."

"No, you haven't. And as you know swimming isn't my favourite pastime, yet you've dragged me here, I'm hoping it's something really special." She tilted her head upwards and tasted the salt on his lips as she kissed him. He didn't linger with the kiss and for some reason, he'd lost his smiling relaxed manner. Maybe pulling her along had taken its toll after all. "You okay?" she asked squeezing his thigh.

"Yeah," he nodded looking downwards. He reached for her wrist and his fingers twisted the bracelet Laura had given her. She sighed; she was going to give her it back if it bothered him so much. She wasn't convinced he was okay at all judging by his expression. His skin had become greyed. Something was bothering him. Where had that jovial laughter gone from minutes earlier on the beach? Somehow that fun-loving man had been replaced by another one with an almost angry look on his face. What could have made him cross? Was it something about his dad and being here on this beach? Maybe his experiences with him weren't as good as he'd led her to believe?

"I wanted to ask you something away from everyone else," he said, "away from prying eyes."

What? He'd already married her so a proposal was out of the question. She couldn't imagine what he was going to say. Was he going to want them to go to Belgium after all for the research on his book? She didn't really fancy it, but maybe it would be better than living in Charlie Parker's old house.

She made a ponytail with her hair and squeezed out the excess water. "Go on then. What?"

"Why did you lie to me?"

Not the sodding bracelet again.

"Lie to you?" she scowled, "What, about the bracelet, is that what this is about, because if it is . . ."

"About the baby," he interrupted. He was staring straight ahead and not looking at her. It was almost as if he was speaking to the water, as he whispered, "I know there isn't a baby."

God, how could he possibly know that? Nobody knew.

"What do you mean, no baby? Of course there's a baby. I've done a test."

He turned slowly towards her, his face looked twisted, almost evil. "No, there isn't, Danielle. Well, let's put it this way, if there is a baby, it isn't mine. And I'm certainly not bringing up another loser's kid."

Unease slithered along her already cold body, which was now beginning to shiver.

"Can we go back and talk about this?" she said, "I'm really cold."

"No, we'll talk about it now," he said firmly, "why did you lie?"

"I didn't lie. I am having a baby." She needed to pacify him. "That's why we got married, isn't it, because I'm having a baby."

His voice became louder, "Why do you persist with this when I know it's a lie, and you know it's a lie. And do you know how I know that . . ." he paused. Panic gripped her entire body. Was she supposed to answer? "Do you?" he growled in a tone she'd not heard from him before.

She shook her head. She was terrified now. His eyes were menacing. And the penny finally dropped. He couldn't have children . . . he was firing blanks.

Oh, my God.

His eyes flashed with hatred. "Cat got your tongue, has it?"

His black expression terrified her. She needed to get away. She tried to move forward so she could ease herself into the water but he was too fast for her. He grabbed her head like a vice with both of his hands. "Stop it, you're scaring me," she squealed trying to grip the rocks but they were too slippery.

"I know you're not pregnant with *my* child," his hands tightened around her head, his thumbs digging deeply into her cheeks, "and do you know why?" He was really hurting her, "Because. I. Can't. Have. Children."

She'd made an almighty mistake.

With the strength that only a man could muster, he almost lifted her head from her neck, and smashed it hard against the rocks.

"Lying . . ."

She heard a crack and knew it was her skull breaking.

"Fucking . . ."

Another smash against the rock and her vision blurred.

"Bitch!"

Pain seared through her whole body.

Then darkness.

Chapter 27

LAURA

As a family depleted by one, the Foleys stood at the bay window in full mourning dress, waiting for the hearse. There wasn't a mantelpiece or windowsill in the house that didn't have a sympathy card on it, and the family home was full of the aroma of flowers, the lilies Laura found particularly sickly. If she didn't know better, she could have been pregnant herself such was the level of nausea she was experiencing. Danielle's *accidental drowning* weighed heavily upon her. She toyed with the idea of coming clean so many times and confessing to her parents how she'd met Cohan in Spain, and explaining how he'd followed her to London. They'd be horrified, first of all because she'd been unfaithful to Matthew, but most of all for allowing such a man into their family. They would have expected her to have spoken up. And if she had done, Danielle would still be alive. It was something she deeply regretted and was going to have to live with because now, Cohan Laity seemed almost to be the son they'd never had. Of course they had got Teddy and loved him dearly, but he would always be the little boy that hadn't grown up. She could see Cohan filling the void in their lives because they'd lost Danielle, and she feared they'd continue to include him for as long as he wanted them to.

"They're here," her dad announced, and Laura followed his gaze as the sombre black hearse slowly approached the front of the house and stopped. Teddy started crying again.

"It's alright, sweetheart," her mum wrapped an arm around him, "it's okay to be upset."

"I don't want to go," Teddy sobbed.

"You have to go, son," her dad said firmly, "this is the last thing we can do for Danielle as a family. It's going to be hard on us all, but we have to do our best and get through it."

"I don't like it." Teddy shook his head and continued to cry.

Laura's heart was full for him. He'd never experienced anyone dying so it was hard to lose his sister, whereas she'd lost loved ones even though she'd only been a child. Teddy's distress gave her an opportunity to dodge the funeral. Anything so she didn't have to be in Cohan's company.

"I could stay here with him," she suggested tentatively, looking at her mum, "and get things ready for when you come back?"

"No," her dad snapped, "we are doing this together."

Her mum sniffed, "Yes, love, but it's not as if Danielle knows who's there," her voice cracked, "I'd rather not upset Teddy any more than he is right now."

"He's coming, Ann," he gave her mum a stern look, "he'll be fine. If it gets too much for him, then Laura can take him outside, but he's going there with us. Now come on, let's do this for Danielle."

Laura took Teddy's hand. "Don't worry, Mum, I'll look after him."

Her dad led them towards the front door and opened it. The undertaker stood in front of them and bowed his head.

As they stepped out of the house, her gaze drifted towards the hearse carrying Danielle. They'd gone for family flowers only so there wasn't an abundance of them, but the pink carnations, red roses and white freesias surrounding the coffin, were beautiful. Her mum's sob was heart-wrenching. She was quickly comforted by her dad wrapping his arms around her. "You're alright, love," he reassured.

Her nemesis, Cohan Laity stepped out of the following car in his shiny black shoes. His stylish suit had designer written all over it, and his chic tie most likely had a label attached to it. As he walked purposely towards her mum and dad, she gave him a fierce glare, making it abundantly clear not to come anywhere near her. Teddy started to tremble, so she tightened her hand around his to reassure herself possibly more than him, that they'd be alright.

"Ian," Cohan nodded at her dad, and then wrapped his arms around her mum and held her. The fiasco was so stomach-churning, Laura had to turn away. Her eyes were drawn to the neighbours who'd come to their gates to see them off. The sympathetic nods from the women, and the men with their slightly bowed heads, said it all. There were no words.

The undertaker gestured for them to move towards the car. Her mum and dad took the first row of seats with Cohan sat beside them. She, Teddy and Matthew sat behind. She loathed being in such close proximity to Cohan. Whatever ton of money he'd spent on his repugnant aftershave, he'd been ripped off. The fruity cedar wood played havoc with her already delicate stomach. She knew she wasn't going to be physically sick, but being so close to him made her want to.

Her skin prickled. Any other time she would have walked away rather than be this close to him, but how could she? She had to get through the funeral. After that, she was never going to see, speak or acknowledge him again. Somehow, she was going to make sure he was out of their lives for good.

They continued by car to the crematorium, each of them immersed in their own grief. The dreadful night they'd heard of Danielle's death was imprinted in her mind. She'd been asleep and was woken by what she thought was screaming. Her eyes quickly became accustomed to the dark and she glanced towards the bedside clock. It was twelve thirty. Muffled voices were coming from downstairs. She got out of bed and reached for her robe off the back of the door. Her thoughts were immediately of Teddy as she descended the stairs. They'd always known that Down's syndrome could weaken the heart.

Please let him be alright.

She opened the door to the sitting room and saw her mum and dad with a uniformed police officer and someone official looking. Her dad had his arms around her mum comforting her on the sofa as she wept. His eyes were full of tears; she'd never seen him like that.

"What is it?" she asked nervously, "Dad, what's happened?"

"It's Danielle, love, there's been an accident . . . she's . . ." he sobbed unable to continue as he clung to her mother.

"What sort of accident, what's happened to Danielle?" she squealed.

The police officer came towards her. "Would you like to sit down, we have some bad news I'm afraid."

She moved towards the chair, "What news . . . tell me," her voice rose, "what is it?"

"I'm terribly sorry to have to tell you, Danielle drowned earlier today."

"Drowned?" she couldn't comprehend what she was hearing . . . "what, in a boat?"

"In the sea. We believe she got into difficulty swimming and it seems likely she hit her head on the rocks."

A sickly ball formed in her throat. "Swimming? But Danielle hates swimming."

"Apparently she was in the water and her husband . . ."

"What about him?" Laura interrupted, "Is he dead?"

"No. He alerted the lifeguard when Danielle didn't come back to the beach. They'd been swimming together but he came back to the shore as he had stomach cramps. He fell asleep so she must have got into difficulty then. The tides can be rough and take swimmers by surprise."

Her mum rushed towards the arm of her chair and wrapped her arms tightly around her, "Poor Danielle," she cried, "poor, poor, love."

She welcomed her mum's arms and leant against her as she tried to comprehend what she was being told. "It can't be right, Danielle doesn't like swimming," she repeated. Was anyone listening to her?

Her mum attempted to wipe her eyes with the tissue she was clutching, "You're right, she doesn't, she's not a strong swimmer at all . . . I mean . . . she wasn't . . . she wasn't a strong swimmer."

The policewoman announced she'd make some tea.

Nobody answered.

They were far too shocked to take anything in.

A gentle squeeze from Matthew's warm hand brought her back from her thoughts to the funeral car steadily following Danielle's coffin. Poor Matthew, today must be an ordeal for him having so recently had to deal with his own cancer diagnosis. A funeral of someone younger must certainly focus the mind. He didn't need this so soon after what he'd been through.

People in the street were nodding their heads respectfully, and one gentleman on a bicycle actually stopped to let them past. The journey to the crematorium seemed endless and all she could think about was the vile man in front of her and the havoc he'd brought on their family. She knew that he'd chosen the isolated beach to lure Danielle to her death. Nobody else suspected a thing, but she was positive he had.

They stood in the crematorium foyer while the funeral directors took the coffin from the car. Teddy was still clinging to her arm as if she was somehow going to abandon him. She'd never do that. There was only the two of them now.

Her mum and dad, along with Cohan had arranged the funeral and decided on everything together. Her dad had asked her if she wanted to do a reading, but she'd declined. She couldn't. Guilt had kicked in hard and wouldn't let go.

Cohan stood directly behind the coffin with her mum and dad at the side of him. If her dad was puzzled as to why she wouldn't walk at the side of Cohan, he didn't say. Her and Matthew stood behind and she made sure Teddy was in between them and both clutched his hand. Her grandparents on her mother's side where behind, and Cohan's mother, his closest friend and an uncle walked behind them. They hardly knew Danielle, she'd only met them all for the first time at the wedding. Oh, how she'd love to tell them exactly what their precious Cohan was really like, and that the tears he was dabbing with a handkerchief, were nothing but crocodile tears.

The undertakers wheeled Danielle down the aisle to the front and they started to follow. Her dad had chosen the entrance music, Elgar's *Enigma Variation –Nimrod,*

which was beautiful, but she never wanted to hear it
again. It would always remind her of today.

She recognised many of Danielle's friends, and
guessed a group huddled together at the back were
some of the staff from *Justin Credible,* the agency
Danielle worked at. She'd done well since joining the
firm and had just started on her first contract before her
death. She spotted Juliet Fleck, Danielle's boss
immediately, even though she'd never met her.
Danielle's descriptions of her were none too polite to
say the least, but extremely accurate visually, looking
at her in her designer black dress and jacket. She'd
even got a fascinator on her head which seemed
inappropriate somehow. Surely they were for weddings
and happy occasions?

They took their seats at the front reserved for
family. Fortunately she didn't have to sit near Cohan.
She sat directly behind him with Teddy and Matthew,
and the rest of the family behind them. The undertakers
bowed their heads and left. They'd placed a beautiful
framed photograph of Danielle next to the coffin. She
didn't recognise it, so wasn't sure when it was taken,
but she knew it wouldn't have been a favourite of
Danielle's as her make-up was smudged slightly below
one of her eyes. She'd hate that. Danielle paid a fortune
for mascara that didn't smudge. No doubt Cohan had
produced the photo, playing the part of the grieving
husband.

The service was simple, but beautiful. Reverend
Short was from her mum and dad's church so knew
them well as a family, but Laura could tell that a lot of
what he spoke about Danielle's life, was by the hand of
her parents'. Poor Mum, Dad and Teddy, Danielle's
death was devastating for them, and even though she'd
often been at loggerheads with her sister, and had
satisfied herself it was just sibling stuff, she wished

she'd been kinder. And she blamed herself entirely; if she'd never been with Cohan, Danielle would be alive today.

She listened to the eulogy and tried to join in with the hymns. Teddy was coping okay thanks to the sweets she'd taken for him. When he became fidgety, she reminded him to be quiet by putting her finger to her lips indicating shush and he kept copying, so he knew it was important not to speak.

Although Cohan didn't speak or acknowledge her, she felt his presence acutely. He'd even managed to spoil the funeral, if it was possible to actually spoil one. She couldn't grieve when her focus had been on him and how she loathed him with every fibre of her being. The vicar's voice became a blur. All she could think about was getting him out of their lives. By marrying Danielle they would have been linked, especially when the baby had been born, but now she'd died, there was no reason for him to be part of their family. But he wouldn't just disappear after a few months, she knew that. And she feared there was more to come from him now he'd murdered once, would she be the next?

The vicar asked everyone to stand and to make their way out of the crematorium into the garden. They'd requested that the coffin remained static and not moved while they were there, her mum had tearfully said she couldn't see it go. Her heart ached desperately for her parents. It was apparent they'd struggled throughout the service, whereas Cohan had done a convincing job of faking grief by dabbing his eyes frequently and blowing his nose. He hadn't fooled her, though.

The undertaker indicated they were to leave the pews. Cohan walked towards the coffin first of all, as the spouse he was classed as the main mourner. Seemingly he'd chosen the music of *All of me,* by John Legend as the final piece for them to leave to. The beautiful lyrics were just another cynical attempt by him to portray himself as the grieving widower. It was almost as if she was seeing it unfold on TV as she watched Cohan reach towards one of the floral tributes resting in front of the coffin and select a red rose. He brought it slowly to his lips and kissed it gently before placing it on top of the coffin. Laura stifled an urge to scream out loud, *you lying hypocrite.*

It was heart-breaking watching her dear mum pass by the coffin and lean forward to kiss it. Her dad, arm-in-arm with her mum, kissed his own hand and rested it tenderly on the top of the coffin, and for a few moments, they stood together, leaning on each other for support.

Cohan watched and waited patiently for them both, and as Laura eased her way out of the pew to move forward with Teddy still clutching onto her, his evil dark eyes momentarily caught hers. She met his stare with utter contempt.

Murdering bastard, I know you killed her.

And one way or another, so help me God, I'm going to make sure you pay.

Part 2

Chapter 28

HAWTHORNE SIDDLEY

Detective Chief Inspector Hawthorne Siddley battled through the Monday morning traffic and arrived at the police station. He found a place to park and applied the hand-brake on his trusted Ford Focus before cutting the ignition. It wasn't a modern ST sports model; it was a basic Zetec and over three years old. There wasn't a new car each year for him despite his ample salary. He was too frugal for that. No point in spending money when you didn't need to.

He released his seat belt, but didn't make a move to go into the imposing building in front of him. He'd been on sick leave for almost five months. Prior to that, he'd spent the last twenty years inside the building solving crimes, and since his promotion to Detective Chief Inspector five years previously, leading on murder cases.

All through his illness, apart from beating it, his focus had been on returning to work. As far as he was concerned, getting back to work meant it was all over. The initial symptoms, the investigations, the bad news, the surgery, the radiotherapy, the chemotherapy and the recuperation period, were all necessities to getting to achieve this moment – how it had previously been before his diagnosis.

He should have a spring in his step as, against all odds, he'd beaten bowel cancer. His latest check-up had been good, and he wasn't being seen again for six months. But more important than that was, tonight after a full day at work, he'd be heading home and someone would be there with a welcoming drink, a loving word and comfort during the night ahead. It had been donkey's years since anyone was at home waiting for him. And even then, he couldn't remember his wife being there with a kind word, and certainly not up for comforting him in bed. She'd have been too busy reading in her own room, buttoned up in her fleecy pyjamas, with the door firmly closed.

For the past twenty-five years, he'd lived alone. Angela, his wife, didn't like the hours he worked, nor the work he did for that matter. He could never talk to her, as a staunch catholic, her whole life was about gentleness, listening and forgiving, so having a police officer whose life was about finding the corrupt bastards and banging them up, didn't fit well.

It was evident from the beginning their marriage should never have happened. They were total opposites which didn't bode well for a compatible union. He didn't find her attractive either so couldn't get it up easily around her. Maybe if she hadn't insisted on being a virgin when they married, he could have sampled the goods and realised they weren't for him. But he didn't, and their wedding night and subsequent couplings hadn't been a great success. He'd frequented whore houses, and used prostitutes most of his adult life, so he'd been naive to think prim-and-proper Angela would cut it for him in the bedroom. Quite why he was thinking about her now, he didn't know, but since his illness, he found himself continually re-evaluating his life and she was a major part of it. Not in an endearing way, by any means. They were bound together by a religious ceremony she wouldn't renounce, and a certificate she wouldn't relinquish, therefore he could never be free of her. And he so wanted to be free of her.

He reached in his jacket pocket for an indigestion tablet. They'd become his essential *must haves* each time he left the house. Women carried tissues, he carried indigestion tablets.

He locked the car door and made his way upstairs, through the main reception area towards his own office, and as he passed through the open-plan area, he spotted his trusted sidekick, Pete Nicholson sat at his desk. Pete had been deputising for him in his absence so he knew he wouldn't be overjoyed at being demoted now he was back. Pete was a good detective, but not as good as him.

"Morning, Pete," he stopped at his desk. He wasn't a great one for smiling or small talk and his team knew that, but as it was his first day back, he thought it prudent to make an effort.

"Welcome back, gov, your office is all ready for you. How are you doing?"

"I'm good, thanks. Time for a catch-up mid-morning?" Hawthorne asked, wanting to be brought up to speed about the ongoing cases. The previous week, he'd met with his superior and HR, and had been told to take things steady when he returned to work, and to let Pete take the load initially.

"Sure," Pete nodded.

"Give me a couple of hours to go through my emails," he glanced at his watch, "shall we say about eleven?"

"Suits me. I've got someone coming to see me first thing, but that won't take long."

"Anything interesting?" he asked placing his briefcase on Pete's desk, hoping there was the prospect of a case to get his teeth into now he was back.

"Doubt it. A female came in yesterday asking to speak to a senior detective. Tracy had a chat with her and then asked me if I would see her today. She's making allegations her sister has been murdered."

"Murdered?" Hawthorne frowned.

"Yeah, on her honeymoon in Cornwall."

"Is it likely?"

"I doubt it. It was a straightforward drowning as far as I can tell, but Tracy said she seemed plausible so I'd better chase it up. Only going to have a chat for now though," he grimaced, "I've enough to do without finding extra work."

"Too right. Okay, see you at eleven and you can fill me in. Good luck."

Hawthorne removed some wipes from his briefcase to clean his PC. He hated dirt and germs and concentrated his efforts on the sticky keyboard. It was filthy. Once he was satisfied the PC was relatively clean, he switched it on and waited for it to boot up. It seemed slow despite IT supposedly updating it to make sure it was all in working order as he'd been off sick for so long. The PC wouldn't have been redundant during his absence, his office would be utilised. But he'd been advised the PC had been personalised with his information and wiped clean of anyone else's.

He stared at the small icon going around in circles on his computer. His back ached and he felt weary already. Getting up at what felt like the crack of dawn this morning for his first day back, had been hard, especially after all the months of not having to. Yet during the radiotherapy and chemotherapy, his one goal was getting back to normal. Whatever normal was. He knew things would never be quite the same, cancer makes sure of that. It focuses your mind on the future and he'd listened to all the self-help paraphernalia from the medical establishment advising that positivity was the way forward.

A tap on the door stopped his *woe is me* thoughts.

"Morning, boss," Tracy Foster, the detective Pete had mentioned gave him a cheery smile, "I'm just making myself a coffee, can I get you one?"

"Morning, Tracy, a coffee would be good, it'll make a change from green tea."

"Ah yes, green tea, I've got some teabags in my desk, would you prefer that? I know it has more health benefits than coffee."

"I'll pass if you don't mind and have a black coffee. One a day won't hurt me, I'm sure," he said with a wry smile.

"Okay, black coffee it is. Great to see you back, by the way."

"Thank you, it's great to be back."

Was it, or had he lied? It certainly felt like an anti-climax from where he was sitting.

The circular icon continued to spin on the screen. He switched the PC off and on again and waited. No joy. He picked up the phone and spoke to IT who promised to send someone immediately; he walked towards the window knowing IT's immediately meant an hour or two.

His office was two floors up and gave him a good view of the front of the building. He watched a couple of police constables leaving with their steady steps, as if things were slack and they were on their way to catching motorists who were flouting the road regulations. A couple of plain clothed colleagues from other departments were arriving for work, clearly not in a rush to get in for nine o'clock. It was just another Monday morning to them; they'd not had to fight cancer to make it in to work today.

He took a deep breath in, already feeling restless and he'd only been back less than an hour. For the first time in years, he wanted to be at home, and all because of the beautiful, Pelo. He wasn't naive, he knew exactly what their relationship looked like, a fifty-year-old bloke with an Asian woman twenty-five years his junior. But she'd captured his brittle old heart and had looked after him all the way through his treatment, and right now, would be waiting anxiously at home eager to find out how his first day back at work had been.

He'd never had anyone care for him. His marriage had been a disaster and it seemed he was doomed to be tied to that forever. He couldn't blame the breakdown of the marriage totally on the force although it suited him to think that way most of the time. He had been devoted to his job and neglectful of her. But it wasn't just that. He wasn't an interactive person; therefore parties and social gatherings weren't for him. His wife would complain endlessly about his lack of enthusiasm for family gatherings, parties or even intimate dinners with friends. He hated socialising, preferring his home comforts with the door closed to outsiders. He strived for quietness so he could devour a good book with a glass of chardonnay or a deep red claret. Even conversing with his wife wasn't something he enjoyed and she'd berate him so often for not talking to her. Yet despite being a quiet and socially inept man, he'd excelled at his job. He could smell a criminal, well, he could before his time off. Would he still be able to? Would he still be as sharp, or would his illness and passage of time, see his detective instincts desert him?

Pete tapped on the door and came in, "How you doing?"

"Exactly the same as the last time you asked when I got here this morning," Hawthorne replied cynically.

Pete's skin flushed slightly, "Sorry, boss, I won't ask again."

He regretted snapping, the staff would be unsure what to say and how to deal with things. Cancer was a small word, with massive consequences.

"No, I'm the one who should be apologising; it feels bloody strange being back, that's all. I'll be okay in a day or so, I'm sure. Anyway, sit down. Tell me, how did the meeting go this morning with the young woman you saw?"

"Quite interesting really." Pete took the seat opposite him, "Basically, she reckons she was being stalked, and when she rejected the bloke, he went after her sister. He got the sister in the club and married her. Then, on honeymoon, she went swimming in the sea, hit her head on rocks and drowned. The death was ruled as accidental, so nothing suspicious until the sister raised it."

"So what's she expecting us to do, charge him with her flimsy allegations?"

"Yes, I think she does. She's persistent, that's for sure, even though she says herself the PM report suggests it was accidental drowning. They've not had the inquest yet."

"What about the stalking?"

"Yeah, maybe there's a grain of truth in that, who knows. Could well be a bit of wishful thinking on her part, I think he's got a bob or two."

Hawthorne frowned, "What would she gain though by making it up now her sister's dead? Did she report the stalking?"

"No."

"I see. How've you left it with her?"

Pete shrugged, "Told her I'd make a note of her visit but for now, without any evidence to substantiate her claims, there's little we can do."

"Right. You say he has a bob or two, what does he do?"

"A writer."

"A good one?"

"How would I know, the last time I read a book, I was at school. He writes about crime apparently."

"What's his name?"

"Cohan Laity."

"Never heard of him."

"Me neither, but she's adamant he's not what he seems. Tracy has done a check on him, and he seems kosher."

"That's his real name, is it, it's not a pseudonym?"

"Yeah, that's his name."

"I see. Best leave it alone then, with a bit of luck she'll move on."

"Yeah, although she seems quite a determined sort of person so I doubt it'll be the last we see of her. There is one thing though, apparently the sister was pregnant, but the PM report says not."

"She probably lost it and hadn't got round to saying anything."

"Yeah, probably."

"If she comes in again, get Tracy to see her and wrap it up."

"Will do."

"Right, tell me about the Fowler case. I can't believe that's still going on, I thought we'd concluded on that before I went off?"

"Yeah, we did, but we're still no further down the line actually nicking him. David Rudd has got his back and you know him, the best brief any lawbreaker can have. Every time we get close, he sticks a spanner in and thwarts us." He gave an ironic smile, "Welcome back to the joys of criminality."

"Cheers, mate."

Chapter 29

HAWHORNE SIDDLEY

Despite suggesting Tracy concentrate on more pressing matters than the woman making allegations about her sister's death, she wouldn't let it drop and had persisted to the point that in Tracy's opinion, the allegations couldn't be dismissed. But she was female and tended to be a bit anal about bloke bashing, particularly in view of anything sexual. Tracy was a good cop, but her judgement could be clouded on occasions, and he couldn't imagine that had improved while he'd been away. Pete and Tracy had plenty of work to be keeping them busy, so the last thing he wanted was their time being spent on a hysterical female with a tenuous allegation. As he was still on his phased return, he advised Tracy he would speak to the woman himself to conclude on the matter. It would be away to ease himself back into work.

He'd asked Tracy to call Laura Foley and invite her to the station at a specific time on the next day he was working. She'd turned up to the station early, he liked that. He couldn't abide lateness of any description. He quickly read through Tracy's notes before the interview. Forewarned is forearmed was his motto, that's why he was a good detective. He didn't like surprises of any kind.

He entered the interview room totally unprepared for the striking young woman sat at the desk. He'd been expecting a young woman in leggings and a tee-shirt, with her hair pulled tight in a ponytail, wearing yesterday's make-up with a bit more added on top.

He'd opened the window earlier expecting she'd be doused in some sort of cheap perfume. He couldn't stand perfume of any kind. But he'd been totally wrong. The woman in front of him was stunningly beautiful. Her eyes were unique, a mix of chocolate and black, if you could have black eyes that is, but more than that, they were determined eyes staring back at him. And not a trace of perfume in the air.

"Good morning, Miss Foley, I'm Detective Chief Inspector Hawthorne Siddley." He held out his hand and she took it, "Pleased to meet you."

He pulled up a chair and sat in front of her with the desk separating them. "I understand you've spoken to my officers and told them you think your sister's death was not accidental?"

"Yes. She was murdered by Cohan Laity, he killed her."

"That's quite an allegation. Have you any evidence to support it?"

"Not any physical evidence, no, but he did. He's been stalking me for weeks now, and when I wouldn't have anything to do with him, he turned to my sister."

"Did you report this stalking to the police?"

She shook her head emphatically indicating no.

He steepled his fingers, "Miss Foley, I appreciate you have been to the station twice now with these allegations, but I'm afraid we're unable to help you. We deal in facts, not hearsay. I've looked at the report into your sister's death, and there isn't a shred of evidence that points to anything other than an accident. She hit her head on rocks which rendered her unconscious and she subsequently drowned. It's all there in the post-mortem report."

"Yes, but don't you see, he wanted it to look like that!"

"Why? What reason would he have for killing her, they'd only just married I understand?"

"To get at me. He wasn't interested in her."

"He told you that, did he?"

"Not exactly. Cohan Laity is more subtle than that. He implied it, though . . . said if I wouldn't be with him, then he'd have my sister instead."

"I see. Tell me, how long have you known Mr Laity?"

He saw it then, quick as a flash, a flicker in her eyes which he'd seen so many times before. She was contemplating telling a lie. He stared directly at her. Would she?

"I met him through my sister," she continued. Her eyes turned dark, and she looked away, as if she was recalling their time together. "I had sex with him, it was a huge mistake, I realise that now. If only I'd known who I was dealing with."

"I'm not sure what your expectations are, Miss Foley, but we can't go accusing people of murdering their spouses without any evidence. You seem like a reasonably intelligent woman to be able to see that."

Anger flashed on her stunning face, which only added to her beauty, "What about the stalking, then? That's a crime isn't it? He won't leave me alone. He's everywhere. I know this sounds far-fetched, but that's why he married my sister, so he could get in with my family. He's a psychopath. It'll be me next," he saw the fear in her eyes as she pleaded, "please do something about him. I'm telling you the man needs locking up."

"You can certainly lodge a complaint about the stalking and it will be looked into."

"What happens if I do that? Do you question him?"

"If we feel the complaint is a legitimate one, then yes he'll be interviewed."

"Then what?"

"Then we'll take it from there. We can't discuss at this stage whether there are grounds for prosecuting him for stalking. But I do need to warn you, charges for stalking are hard to prove, and even more difficult with a relative as, by the very nature of that connection, he is likely to be in places that you would be."

"He's no relative of mine," she snapped, "he's fake . . . the whole thing is fake. He wasn't bothered about my sister. It was all to get at me because I didn't want him." She paused for a moment as if considering something relevant, then continued, "If I put in a complaint about the stalking, is it confidential?" She fiddled with her engagement ring, turning it around on her finger, "I really don't want my family to know. They're grieving for my sister and my father's blood pressure isn't good since . . . Danielle's accident."

"There isn't any reason to inform your parents, but it might be helpful to you to involve them for support."

"I don't want to involve them," she said.

"So, do I take it you haven't shared any of your concerns with them relating to Mr Laity?"

She shook her head, "No."

"Anybody else? I see you're wearing an engagement ring. Does your fiancé know about these allegations?"

"They are not allegations, they're facts," she replied emphatically, "Cohan Laity is stalking me. He's everywhere, outside of my place of work, in the pub I use, and more recently at my home. The man won't leave me alone."

"And he managed all this while in a relationship with your sister?"

"Yes. I'm telling you, the man is unhinged. He's obsessed, talks about us being together all the time. I told him there wasn't a chance and he threatened he'd go after my sister, and he did just that."

"Did your sister know you and he had sex?" he asked, already knowing the answer. Having sex with someone's husband wasn't something that was readily discussed with the wife.

A pained expression passed across her face. "I did try and talk to my sister about him but she thought I was jealous of her and Cohan. She then told him what I'd said, and he dismissed it as me being after him." She screwed her face up, "As if. I detest the man."

"You didn't answer the question," he raised an eyebrow, and asked again, "did your sister know you'd had sex with him before she married him?"

A wave of sadness passed across her face, he was right, the sister didn't know.

"No, I was too ashamed to tell her."

"I see." He took an exaggerated breath to convey he wasn't there to absolve her guilt. If she'd come hoping for him to tell her to say ten Hail Marys and all would be forgiven, she'd come to the wrong place. His abdomen hurt; he'd been warned to expect it initially when becoming more active. Sweat trickled down his back, he required some analgesia so needed to conclude on things. As he suspected, it was most probably something and nothing, a woman scorned and all that, best to get rid of her.

"I'll get someone to come in and take a formal statement from you in relation to the stalking and we'll take it from there."

"Thank you," relief spread across her face, "I just want the man stopping. He's actually rented a house at the back of our family home. That's how hard things are. He's mad. I'm really scared about what he'll do next."

He'd heard enough. He lifted Tracy's notes from the table and stood up. "We'll find out more about the stalking issue and then decide a way forward. If you wait here, I'll send someone in."

"Thank you, I feel better knowing someone is going to do something. The man's dangerous."

He nodded and closed the door behind him. The young woman seemed articulate and quite believable, but in his experience, the devious ones always were. And she was already telling lies. It'd be no more than *guilty shagging syndrome*. She'd been at it with him behind her sister's back, and now she'd died, he was keen to take up where they'd left off. She was just concocting a story based on that to get rid, no doubt ashamed about what the two of them had been up to.

He reached inside his trouser pocket for his hand gel and squirted some liberally on his hands and rubbed them together. That table he'd used for the interview was covered with dirty fingerprints.

The bloody cleaners wanted sacking.

Chapter 30

HAWTHORNE SIDDLEY

He set off from the station for the thirty-minute drive home. He'd texted Pelo and pictured her beautiful face eagerly staring at the screen of the pay-as-you-go phone he'd bought her. He didn't want her to have anything fancy like an iPhone where she'd have access to Facebook and Instagram, she was his and he wasn't going to share her with anyone. And why pay for a contract when all her needs were provided by him?

Pelo would have everything ready for him coming home. The house would be hoovered and dusted, the kitchen floor mopped, and the work surfaces would sparkle, just how he liked it, and she'd have a delicious home-cooked meal on the stove. She was all about pleasing him and he loved her for it. Never in his whole life had he expected to find such a woman, her eagerness to make sure everything was just perfect for him, was delightful. As the saying went, *a cook in the kitchen and a whore in the bedroom – everyman's dream,* and it certainly was his. He couldn't wait to get home, eat a fine meal, and then go to his own sitting room, close the door and put the radio on. He could read a book and do the Times crossword in the seclusion of his room while Pelo stayed in the lounge and watched the soaps. She seemed content with that, which suited him. He wasn't with her for intellectual stimulation and her ever-ready availability in the bedroom was an added bonus. It felt like he'd won the lottery after spending so many years paying for sex.

The traffic was heavy, and the traffic lights had a contra flow in place, so he cut the engine so as not to waste fuel. While he waited, his mind drifted back to work as it invariably did on his way home. Solving crime occupied his thoughts most evenings. He'd always found it hard to switch off and he'd missed the mental stimulation and challenge of crime during his illness. He thought about seeing Laura Foley earlier, she'd lied so wouldn't get any quarter from him – once a liar, always a liar as far as he was concerned. He hadn't believed her story about the stalking one bit, but she had a level of vulnerability about her when she'd talked about the writer, and Pete mentioning her genetic father being a murderer had sparked his curiosity. His copper instincts kicked in and he'd pulled the file on small-time crook Frank Milton, and, reading through his record, it was fairly evident a period behind bars had been inevitable. The report gave details of him being sentenced to life for killing his wife and he'd been viciously stabbed inside after an altercation with another lifer. He'd worked collecting debts for gangster, Tommy Whattam, and part of the report identified several brutal beatings of victims, but evidence to prosecute had eluded the police. Two particularly violent murders were linked to the gang he'd been part of. Both unsolved, but that wasn't unusual, the criminal fraternity who spent their time avoiding the law, rarely snitched . . . honour amongst thieves and all that. And even though Frank Milton was convicted of the murder of his wife and sentenced to life, he was pretty sure from what he'd read, it wasn't the first time he'd killed.

He let himself into his Georgian semi and made his way towards the kitchen. Pelo had placed some tea lights in the lounge and dimmed the lights.

Normally he wouldn't even be home from work at this time, prior to his illness, he rarely arrived home before eight.

She hadn't heard him come in because of the wretched radio blurting out the latest crap she listened to, but she turned around as he reached forward and switched it off. Her face lit up with a beautiful smile as she put the salad knife down and rushed towards him. He wrapped his arms around her, inhaling her clean hair which she cutely wore in a ponytail. Due to his huge stature and her slight height, she barely reached his chest, but couldn't care less about their height difference, she was his little pocket-rocket, and he hugged her tightly. He'd missed her and he'd only been gone eight hours.

How did life ever get this good?

She stood on her tiptoes and he bent and kissed her inviting lips. She had the most enticing lips. "How your day go?" she asked having to crane her neck to look up at him, "it too long without you."

"It was too long without you, too," he smiled lovingly, "you have no idea how pleased I am to have you waiting for me." He daren't tell her every bone in his body ached, and he'd been ready for home about an hour after he'd got to work. She worried and he didn't want everything to be about him. They had precious enough time together as it was. The clock was ticking on two counts, his health, and her returning to Thailand in little over a month. Anxiety gripped his chest, he couldn't comprehend going back to being Billy-no-mates and alone again.

"Come, sit down, I fix you drink?" He took her outstretched hand and let her pull him towards the kitchen table and ease a chair out for him. "Here, sit, food nearly done," she walked towards the kitchen units and took the bottle of scotch from the cupboard.

He watched her running the ice cube tray under the hot water tap. Even her delicate tiny hands were pretty. Everything about her was attractive.

"You no work tomorrow?" she asked, "you still . . . phase back?"

"Yes, that's right, increasing by a day each week, and providing I'm okay, I'll go back to full time hours in a couple of weeks."

She handed him the glass, "You enjoy," she turned to the cooker and began to stir the latest concoction she'd made. It felt good just watching her. All the years he'd been on his own and having to make do with a microwave meal, or in most cases, cheese and biscuits washed down with a bottle of wine, yet now he had her.

"How was your day?" he asked, "did you go out?"

"Yeah, I went to shops and walked back through park. It nice and sunny. Long day," she turned towards him with genuineness written all over her face, "I miss you. I like you being here."

Her love for him gave his libido a kick, thankfully that hadn't been affected by his illness. "Come here."

He made room for her on his knee, she fitted perfectly as she cuddled up to him. She'd be able to feel the evidence of how much he wanted her.

He kissed her head. "I'm going to do everything I can to get you over here permanently. I promise you, I'll do it. My life is nothing without you in it."

"I know you do everything. You honourable man and I love you."

He'd never been loved like she loved him. Her life in Thailand was crap, she was one of six and they barely had enough food for them all. She'd have a much better life living with him permanently in England. He'd been sending the family money since he'd met her. While she was in the UK, she'd not been earning. And the thought of her going home and having sex with other blokes, crucified him. She was his now and he couldn't bear to share her.

She smelt clean. He'd told her how he hated perfume of any kind, Tracy at work was always covered in it and he found it nauseating. Pelo was fresh, just how he liked her to be.

"Have I time for a quick shower before dinner?" he asked polishing off his scotch in one. No point in trying to save his liver now, the damage to his body was done. As far as he was concerned, all the stats he'd read about life after cancer were estimates, some people were lucky and got over five years after diagnosis and surgery, others weren't so lucky. And he felt he was destined to be one of the unlucky ones. His purpose in life now was to enjoy what time he had, working for as long as he could, if he still had the ability to solve crimes – time would tell on that score, and he wanted to enjoy Pelo. He had to somehow think of a way to enable her to stay in the country.

"You no want dinner first, before shower?" she rubbed his tense muscle in his shoulder, "I give you massage."

"I'd prefer a shower now, and save the massage until later?" He wanted to wash the station off even though it didn't actually smell. It was more symbolic. He was home now and wanted rid of it until he had to go back.

"Okay. You no want bath? I can run one for you?"

"No need, a shower is good. You stay here, I won't be five minutes."

He made his way upstairs to the bathroom. He meant it. He was going to do everything in his power to keep her in the country. If only he could marry her, then they'd be fine. Her visa would be extended and they could apply for permanent residency. But sodding Angela would never hear of a divorce. He'd pleaded with her, but she was having none of it. Said their vows were until death. If only she knew how close she was to death. And he could easily do it if he wanted to. He knew how to commit the perfect crime and get away with it.

Chapter 31

LAURA

Her mum walked into the kitchen. "Hello, love, you making tea?"

"Yes, that's timing," she smiled at her dear mum, she'd have been out and about helping someone in need, "you're back early?"

Her mother opened her shopping bag and began to place some Tupperware containers in the dishwasher. "Yes, earlier than I thought. Old Mrs Jacobson had gone into hospital, so that was a wasted journey. I've dropped the cakes off at the church for their coffee afternoon, and I called at Cohan's. I made some extra cakes for him."

Laura's stomach clenched, *that would be the man who murdered your daughter.*

Her mum closed the dishwasher door, "Because of his nut allergy, he doesn't eat a lot of cakes, so the only pleasure he has at the moment is when I take him some." Her mum's eyes became glazed with tears, "He says it's his evening treat with a glass of milk, can you remember Danielle used to tease him about his regimental evening shower followed by a glass of milk, watching the news, and then bed?"

Laura didn't answer. She had no interest in Cohan Laity's daily activities and it wasn't really a direct question, more reminiscing. Her mum carried on, "I've been treating him to some Jersey milk, he loves the full cream," her lip quivered, "he is struggling, but it is still early days, I keep telling him."

God, Mum, if you only knew. The bastard's fooling you all.

Laura rushed forward and threw her arms around her. "You're doing brilliantly, and keeping busy's the key, I'm sure." She hugged her mum tightly; she didn't deserve such pain.

"Thanks, love," her mum smiled, "I needed that."

"Me too," Laura said as she moved away and reached for the teapot. She poured them both a cup and handed her mum one as she stood by the sink.

"Your dad's doing his best to keep busy too, but Teddy's such a worry, it's hard for him to make sense of it all." She looked around the kitchen, "Where is he anyway?"

"He went up to his room and last time I looked in, he was asleep."

"God love him, it'll do him good. He's not been sleeping well. Dad says he's tempted to take his binoculars off him to stop him sitting in the window at night with them when he should be sleeping."

"Aw, don't do that. Sadie at school told him Danielle is a star in the sky so he keeps looking at them. He's got an astronomy book from the library, we might have to get him a telescope if it helps."

"Mmm, we'll see. Anyway, what time's Matthew back tomorrow?"

"About seven," Laura took a sip of her tea, "he seems to have been gone ages."

"I think that company of his have got him earmarked for promotion sending him to Le Havre to look at a refinery." A shadow fell across her mum's face, "I'll be sad if you both go and live there when you're married."

She'd be sad too having to leave her family, but she was going to have to if it meant getting away from Cohan, although she hadn't seen him since she'd been to the police. She secretly hoped he'd been following her when she went into the police station, and that it had put the wind up him. Or better still, they'd interviewed him about the stalking and it had scared the shit out of him.

"We'll see, Mum, who knows. It is exciting for Matthew though to be taken to the refinery, it sort of shows they think he has potential. He doesn't say much, you know what he's like, but I reckon he's secretly pleased to have been selected to go."

"I'm sure it would be a marvellous opportunity if he did get a chance to work there, and don't worry about me, I just get a bit maudlin. Some days are better than others." Her face clouded with sadness, "Today hasn't been so good. I wanted to see Cohan, but there's another part of me that reminds me everything that's happened is because Danielle met him. If she hadn't, she'd still be here now. I've spoken to Reverend Short about it and that's helped. He keeps reminding me of how happy Danielle was with Cohan, and he's right, she did really love him."

Guilt thumped hard in Laura's gut reminding her she was to blame. She stifled an urge to cry out loud, *yeah, but he didn't love her*.

"I don't think he'll be here long, if I'm honest," her mum took a sip of her tea, "nothing really for him to stay around for anymore. Reverend Short says it's right to encourage him to make a fresh start. He can't spend his life mourning Danielle, it's not as if they were together that long, it was all such a whirlwind really."

Laura couldn't stand the focus being on Cohan any longer. "I was just about to get changed; I thought you said you wouldn't be back. Do you still want me to take Teddy for his appointment?"

"Do you mind? I'm worn out today. I'll sit down for a few minutes and close my eyes, I think."

"You must, Mum. I can take him, I'm glad to help. It's been nice having a few days' leave. How was Dad's check-up, by the way?"

"Fine. I think the cutting down on the salt and increasing his exercise are helping to bring his blood pressure down. I hope so as I don't want him having to go on medication."

"Yeah, and maybe he needs to stop rushing about so much too."

"You're right, but he can't help it. He didn't really want to go on the scout trip right now, but one of the leaders dropped out and it couldn't go ahead if they couldn't find another adult, so your dad being your dad, stepped in."

"It might do him good to have something to focus on, maybe?"

"Yes, I think so too."

"Okay," Laura glanced at the kitchen clock, "I'll go and get ready and give Teddy a shout."

"Remember it's the counsellor he's seeing today, not Dr Meadows."

"Yeah, you said. I've got my Kindle to read in the surgery while I'm waiting."

"I hope she can help him," her mum's expression was full of concern, "he's become quite withdrawn lately."

"How many counselling sessions has he got?"

"Six. Dr Meadows thinks that will be enough and says we should see an improvement after that with Teddy being more like his old self."

"He'll be fine, I'm sure. He's got us to support him, we just need a bit of time. Losing Danielle has been a massive shock to us all. It's no wonder he's struggling."

"I know. Thanks, love, you're a good girl."

Laura sat with Teddy in the health centre waiting room. It was Thursday afternoon and the rush must have been over as the surgery wasn't crowded. The occasions she'd ever had an appointment were after work and it was always manic.

"Can we go to McDonald's after?" Teddy asked.

"If you want to."

"Yeah."

His momentary joy at the treat was short-lived as he started rubbing his hands together and inadvertently shaking his head which he did when he was nervous. She thought at first he must be worried about the counsellor until he whispered, "I don't like, Cohan."

She needed to be careful with her response; Teddy had a habit of repeating things that were said to him.

"I don't either very much," she whispered truthfully, "why don't you like him?"

Teddy shook his head from side to side, "Mum says if you can't say anything nice, you shouldn't say anything at all."

She nodded as if she was in agreement and her mother was absolutely right, but she wanted to know more. Despite all the education he'd been given at school and home about various people not *being nice,* Teddy was enthusiastic about everyone from the postman to the vicar. He loved people.

"Tell you what. I'll say why I don't like him, and you tell me why you don't, deal?"

He nodded several times but wouldn't look at her. He stared at the floor.

She leaned towards his ear, "I don't like him because he doesn't like me."

Teddy turned his head and his eyes widened, "Why?"

"I don't really know why," she lied, "but I know he doesn't."

His bottom lip came out as if he was going to cry. "He doesn't like me, either. He called me a name."

"What name?" Fury gripped her chest at the thought of him upsetting Teddy. When had he managed to do that? "Tell me what he's said to you," she asked gently, as if it was an entirely normal conversation, but inside she was raging.

"It's swearing."

"It won't matter just this once. It's not you saying it, you're only telling me what someone else has said, so that's okay."

Teddy's eyes filled with tears, "He said I'm a fucking retard and to keep my mouth shut."

Her heart constricted. *Bastard.*

She calmly asked, "When did he say that?"

Teddy shrugged, "When he was in your bedroom . . . after Danielle's funeral, I saw him looking in the drawer next to your bed. Dad says it's private business in the bedrooms, doesn't he?"

"Yes, he does." She kept the tone in her voice light so Teddy didn't clam up. "I wonder why he was looking in my drawer?"

He didn't answer.

"Do you know what he was looking for?" she touched his arm, "you must say, Teddy, if you do know."

He shook his head fast. Too fast. It usually meant he wasn't telling the truth.

"What did you see? Tell me, it's important."

"I think he had your passport in his hand."

Christ. Why would he want her passport?

"Have you told anyone, Mum or Dad?"

"No." A tear escaped and rolled down his cheek, she caught it with her thumb.

"What is it? Did he say anything else? You have to tell me."

"Promise you won't say."

"I promise."

"He asked me if I knew who Guy Fawkes was and when I said I did, he said he would make sure Mum and Dad burned like him on a bonfire if I said anything."

Oh, my God. The man was insane.

Teddy's face was crestfallen and her heart ached for him. She took his hand and just as she was about to reassure him, his expression turned from sadness to fear as he gazed over her shoulder. She turned to see what had caused the transformation.

Cohan Laity.

He'd come through the automatic doors and was making his way towards them.

"Hello, Laura," he beamed as he stood in front of her, greeting her as if somehow they were friends. He nodded an acknowledgment to Teddy, "Nice to see you both, how are you doing?"

Her chest was so tight, she struggled to breathe. If hate could kill, he'd be a dead man. Totally oblivious to the havoc he was causing her and Teddy, he gave the smile she loathed, "Your mum was telling me how good this surgery is and encouraged me to register so I've just called on the off chance I can get in here."

Off chance? Liar. He must have followed her.

Teddy's grip on her hand became tighter, anxiety oozing from all his pores. She gritted her teeth and hissed, "Why don't you do us all a favour and move on?"

He shrugged, "I will do eventually, but there's no rush. I thought I'd stay around for a while . . . you know, grieving with the in-laws," he put on a wistful expression, "I'm finding their support helpful."

"Teddy Foley," a female voice called from down the corridor. Teddy let go of her hand, eager to be away, judging by his relieved expression.

She nodded, "You go, I'll be sitting here when you come out." She waited until he disappeared with the counsellor before standing up. Her blood pressure must have been off the scale as she felt giddy. She faced Cohan and lowered her voice. "I don't know what you think you're playing at," she snarled, "but you'll not get away with it. You're a psycho. I know what you did to Danielle, and now threatening Teddy. With a determination she didn't actually feel, she added, "I'll make sure you pay for that."

"Tut, tut, tut, Laura, I can see you're upset but you need to calm down. Grief can make us all say things we don't really mean. What does the bible say, *"Bear with each other and forgive as the Lord forgave you,"* he widened his eyes, "it's understandable you want to lash out, I feel that way too. Danielle was too young to be taken. I'd like to comfort you, if you'll let me."

"Get out of my sight," she spat. Her shaky legs propelled her towards the automatic entrance door. The outside breeze was welcoming as her heart was hammering and sweat was running down her back. She hastily headed towards her car, wishing she'd been able to park closer to the health centre. Regrettably, he followed her. His ability to match her pace, scared her. She wouldn't look back, she just kept briskly walking. She was almost at her car, when he reached for her arm to stop her. "That's not a nice way to speak to your brother-in-law, Laura. I told you, I want us to be together, and we will be, I'll make sure of it."

She spun round and forcibly shrugged his arm off hers, "You're mad, fucking mad," she shouted regardless of who might hear, "and I'm telling you to leave me and my family alone, or else." She hurried on, trying to quicken her pace and get to the safety of her car.

"Or else what?" he carried on beside her, "You know we're meant to be together. I can see you found that difficult at first, but now we can legitimately become close through our grief over Danielle. We'll give it a reasonable period of time for the family get used to that, and then you can ditch Matthew. We'll be able to begin a new life together then, just the two of us."

She reached her car and stopped at the door. "As if I'd ever be with you," she snapped, "I'm telling you now, I will get you out of my life. Whatever it takes, I'll make sure you go. I'll tell Matthew and my family what happened between us then we'll see how much power you have."

"Sure you will," he sneered, "imagine what your precious mother would think of you then. It most definitely would destroy your mummy daughter bond, don't you think?"

What could she say? He was right. Her heart felt as if it was coming through her chest into her throat. She glared at him with venom in her eyes.

He glanced down at his watch and his mood changed completely. "Right, I'd better go back in and see if I can register. Be seeing you around no doubt, Laura. Keep smiling."

He turned and made his way back towards the health centre. The man was deranged. None of them were safe. And the threat to Teddy of burning her parents on a bonfire really frightened her. Who would have any idea what he was capable of?

Her legs were shaking, and her head throbbed to the same heavy beat of her heart. She was relieved to sit down inside the car and hastily pressed the lock as if it would protect her from him. The water bottle was where she left it and she took a large gulp and tried to take some deep breaths to calm herself. She wiped her sweaty hands along her jeans. She was going to have to go back into the health centre at some stage, she'd told Teddy she'd be there when he came out. He was frightened enough as it was seeing Cohan there. Hopefully he'd be long-gone by the time Teddy was ready, she couldn't face anymore of him right now. She was going to have to contact the police again and tell them he was now issuing threats. Better to get it out in the open then he wouldn't dare harm her mum and dad. Or Teddy, he must have been terrified, bless him. Mum and Dad were his life. He struggled enough with his own challenges so he didn't need the fear of losing them on top of things. That could well explain why he was becoming so withdrawn, Cohan's threats were probably affecting him as well as Danielle's death. What a despicable excuse for a human being. The man was stark raving mad.

The tears that threatened, gave way to a sob. Would she ever be free of him? She recalled Ed's remark when his wife left him for another man, *Can you imagine what it's like to hate someone so much you want them dead?*

Now, she understood perfectly.

That Hawthorne bloke better do something about him, or she'd be forced to do something herself. She hadn't been able to stop him killing Danielle, but she could make sure he didn't hurt anyone else.

She had to protect her family from the monster.

Chapter 32

HAWTHORNE SIDDLEY

"I thought you wanted to see me about my wife's death," Cohan Laity frowned and nodded towards Tracy who was sat at the table opposite him, "The officer says it's not about that at all?"

"No, Mr Laity, it isn't," Hawthorne Siddley said, taking his seat next to Tracy and placing his paperwork on the desk. "We've invited you here to talk about something entirely different and appreciate you giving up your time and coming in this morning."

He'd asked Tracy to meet Cohan Laity and take him to the interview room. He could see by the remnants in the paper cup on the sticky table, she'd given Cohan one of the dreadful concoctions from the corridor coffee machine. He'd been justified in not finishing it.

Hawthorne looked directly at him, "I'll come straight to the point. We've received an allegation relating to you from Laura Foley."

"I see," Cohan Laity rested back on the chair, "what's she saying this time?"

"This time?"

"Yes, this time. She has made *allegations* as you put it to my late wife about me before."

"Really? Well, the allegations she's made to the police are that you have been stalking her."

"Stalking her?" Cohan repeated, and shook his head, "she can't be serious. I can assure you, I have not been stalking her. Why would I do that?"

"She says you and she had a brief affair."

"Yes," he nodded, "that's correct."

"And these liaisons happened while you were in a relationship with her sister?"

"Is that what she said?" he gave a cynical smile, "another one of her lies, then. We met in Spain when she was over there in April. She was cat-sitting for a relative. We were together for about five days."

"I see. So you'd had a relationship before you came to the UK?"

"Yes, that's right. We only had that short time together in Spain and Laura had to get back for work. I asked her to stay to see how things worked out between us. Five days wasn't long, so I wanted to see if the initial attraction would turn into something more."

Hawthorne raised an eyebrow. "She didn't feel the same way?"

"I think she did, but was torn. She is very dependent on her family. After a few days I realised that I wanted to see her again, and I needed to do some marketing for my book in London, so I sort of opportunistically came over and thought I could combine the trip with doing some research for my next book."

"And you made contact to let her know you were here in London?"

"No, I didn't. That was my intention once I settled, but the next thing that happened was more of a coincidence. I engaged a small PR company, Justin Credible, to help with the promotion of my book, and as luck would have it, Laura's sister, Danielle, worked there. That particular day she was forced onto reception duties due to sickness and I met her then. The chances of us meeting were so remote as Danielle was a junior design artist and it was a relatively new job so she wasn't actually involved with clients. Anyway, to cut a long story short, Danielle helped me out when I'd got coffee spilt on my jacket, and as a thank you I invited her to join her boss and I for lunch."

"So you had no idea that this was the sister of the woman you had come to England to pursue?"

"No. How could I know?"

"Maybe Laura had told you her sister worked at that particular company?"

He shook his head, "No, I don't believe we discussed much about family. Our," he held his hands to show air quotes, "affair, was very brief and we didn't get chance to do a lot of talking if you get my drift."

Hawthorne sighed purposely, "Yes, I understand. So when did you find out they were sisters?"

"When Danielle invited me to Laura's twenty-first birthday party. I couldn't make the actual party as I had a prior dinner engagement but managed to call on my way home for a drink. It was then I was introduced to Laura just after her boyfriend Matthew had gone down on one knee and proposed. For obvious reasons we both kept quiet. It didn't seem right to announce there and then we knew each other."

Tracy interrupted, "When Danielle invited you to call in at Laura's party after your dinner engagement, didn't she give the name of her sister?"

He shook his head, "I'm not entirely sure. Anyway, even if she had, I don't think I'd have made the connection to be honest. It's quite a coincidence."

"Yes, it is," Tracy agreed, "and what stage did you move your affections from Laura to Danielle. You say you came here to pursue Laura?"

"That's right, I did. But only with a view to seeing her again and carrying on with our affair, but once I met Danielle, she was something else. I knew straight away she was the one for me," a shadow passed across his face, "hence asking her to marry me."

"How did Laura take it, you pursuing her sister?" Hawthorne asked, "Was she jealous?"

"She wasn't happy, is putting it mildly." He shuffled in his chair, "Look, can I be honest?"

"Please do."

"I think . . . well, I know, there was a lot of rivalry between the sisters. Laura is a bit headstrong and has a massive chip on her shoulder about being adopted. I'm not sure if you are aware, her father killed her mother when Laura was nine and subsequently died in prison? She's actually adopted by the Foleys."

Hawthorne nodded indicating they knew.

Cohan continued, "My late wife told me Laura lives her life in a sort of fantasy way. She makes things up. She adores her adoptive parents and seems to spend most of her time trying to curry favour with them. I don't know how much truth is in this, but Danielle felt she was only marrying Matthew to please them."

"That may well be, but marrying him seems highly probable as they are engaged. So I'm curious as to what she would be likely to gain by making up allegations about you? They are very serious."

"I really have no idea," he shrugged, "maybe a woman scorned, who knows?"

"Did you tell your wife about your previous relationship with her sister?"

"No, I did not."

"Why not?"

"Because Laura asked me not to. I suggested we needed to come clean, but she didn't want to. Said it had just been a holiday fling and she didn't want her parents and Matthew finding out."

"So why is she pursuing this stalking thing now do you think?"

Cohan Laity remained silent.

"You must have an opinion?"

"I can only assume she has had a change of heart." He took a deep breath in, "I wasn't going to say anything, but perhaps it's best if I do. All this talk about me stalking her, is a complete red herring, it's Laura that has started to follow me. She seems to be around places I am. She also keeps texting me."

"Texting you? Have you got any texts you could show us?"

Cohan took the phone out of his pocket and scrolled down it.

"This is the last one she sent yesterday."

The text had the name Laura on it.

When can I see you? Please can we meet? Xx

Hawthorne flicked onto the contacts and jotted down Laura's number.

"I don't think that's going to be any good to you. I think she uses a pay-as-you-go phone or something as that isn't her number. Not her official one anyway, I know that from Danielle's phone."

"So you're saying she's using a separate phone to text you on?"

"She must be, yes."

"Why do you think she would do that?"

"I have no idea. It's all very odd. And with respect, I've more to do with my time than answer questions about a highly-strung female I had a brief fling with several months ago. I'm finding it hard since my wife's death, and I'm trying to support her parents. They've been marvellous, I have to say, considering I haven't known them long."

"Yes, I do understand, and you coming in today has helped clarify things."

"That's good. I've told you all I'm able to. Could I ask, if you are talking to her again, do you think you could have a quiet word? I know it isn't your place, but I don't want this getting out of hand."

"Thank you, Mr Laity, we'll do our best. Now, we've taken up enough of your time," he smiled, and then added, "there is just one more thing before you go. Did you see Laura Foley outside of North Carlton health centre yesterday?"

"Yes. I went to register there. My mother-in-law recommended it. Laura was there with Teddy in the waiting room."

"You spoke to her and followed her out to the car I understand."

"That's correct, I did. She seemed upset and I didn't want her driving home like that."

"I see. Miss Foley says you have been issuing threats to her brother," he glanced down at the papers on the desk, "seemingly you have also made threats against their parents to the brother and frightened him."

"I can assure you that isn't correct at all," Cohan replied indignantly, "if he's suggesting that, then it sounds to me as if some of Laura's over-active imagination has rubbed off on him. Has he actually said that, or is this all from Laura?"

"We haven't had an opportunity to speak directly to the young boy yet, but we may try and get his version."

"This is all very worrying," he frowned, "if this sort of slander continues to be spewed out by the two of them, I might have to take action myself. I can't have my reputation tarnished in any way; I earn my living as a writer so can't afford to alienate readers." He raised an eyebrow, "I do understand you have procedures to follow, but you do know the boy has a level of mental retardation?"

"Yes, we do." Hawthorne shuffled his papers, "I think that's it for now, Mr Laity, Tracy will show you out unless there's anything else you want to add?"

Cohan Laity stood and reached out his hand which he shook. "Only that I hope this all blows over. My late wife's parents are lovely people, they certainly do not need any more stress. We are all grieving over Danielle's death, that's more than enough to cope with."

"I do understand," Hawthorne nodded. "Thank you again for coming in."

Tracy led Cohan out and he moved towards the window waiting for him to come into view as he left the station and got into his car. He'd given a good account of himself and confirmed Laura Foley had lied. They had met before.

The interview room door opened and Tracy came in and let it swing behind her. "What do you think?" she asked.

"It all sounds plausible to me. What did you make of him?"

"Now I've met him, I think it most probably is her stalking him," Tracy replied, "but why come to us? It doesn't make sense. It was interesting what he said about Laura always trying to fit in and please her parents. I bet they'd be pretty pissed off if they found out about the affair between the two of them."

He widened his eyes, "Yeah, not to mention the fiancé. It does lead you to think her course of action would be to lay low, though."

"And what about the texts, do you believe they're from her?"

"Not sure. As you know, anyone can buy a pay-as-you-go phone and send themselves texts. That proves nothing."

"And the threats to the brother? Do you think she's making those up?"

"Maybe, but right now, over-egging the pudding springs to mind. And she's already proven to be a liar. She reckoned she met him through her sister yet it sounds like they've been at it for ages."

"So where should we go with this?" Tracy asked, "do you want me to speak to the brother?"

He shook his head, "She doesn't want the family involved and we couldn't take anything he said as accurate."

"What about checking she was in Spain in April?"

"Nah, no need, I'm fairly sure she would have been." He picked the documents up from the table, "I think we've wasted enough time on this now. If you could do a report on the interview with him, I'll ring Laura Foley and tell her we've looked into it, blah, blah, blah, and there isn't any evidence to pursue a case. Then we can close it."

"Okay," Tracy agreed, "I still feel a bit sorry for her though. She does seem genuinely scared of him. I found her account believable and that was before the so-called threats he made yesterday."

"Sounds like six of one, and half a dozen of the other to me." He glanced at his watch, "Anyway, I'll go and ring her now, before the superintendent gets here."

"The super's coming here, today? What's that all about?" Tracy asked as they walked towards the door.

"Seemingly to see how I'm getting on. I can only assume it must be a new HR initiative and he's got to do the rounds."

"Christ, you're honoured, then."

"Quite," he smiled wryly, "so I keep telling myself."

Chapter 33

LAURA

Laura walked from the changing room into the gym, busy as always on a Saturday morning. Her eyes skirted towards the segregated weight-lifting area, checking anxiously around to see if Cohan might be lurking. Even though it was a membership only gym, she knew they offered taster sessions and she wouldn't put it past him to sign up for one of those while she was there.

Exercise was the last thing she felt like doing but she needed some time alone to think what to do next. She stepped onto one of the treadmills, programmed twenty minutes in and began walking as it started up. Cohan Laity occupied her mind every waking moment, and of late her thoughts were becoming more and more sinister in relation to him. She'd tried the police but Hawthorne Siddley had telephoned the previous day and said there wasn't enough evidence to bring forward a case about Cohan Laity stalking her. They'd interviewed him and were satisfied with his account of events.

Account of events? That would be the pack of lies he'd spun them. Now she wasn't sure which way to turn. Even though she had a long-term plan to marry Matthew and move away, the threats to Teddy and her parents had strengthened the need to do something now. She'd lost one family member, she couldn't lose another. The nausea she'd been experiencing had intensified and she'd actually been physically sick when she'd returned from the health centre the previous day. Not that there was anything to be sick with, she couldn't keep food down lately.

Her phone pinged in her pocket. It was a text from Matthew.

Can you come now? I need to see you

There was no kiss at the end of the message, which seemed strange. She was supposed to be going to Matthew's flat after the gym as per usual on a Saturday as they always spent the day together. Why would he want her to go now? She'd been with him the previous evening so he knew she was coming at 11.30.

Abandoning the workout was no great hardship. She picked up her water bottle, stepped off the treadmill and headed for the changing room. She had hoped a vigorous session might somehow ease the tension, but Matthew's text had cut short any chance of that. She sent him a quick message to tell him she was on her way.

Traffic was slow and her thoughts drifted to the conversation she'd had with Matthew about holding off speaking to her dad about them moving in together. Although he was a bit miffed, he was agreeable when she'd asked him to wait a while because of Danielle's *accident*. Her mum and dad had enough on without her leaving home at the moment.

She exited her car and, as usual, looked around the immediate area. It had become a habit, looking over her shoulder seemed the norm now. She couldn't remember what it was like before Cohan, as now everything in her life was tainted by him.

She took the lift up to Matthew's flat and let herself in as the front door was unlocked. "It's only me," she called as she made her way along the hall and into the kitchen. She'd usually find him facing the panoramic view overlooking the bustling shops and street. And normally, he'd have a pot of coffee burbling away and they'd have a chat about what they were going to do before heading out, but there was no coffee today. He was sat at the kitchen table, still in his boxers and tee shirt, with a bottle of whisky and a glass in front of him. Something was wrong.

"What's the matter?" she asked, slipping off her jacket but not taking her eyes off his face. His eyes were red-rimmed and his cheeks flushed.

Please not the cancer.

"I've had a phone call."

"Who from?"

Angry eyes looked directly at her, "Your brother-in-law."

No!

Not him. Please.

Rage spewed out of him. "Tell me he's lying and you haven't been having sex with him?"

She felt the colour visibly draining from her face. She'd lied. Lied by omission, and it had all been a complete waste of time. Cohan had exposed her as she'd always known somehow, he would.

"Is it true?" Matthew glared.

She swallowed the lump in her throat. "Okay, calm down and I'll tell you."

"I don't want fucking details," he snapped, "just a yes or no."

"It's not as simple as that."

"So it's yes, then. You have been shagging him."

He stood up from the table and walked across to the sofa and sat down. She followed him and sat down next to him reaching for his hand but he pushed hers away.

"How could you?" he spat and ran his hands through his hair, "I thought you loved me. I'd never do this to you," he raised his voice as if to make his point, "never!"

"It's not what you think, Matthew."

"And how do you know what I'm thinking?" His voice was becoming louder, "I thought our future was all mapped out. I thought you wanted the marriage and kids thing."

"I do want that, I love you, you know I do."

"You love me, do you?" he snarled, "how the fuck does that work then when you've been shagging your brother-in-law behind my back. That's how much you love me, is it?"

"That isn't true," she denied, "I haven't been doing that behind your back. It happened when I went to Spain and you couldn't come. It was just a fling, nothing more. It meant nothing. I'm not trying to make light of it. It happened and I was sorry it had. I wasn't sure what to do. I wanted to tell you, and I realise now I should have. But I was scared I'd lose you, and I couldn't bear that."

"Oh, yeah, I can see how scared you were about losing me. You had an affair for God's sake. What did you think would happen, eh? That I'd brush it all under the fucking carpet and we'd start afresh."

"It wasn't an affair, it was a couple of days. Then when I got home, you got your cancer diagnosis so I couldn't say anything then."

"Ah, I get it. You were going to come back and tell me you'd been shagging someone else, hoping I'd forgive you, but the cancer diagnosis got in the way. Sorry about that."

"It wasn't like that. I was scared to tell you. I didn't want to lose you."

He wasn't listening, "And as if that's not bad enough, you let me make a complete fool of myself by asking you to marry me, in front of all your family and you said yes, knowing you'd been with someone else.

What type of person does that make you, Laura, for fuck's sake?"

"I know it looks bad," tears threatened but she held them back, "but I wanted to marry you . . . I still do. I had no idea you were going to ask me then. I honestly didn't. I thought it would be in another couple of years. But as soon as you asked, it seemed right. You're all I want, you have to believe that."

His expression smacked of disgust. "I don't believe a word you say. Did Danielle know you'd been with him?"

"No. I did try to say something but she said I was jealous and causing trouble."

His face twisted with pain, "How could you? While I was having surgery, all I could think about was getting back to normal so we could make plans for our wedding, freezing the sperm so we could have kids. I did it all for you, and what for, eh? So you can humiliate me? God, Laura," he spat, "I thought I knew you, now I realise I know nothing."

"You do know me, better than anyone. And I'm so sorry I didn't come clean in the beginning. I should have, and I wish now I had, then he wouldn't have had this hold over me."

"What hold? What are you on about?"

"Cohan's been stalking me. He came over to the UK to find me and when I wouldn't have anything to do with him, he threatened me. Then before I knew it, he'd taken up with Danielle."

"How did he threaten you?"

"He kept saying if I wouldn't be with him, he'd take up with Danielle which he did do. I know it all sounds far-fetched, but I think he killed her on their honeymoon. I don't think she died as a result of an accident. I think he did it."

"Are you mad?" he barked, "of course he hasn't killed his wife, he loved her. Anyone can see that."

"He didn't love her, Matthew, it's me he wants. You've got to believe me. I'm not making this up. I'm scared. He keeps turning up everywhere I go. He's watching me all the time. I've even been to the police."

"Hang on a minute; you've been to the police? Didn't you think to tell me about all of this?"

"I couldn't. I thought I'd lose you. I just wanted it all to stop. I wanted to get him out my life."

"You could have done that in an instant. You should have been honest, then he wouldn't have been able to do anything to you, if that is the case. I'm finding it hard to understand all of this. It sounds like something you read about in a crap women's magazine."

"It's true. Why do you think he's told you? After all this time, why has he suddenly decided to tell you now, ask yourself? It's to get at me because the police questioned him. He wants us to split up."

"He's definitely got what he wants, then, 'cause we are well and truly over. There's no going back after this."

"Please don't say that, we're all entitled to one mistake. We can work through it."

"No, we can't," he snarled, "I don't want to work through anything. All this stalking rubbish you're churning out, which I don't believe by the way, but whatever's going on, you'll have to deal with it yourself. If it's as you say it is, now it's out in the open, he'll most probably clear off."

"Do you think?" she asked hopefully. She wanted that more than anything.

"I've no bloody idea, but do you know what? I couldn't give a stuff. We're done. And much as I love you, I can't make a life with you now."

"Don't say that," she pleaded, "we can put this behind us. Please Matthew, I love you. I want us to get married and all that goes with it. I made a mistake, and I promise I'll make it up to you. Just give me a chance."

"Does your mum and dad know you've been with him?"

"No."

"So what about all this supposed stalking. You say you've been to the police?"

"Yes, but I didn't tell Mum and Dad."

"Why?"

"Why do you think? They're grieving for Danielle, you know that. What good would it do telling them now?"

"What good would it do you, you mean. You haven't told them because you're scared they'll think less of you. I know you Laura, your whole life is about gaining their approval."

"No, it isn't. Don't be stupid. I don't need their approval, they love me, I've always known that."

"Yeah, well, regardless of that, everything you do is to gain favour with them. Deep down you're that little girl with shit parents that they took in. The little girl that was different from the rest. That's why you love Teddy so much, he's like your child. And the reason you didn't get on with Danielle was because you were jealous of her as she had the one thing you craved . . . she was their genetic daughter whereas you aren't."

"That's ridiculous," she stood up and walked towards the chair to retrieve her jacket. "I'm not listening to any more of this rubbish."

"Yeah, go, run off when you don't like hearing the truth."

"I am going. I know what I did was wrong, and I'm hoping in time you'll forgive me. I meant it when I said

I love you and I'm sorry. If I could turn back time, then I would. I wish I'd never met Cohan Laity, but I have and what's done is done. Please try and find it in your heart to forgive me and we can move on and have that future we both want, otherwise he's won."

"It's too late. It's over between us. I don't want to see you ever again. I need to get on with my life."

"Please, Matthew, don't leave it like this?"

"Just go, it's over, we're done." He stood up and turned away from her, "And leave the ring," he said with his back to her, "I might as well get some compensation out of this bloody fiasco."

She made it to the car before the tears exploded. Sobs racked her body for her future cruelly snatched away. All the plans to get married in March, enjoy a couple of years of married life with nice holidays, and completing the academic course work was facilitating for her. After that, they would have started a family. Her mum would have been the most marvellous grandma, and her dad would have been a great grandpa too. They were both brilliant with Teddy, he was like a child, but they'd have been just as loving towards her baby or babies. Any additions to the family would have brought them such joy.

Reality kicked in, looking down at the bare third finger of her left hand; no happy-ever-after now, Cohan Laity had seen to that. He'd brought heartache to them all. When Teddy had told her he'd called him a fucking retard, her fury was intense. And to threaten that her mum and dad would burn on a bonfire, was sickening. She was scared, so goodness knows how frightened Teddy must feel.

She reached in her bag for a tissue and blew her nose. The back of her tongue felt swollen and she rubbed her itchy eyes. Cohan Laity had to somehow be stopped. But how? She'd tried the law and that hadn't worked.

She pulled the visor down and looked at herself in the mirror. Staring back was a sleep-deprived nine-year-old girl, with pale skin and lank greasy hair.

What the hell can I do to make sure he never bothers us again?

Georgie girl didn't flinch.

Kill him.

Chapter 34

LAURA

"Hello love, you're late," her mum said as Laura walked into the lounge. A warm feeling engulfed her at the cosy sight of her mum sitting in her favourite armchair with her knitting needles clicking away on the Aran jumper she was making for her dad, and Teddy sitting with his pencil crayons at a small table creating a picture. He was talented and spent hours and hours doing endless drawings.

"I stayed back at work and had a quick drink with Ed. Bless him, I was telling him about my car being in the garage, and he's lent me his while he's away this week. I told him I could manage with Dad taking me to the station each day, but he insisted."

"That's kind of him. Be careful with it though whatever you do."

"Oh, I will, don't you worry."

"Where has Ed gone?"

"He's taken his son to Sweden to see his grandparents."

"That'll be nice for them both. How's he doing? Sounds like much better if he's going on holiday."

"Yes, he's been much better lately."

"Any chance of him and his wife getting back together?"

"I doubt it. She sounds happy with her new chap."

"Mind he doesn't transfer his affections towards you. You're vulnerable right now after falling out with Matthew."

She hadn't told her mum and dad exactly why her and Matthew had split up, only that they had. How could she? Thankfully they were supportive enough to wait until she felt ready to share the break-up with them.

"Don't be daft, Ed's not interested in me," she pulled a face, "he's too old anyway."

"Yes, well, stranger things have happened. You're an attractive young woman and I could easily see him falling for you. And I still think whatever it is that's gone on between you and Matthew, and I'm not prying," she added, even though Laura knew she desperately wanted to know, "will sort itself out. These things usually do, but it'd be much harder if there was someone new on the scene."

"Well, there isn't, but I can assure you, Matthew and I are definitely over." Tears threatened. It hadn't even been a week and she missed him terribly. "I will explain, but it hurts too much right now."

"I know, love, there's no rush. But you see if I'm right, just give it time," she eased herself out of the armchair, "I'm just going to make a drink. We've already eaten, but there's some lasagne left if you want me to warm it up?"

"No, I'm okay thanks. I think I'll nip to the gym and maybe have something when I get back."

"I'll have some more lasagne," Teddy said eagerly.

Her mum turned to look at him with a loving but stern expression on her face, "I don't think so considering the portion you ate less than an hour ago with all that garlic bread. There's no more for you tonight that's for sure."

"Aw."

"Aw, nothing, I mean it, nothing else tonight." She turned back to Laura, "Are you sure I can't get you anything, love?"

"No, honestly Mum, I'm fine. Is Dad at church?"

"Yes, he was in a rush tonight. He's planning for the church art exhibition they're putting on next month. You've got the date haven't you?"

"Yeah, definitely," she smiled at Teddy, "I'm looking forward to seeing my talented brother's pictures."

Teddy grinned back. He loved praise. Each year he exhibited his amateur drawings at the annual art exhibition and managed to make a few sales and a bit of pocket money. Dad patiently framed them all for him in the workshop at the bottom of the garden next to their little allotment. He did war-themed sketches which the church-goers seemed happy to support.

"Right, I'll get off to the gym."

"Laura," Teddy stopped her, "we're doing a time capsule at school. Mrs Clegg says we can put anything we like in it, it's up to us."

"Really? What a fabulous idea."

"We are going to dig the hole, and she has a big chest. It's not going to be dug up for a hundred years, then we can look at all the things that will be obs . . ." he frowned, "something or other?"

"Obsolete, Teddy," her mum chipped in, "all the things in the chest will seem really dated in a hundred years from now. But we won't be here then, remember, it's for the next generation to find."

Teddy pulled a face, "I want to see it, though."

"Well, unless you live for another hundred years, son, that isn't going to happen."

Laura smiled tenderly. She couldn't put into words how much she loved them both. "Sounds like a marvellous idea to me. I'll have to give you something to put in it. Right, I'll get off and see you both in a bit."

She headed upstairs and changed into her gym kit, calling goodbye as she let herself out of the house. Ed's Volkswagen was much bigger than her Mini so she took her time reversing it out of the drive. As always, before she pulled away, she glanced in the rear-view mirror for any signs she was being followed.

Tonight, her usual routine would have been to have met Matthew after work. *Was he missing her as much as she was missing him?* She'd stared at her phone endless times since they'd split up, willing him to text, but nothing came through.

Determined to push all thoughts of him out of her mind, she set off. Right now, there were far more pressing issues she had to deal with. She had no intention of going to the gym as she'd told her mum, she was going back to the street where Cohan lived as she'd done the last four evenings in a row. Her objective each night had been to watch his movements inside the house as best she could. Danielle had teased often enough about his evening routine when he was at home. By nine-thirty each night, he would shower and be downstairs for his glass of milk and the BBC news at ten. After that, he would go to bed as he was an early riser.

Her dear mum, bless her, had been keeping a close eye on Cohan. Only she could be busying herself while trying to mourn her daughter. Most days her mum would mention having a telephone conversation with him, or calling round with some tasty delights she'd baked. Laura wanted to scream at her, *don't you realise he killed your daughter,* but neither her mum or dad would see that. They were kind, deeply religious people who only saw good in everyone they came into contact with.

She drove down the leafy lane and parked a distance away from Cohan's house so she couldn't be spotted.

There was a parked car she slipped behind and cut the engine. It didn't appear Cohan was home as his car wasn't on the drive, so she fiddled around with the radio, determined to wait. Amy Winehouse came on which was a blast from the past as she recalled happy times at college when she used to listen to her. It seemed such a long time since she'd enjoyed music and the light-hearted aspects of life; her days currently were filled with thoughts of her demon. And the tickets Matthew had bought to the Cold Play concert would be redundant now. She couldn't use them and take a friend, not when they'd been going there together.

Patiently waiting paid off after an hour when Cohan's silver-grey Mazda came into view down the bottom of the leafy avenue, and she watched as he indicated right and turned onto his drive. Even though she was quite a distance away, she ducked her head just in case. If he looked down the road, he wouldn't recognise the car, so there was really no need to worry. But she did. Worry had been her middle name ever since she'd met the bastard.

She waited until he went inside the house and closed the door before moving the car closer. According to her mum, he spent most of his time at the back of the house where it was cosy and more practical with a log burner in the kitchen, and his study was adjacent to that. As far as she could ascertain, he never used the rooms at the front with the huge bay windows.

Her eyes were glued to the house, and sure enough, at twenty-eight minutes past nine, the hall and landing lights went on. It was helpful there was a big window alongside the stairs. Although it was frosted and she couldn't see anything, when the light went on, it was an indication he was going up the stairs. No less than fifteen minutes later, the hall and landing lights went off. So it appeared his pattern each evening was exactly the same. Nothing seemed to have changed since Danielle's death. The difficulties were going to be, which nights he'd be out. She had no way of knowing exactly, but he'd only been out one evening when she'd been watching, the other three he'd been in. *Probably still playing the grieving widower.*

He was nothing more than a wolf in sheep's clothing, and a smiling assassin. Her first mistake had been opening the door and allowing him in. She should have run away in the opposite direction as soon as she saw him coming. But she hadn't and the consequences had left her whole family paying the price. Her second mistake had not been telling the truth. If she had faced up to the consequences of her actions, Danielle would still be alive. All the months of uncertainty, tears, pain and suffering, were all because of her stupidity. The future with Matthew was gone now. Their plans to have children and grow old together, were now in the past. Cohan Laity was poison. It was time to put right the wrong she'd inflicted on her family.

She started the engine, put the car into gear and moved away. Could she do it? Could she eradicate Cohan Laity completely from their lives? Anger thumped hard in her chest when she thought about him frightening Teddy. The threats of her parents burning on top of a bonfire had scared Teddy and terrified her. What if the crazy bastard carried out his threats? How could they live without their precious mum and dad? He needed stopping, the question was how?

A plan was beginning to whirl around her head. Could it become a reality? She'd tried the police and they were hopeless. But could she take the law into her own hands? What if she was found out, what then? She could end up spending years in jail. However, what if there was a way, and if it all went to plan, the likelihood of getting caught was minimal? Laura Foley, the kind and thoughtful daughter could never commit murder. But Laura Foley knew someone who would do it; someone who would make sure Cohan Laity never bothered them again.

Georgie girl. She could do it. But would she want to?

Yes, a tiny voice whispered, *I want to, and I know a way to do it that will outsmart them all.*

Chapter 35

LAURA

Laura arrived at the small private hospital for the cyst to be taken off her eye, and was directed to a waiting area and told to take a seat and a nurse would come for her. Her eyes flitted around the plush waiting area with the contemporary chairs and lavish carpets. The latest designer coffee maker burbled away with a sign suggesting those waiting could help themselves. It was a far cry from the NHS hospital where she'd sat with Matthew in the cold clinical waiting room when he'd been diagnosed.

She stared to her left at a door with a no entry sign and guessed that was where the procedures were carried out. Having minor surgery didn't worry her, but her heart ached with the memory of being at the hospital only weeks earlier with Matthew at the time he'd had the prosthesis fitted. It stung terribly. She fiddled with the bracelet he'd given her with the *Linchpin, I love you* inscription; she should really take it off as they weren't together anymore, but she couldn't. It reminded her of happier times, although there had been a big cloud hanging over her even then, but it was all she had of their time together as he'd taken back the engagement ring.

It was her own fault, she couldn't blame Matthew for calling their engagement off. He was hurting just as she knew he would be. It was Cohan she blamed, and Georgie girl telling her to get rid of him, was becoming more frequent. It was a great fantasy, eradicating him from their lives so that she never had to look over her shoulder again. The past few days formulating a plan had made her feel much better, but the practicality of executing it, was easier said than done.

The *no entry* door opened and a patient with an eye patch on was escorted into a room opposite which Laura assumed was a resting area following surgery.

Another nurse came out a few minutes later, "Laura Foley?" she asked. Laura smiled and nodded and she was escorted into the room and offered a seat. The nurse introduced herself as Kay, and checked her date of birth, asked her if she had any allergies and identified which eye they were operating on.

"I'll just explain what's going to happen when you go inside. The surgeon will inject some local anaesthetic into your eye to numb it. It might be a little uncomfortable, but nothing too bad. When it's numb, Mr Haith will remove the cyst, which will only take a few minutes. We don't usually apply a dressing, unless there is any bleeding, but it's unlikely."

"That's fine," Laura said.

"Okay, well you'll be pleased to know you don't have to get undressed or anything, but you do need to put a gown on over your own clothes. If you could remove any jewellery and put it in your handbag, then you can put that in this locker," she nodded towards a small locker in the corner, "take the key in with you, and then when we're done, we'll bring you back out and you can collect your belongings. We'll take you across the way for a drink and a biscuit, check your eye is fine, and then you can go home. Hope that's all okay for you, is there anything you want to ask me?"

"No, I think you've covered everything," Laura smiled.

"Oh, I forgot to mention, when you get inside, Mr Haith, will get you to sign a consent form, and we'll give you a minor surgery sheet to take home with you explaining . . ."

The door opening interrupted her. A nurse with a concerned expression spoke directly to Kay, "Can you come, quickly?"

"Excuse me, I won't be a moment," Kay said, and Laura watched as the two nurses rushed off together, leaving her alone.

Must be the lady they took out earlier.

Her gaze wondered around the adjacent clinical area which was tiled with clean white surfaces and cupboards no doubt containing endless medical devices and equipment. In the corner was a small trolley with equipment on it, and what looked like a microscope. Laura guessed the room was maybe used as a clinical outpatient room, or maybe some sort of storage room. Adjacent to the trolley were some shelves with baskets in a neat row. Inside each of the baskets was an assortment of different sized syringes, and boxes containing an assortment of needles. Her gaze moved to her left and she saw some boxes labelled *sterile surgical gowns*, and an array of different sized surgical gloves. There was an open box containing what appeared to be paper hats, rather like those staff wore working on delicatessen counters in supermarkets to prevent loose hairs straying. Her gaze drifted towards the top of the room, to see if there was any CCTV cameras, guessing there wouldn't be. She couldn't imagine you could have anything like that in rooms used for procedures of any kind.

Georgie girl's voice jumped into her head, *That sterile surgical stuff would be perfect to hide any forensics. Take some!*

She looked down at the large Michael Kors handbag her mother had insisted she had of Danielle's. It was a bit big for Laura's liking; it was one of those bags that you could fit absolutely everything in.

Quickly, she reached across and took a handful of assorted syringes and needles and hastily tossed them in her bag. She then reached for a sterile gown, a couple of packets of sterile gloves and paper hats, stuffing them all into her oversized bag. Some plastic overshoes caught her eye and she took some of them also. The bag was bulky so she squashed it all down as best she could and zipped it up. She added her watch and bracelet then put it in the locker as she'd been instructed to do, and turned the key. As she sat down again, she took a deep breath and tried to calm her racing heart.

Seconds later the door opened and Kay returned. "I'm sorry about that," she said.

"It's okay. Is everything alright?"

"Fine, nothing for you to worry about. You've locked your bag up, have you?" she asked glancing at the closed locker."

"Yes," Laura held up the key.

"Great." Kay handed her a gown and a paper hat, "Put this on over your clothes, and pop the hat on, and then I'll take you through. While you're doing that," she walked towards a PC, "I'll just sign on your notes that I've explained everything about the procedure."

Laura placed the locker key in her trouser pocket and Georgie girl whispered, *Well done. No forensics, no proof.*

Chapter 36

LAURA

They were all in the lounge watching television. Teddy was munching on his sweets, and her mother was knitting. Dad was in his study as normal, no doubt reading his latest novel. He certainly wouldn't be watching the current soap they had on. Documentaries were more his bag.

"I'm going to go to bed, Mum, I've got a splitting headache."

"Oh, bless you. Are you going to take anything?"

"I'll grab a couple of aspirin. I'm sure a good sleep will clear it."

"I hope it's not the start of a cold. There's so much of it at the church. Loads were missing from the coffee morning this week."

Laura stretched her arms above her head. "Let's hope not." She got up from the chair and kissed her mum on the head, "I'll see you in the morning."

"Alright love, sleep tight. Hope you feel better in the morning. If not, don't go into work."

"I'm sure I'll be fine. Night, Teddy."

He jumped up for a hug. She wrapped her arms around him tightly, she loved him so much.

"Night night," he said, "make sure the bed bugs don't bite."

She smiled, "You too." She headed for the kitchen to the medicine cupboard and made a pretence of looking for some tablets and running the tap for some cold water. She opened the drawer where her mother kept the key to Cohan's house. It stared back at her with its leather key ring denoting a flag of Spain. How ironic, the country where she'd met him. She opened the door of the huge Smeg fridge and removed the two cartons of Jersey milk she'd bought earlier and hidden at the back. As she made her way from the kitchen towards the stairs, her hand tightened around the key in her hand. There was so much at stake about what she was intending to do, and for her plan to work, there was no margin for error. She'd considered the possibility of getting caught and the ramifications of that. Of course that would bring terrible shame on her family, but they'd be alive. If she did nothing, Cohan might kill them. If the worst did happen and she was caught, she had a back-up plan. She was going to plead the mental health condition of a personality disorder due to her alter-ego. Lately, libraries had become her most frequent places to hang out. She used their internet booths to do her research. She'd looked up numerous cases about alter-egos and knew it was a credible defence.

At the bottom of the stairs, she paused and looked at her reflection in the full-length mirror. Same dark eyes, same dark hair, but it wasn't the twenty-one-year-old Laura looking back at her. It was a nine-year-old-girl in a grubby tight dress, lank unwashed hair and long socks which didn't quite reach her knees.

It was Georgie girl grinning back at her.

And tonight, Cohan Laity was going to die.

Laura made her way upstairs and once inside her bedroom, she opened the drawer underneath her bed and fished out an extra blanket and a couple of pillows. She needed to make sure the bed looked as if she was in it if anyone came to check on her. It was most unlikely, but she wasn't taking any chances. She pulled the duvet back and placed the pillows on the bed so it looked like a body and rolled the blanket up to give the shape of legs. She pulled the covers up and even placed an old wig she had from a 70's night, jutting out slightly so it looked like her head. Once she was satisfied it appeared as if she was sleeping at a casual glance, she took the rucksack she'd prepared earlier from the wardrobe. In it was the sealed sterile surgical gown and cap she'd stolen from the hospital, and a pair of overshoes. She carefully checked everything she needed was there and put the two cartons of Jersey milk inside. One contained a black dot which she'd put there so she didn't muddle the two of them up. The black dot identified the one she'd added the most almond milk to. The second carton had the tiniest trace.

Her next step was getting out of the house without disturbing anyone. Fortunately her mum was a great one for closing curtains in every room as soon as nightfall came. Even the blinds in the kitchen were closed. Her dad always said it was ridiculous each morning opening them all again, but her mum liked cosy.

Quietly, she opened the bedroom window. It was a modern window which you could tilt for fresh air, but would open fully in case of a fire, so could be used as an escape route. Directly outside her room was the kitchen extension, and adjacent to that was the garage, so she was going to climb onto both roofs. She couldn't close the window from the outside because there wasn't an outside handle, but she'd considered that and reached in her pocket for the Blu Tack. She precariously balanced on the roof outside her bedroom window and placed blobs of Blu Tack along the frame and pulled the window to with a suction plunger she'd taken from her dad's shed. She left the plunger on the roof.

She carefully crawled down the sloping roof, grateful it wasn't raining as it would have been too slippery. She eased herself onto the garage roof. It wasn't as easy. She recalled doing it as a teenager, but she'd been much lighter then. There was a bit of a drop from the garage roof, but she managed to hold onto the drain pipe to help her leap down. Time was of the essence. She'd done a dummy run and knew how long everything would take.

She crept along the garden at a fast pace towards the wall with her eyes nervously scanning the surrounding area, checking nobody was about. At the bottom of the garden, she climbed over the wall and into Cohan's garden, and quickly made her way towards his house. She kept close to the outside wall as she moved along, although it was unlikely she would be spotted if he'd been at the window. He'd have to be specifically looking at the peripheral walls of the garden. She'd dressed in dark leggings and jumper, and even had black shoes on. If it wasn't so serious, it would be funny. Success would only happen if she wasn't seen, and it was vital she was in the house when Cohan showered. Thankfully there weren't any of those blinding security lights that would have lit up the garden as the slightest movement activated them. The darkness gave her the anonymity she needed.

At the side of the study, there were two tiny ornate windows. She was terrified to look in case he spotted her. She squatted down underneath them and waited. He could quite easily change his routine, nothing was to say he wouldn't receive a phone call or something and that might delay things. He might not even have a shower. Fear snaked through as she prayed that he would. It was just a question of waiting. She felt sick, and her tummy was swirling in turmoil. But she'd come this far, there was no turning back now.

It seemed like forever, but eventually the hall light went on and, thanks to the large window at the side of the property, she saw his shadow mount the stairs. This was her opportunity – it was now or never. She held her breath, waiting for the bathroom light to go on before she made her move. There was an open porch at the side of the house which she nervously crept into. If he'd opened the door, it would have all been over. She opened a pair of the surgical gloves she'd stolen, stuffed the wrapping in her rucksack, and put on a pair of the plastic overshoes over her own shoes. She took the key she'd taken from the drawer at home, opened the front door, stepped inside, and closed it quietly. Adrenaline spurred her on as she crept through the hall and into the kitchen. She had to do it silently, but swiftly. It was vital she got his emergency EpiPen that she knew from conversations she'd overheard, he kept in the kitchen drawer, which would be the obvious place near to any food. Did he still keep it there? She couldn't be certain. So much depended on him not changing anything. She'd wanted to do a recce and go in the house to check the previous day, but she hadn't dared. If there was no EpiPen in the drawer, then she was out of there. She'd have to abandon everything as the adrenaline it contained might save his life.

As soon as he realised he'd been exposed to nuts, he'd reach for the EpiPen. She heard the sound of the old boiler kicking in and the shower running and hastily opened each drawer, eventually locating it in the third one she tried. She placed it in her rucksack. The next step was taking the second rescue EpiPen which she was confident would be in his rucksack he carried everywhere with him. She quickly located the rucksack next to the coats and fished around until she found it and placed that one in her bag also. Both EpiPens were now in her possession. *Game on.*

She reached for his iPhone from the kitchen table next to a newspaper and put it in her pocket praying he wouldn't realise it wasn't there when he came down. He used to say he liked the internet for research but couldn't understand why people spent endless time looking at their phones. She was banking on it still being the same.

Next, she headed towards the fridge. The Jersey full cream milk was there on the shelf. *Thank you, Mum.* She removed his carton and replaced it with her carton of the same brand – the one with the black dot that she'd added the most almond milk to. She'd had to get the balance right. Too much almond milk and he'd taste it and stop drinking, not enough, and he might live to tell the tale.

Everything was in place. Now she needed to get out of the house, and pray. If all went to plan, Cohan Laity would be dead shortly, if not, he would know what she'd tried to do and very likely go to the police.

She left the house by the front door, locked it again and waited in the porch. Thank God he wasn't like her mother with all the curtains closed, she could never do it if she couldn't see what was going on in the house. She'd done her homework. Although she knew his routine as her mother filled her in endlessly about how she thought he must be a little autistic as he had habitual routines such as showering the same time, and then enjoying a glass of milk. She remembered when she had a fling with him how he consumed milk, he did seem to drink plenty of it. How ironic then that very shortly, milk was going to kill him.

She could just see the kitchen from where she was hiding. The light went off from the stairs, and he came into view through the window as he entered the kitchen in his towelling dressing gown.

Come on, you bastard, drink your milk.

It seemed like the scene in front of her was playing out in slow motion. He reached for a glass from the overhead cupboard and filled it with milk from the carton she'd placed in the fridge. A screech from a cat startled her, and must have startled him, too as he turned suddenly and looked towards the window. For a second, she thought he was looking directly at her. She held her breath. He turned back, and then, painstakingly slow, she watched him lift the glass of milk to his lips and glug back three quarters of it. He stopped drinking and stared at the glass in his hand. *Had he tasted the almond?*

He put the glass to his nose and smelt the remainder of the milk.

Yes, he had.

He placed the glass down, and swiftly opened the drawer she'd taken the EpiPen from, quickly rummaging about.

He knew.

Her breath caught in her throat. All being well, next, he'd be rushing to his rucksack for his second EpiPen. He did exactly that. He reached for his rucksack and tipped the contents out on the floor. No EpiPen. He'd told her when they'd first met what the process was, that if he had inadvertently taken nuts, he had to ring for an ambulance, and give himself a dose of adrenaline. Seemingly, the rescue dose would help until the ambulance arrived and they could give him more. At the time she remembered thinking how awful it must be for him to be on his guard the whole time against inadvertently consuming nuts and felt sorry for him. But right now, she was relieved she'd listened to his every word.

She held her breath. He'd realised both his EpiPens were missing. He'd have to go for his phone to call

999. She felt for it in her back pocket, as if she needed to reassure herself she still had it.

She waited. The neighbouring properties weren't adjacent to the house, they were too far away to get to. She'd read that during a severe reaction, there would be a sudden weakness due to the drop in blood pressure and the alteration of the heartbeat, but she feared he might try and make a dash to their house by climbing over the back wall to her mum. She had hidden a spade close by the previous day so she could whack him with it if he tried to get from the house. But that was a last resort. Any wound to his head or body would draw attention.

She hardly dared breathe. Something clattered inside, a table or chair, she wasn't sure which. It was too soon to go into the house. She checked her watch. It had only been three minutes so far, but she had done extensive research in the library and read that in a severe allergy case, as in Cohan's, the symptoms would be instantaneous. Even he'd told her any exposure to the smallest amount of nut and the reaction was immediate.

She couldn't see him in the kitchen, but still waited. Her heart thumped so hard she was certain she could hear it in her head. She wanted to watch him die, *but what if it hadn't worked?* If he was okay, he could attack her. The house was eerily silent, she checked her watch again and decided she needed to go in. Her chest was bursting with anxiety as she applied the sterile surgical attire, and tentatively eased herself slowly through the front door, half expecting him to jump out and grab hold of her.

But he couldn't. He was on his knees in the hall, crawling. She hadn't expected his face to be as blue. His lips were navy, and his eyes were bulging so much they looked almost ready to pop out. His lips were swollen, almost like they'd been cosmetically enhanced.

He raised his head to look at her.

What must she look like facing him in her surgical clothing? Could he tell it was her?

"Help me," he croaked ". . . please help me." He fell forward and rolled onto his side.

His breathing was fast and shallow. In barely a whisper he pleaded again, "Please . . . help . . . me."

His airway would be almost closed with swelling, she'd read that happened quickly in severe allergic reactions. He was puce so very little oxygen was circulating. She pulled down the surgical mask so he could see her face as she stood over him. "You killed Danielle," she spat, "and what goes around, comes around."

There was a flicker of recognition in his bulbous eyeballs.

She tilted her head slightly and chanted, "Do something bad and you will find, Karma's lurking right behind."

He tried one more feeble attempt to speak, but couldn't. He was gasping for every last breath and clutching his throat. His airway was closed. The information she'd read about people dying all said that hearing was the last sense to go. She so hoped that was true as she crouched down and said in a voice loud enough for him to hear, "So, who's smiling now, Cohan?"

His chest became static. He'd stopped breathing. His colour was a purplish navy, and his huge globular eyes didn't close as she'd expected they would. He lay motionless. There was nothing.

Only stillness.

He'd gone.

But it wasn't over. She had work to do as so much depended on the next part. She reached in her bag, took out one of the EpiPens, injected it as if he'd missed his leg, and carefully placed it in his hand. She'd take the other EpiPen away with her and the police would deduce he'd only had one. Health professionals would of course confirm that he would have had two pens, and the police may even search for a second one in the house, but they would most likely conclude he'd left it somewhere he frequented regularly.

The realisation of what she'd done was kicking in and her body began to tremble.

You have to finish it off, Georgie girl urged. Her fingers were shaking, and wearing the surgical gloves made it difficult to press 999 on his phone, but she managed by pressing firmly, and then tossed the phone down on the floor next to him, knowing the call handler would pick it up and try and talk to the caller. They'd have to trace the call and then dispatch an ambulance, but it would take time and she needed a few minutes more before she could leave.

She tiptoed towards the kitchen so she couldn't be heard by the call handler. The last thing she needed was anyone to realise there had been someone in the house when he'd died. She reached the fridge and removed the milk carton with the black dot on that he'd drunk the milk from. She took some tape from her bag and secured the top so it didn't spill and put it in her rucksack. She replaced it with the second carton she'd brought which only contained a small amount of nut residue. She poured some down the sink so it looked half used and ran the tap to disperse it.

She took the glass he'd drank out of and placed it in her bag, and reached for a fresh glass from the cupboard and poured some milk from the new carton into it. She strategically placed the glass on the side of the draining board with the remainder of the milk still in it. They would think he took a large mouthful before realising he'd been exposed to the nuts. When they examined it, it would contain minute traces of nuts and the finger of suspicion hopefully would be traced back to the manufacturer.

Everything was done. She needed to get out of there quickly and made her way towards to the door purposely not looking at Cohan's body. As she reached for the handle, Georgie girl stopped her.

There'd be none of Cohan's saliva around the glass he'd supposedly drunk the milk out of. Nor would there be any fingerprints.

There was no choice, she had to turn back.

Again she passed his lifeless body on the way to the kitchen. She picked up the glass from the draining board and moved back towards Cohan's motionless body, scared shitless he would sit up even though she knew he was dead. As she knelt down beside him and eased his head up so she could rub the glass along his bulbous blue lips which had plenty of saliva oozing from them, her stomach retched, making her want to vomit. She had to swallow down the lump at the back of her throat as she picked up his limp hand, and folded his fingers around the glass and milk carton, just enough to leave fingerprints.

It was done.

She returned the glass to its place on the draining board, put the carton of milk in the fridge and quickly made her way towards the front door, passing the body one last time. She left the house and locked the door behind her. At speed, she removed all the surgical attire and bundled it in her rucksack. Only then did she breathe out and hastily begin to retrace her steps back home. She moved forward positively, creeping back along the property wall and over the smaller wall into her garden, not pausing once as adrenaline helped her climb the drainpipe with ease. She crossed the roof to her window, eased it open, dropped the plunger inside and climbed in after it, quickly removing the Blu Tack and bundling everything into her wardrobe along with the wig and the duvet and pillows she'd used in the bed. She changed into her waiting pyjamas, climbed into bed and pulled the covers up, just as the sound of sirens wailed in the distance.

She closed her eyes to it, smiling in the darkness. Cohan Laity was dead, never to bother her family again.

You did real good, came a whisper in her ear.

Of course she did.

She was the daughter of a killer after all.

Chapter 37

LAURA

Mornings in the Foley household were always chaotic with them flying round at different times and her mother trying to make sure they had enough sustenance to see them through the day.

"I've made tuna and mayo today, love," her mum smiled, "and yours Teddy, don't leave it on the side like you did yesterday."

Christ, as if she could eat anything after last night.

"Can I go to the football match with Sid on Saturday?" Teddy asked, "just me and him?"

"Not on your own you can't," her mum answered, "you'll have to ask Dad to take you."

"Aw, me and Sid want to go on our own."

"You can't. There's too much fighting going on with the rival teams, you could get hurt." She handed Teddy his lunch box, ignoring his mardy face when he didn't get his own way, "There you go."

Teddy took it from her and put it in his schoolbag.

"Quickly go and do your teeth, Mrs Davis will be here shortly with Sid to take you to school."

As Teddy left the kitchen, Laura followed him upstairs. "Is it today you're putting the time capsule in the ground?"

"Yeah, at eleven o'clock and some special people are coming from the council, and the mayor. Miss Clegg says it's not full so we can take more stuff in today," he scrunched his face, "I can't though 'cause Mum says I've put enough in."

"Did you say Miss Clegg had asked for some clothes so that when they dig it up eventually they can see what the fashions were like?"

He nodded enthusiastically.

"I might put one of my skirts in, then. Have you got anymore of those bags you seal everything up in?"

"Yeah, I have. You have to wrap the stuff up before you put it in the bag, then we have to seal it and write on the label what it is and put the date on it."

"Okay, I'll have a bag then and I'll go fish out one of my old skirts and wrap it."

She followed Teddy to his room and took one of the thick brown packages from him. "Do your teeth quickly and I'll be back in a second."

He smiled eagerly, "Miss Clegg will be pleased to have extra. Dad's put some of his flat caps in."

"Oh, has he? He's got stacks of those so won't miss a few. I won't be long."

She closed her bedroom door and listened to the tap running in the bathroom. Her heart-rate increased with the previous night's images flashing through her mind and she could almost smell Cohan's house as she retrieved the surgical gown, gloves, overshoes and hat from her rucksack, squashing them together as tightly as she could, and wrapping them in brown paper and taping them up. She opened the bag with the seal and placed the bundle in it, sealed it up and added some Sellotape for extra security. Any evidence that she'd been in Cohan's house wouldn't be found in a time capsule underground. If the police suspected foul play, it was highly likely she'd be a suspect. She knew they'd quickly deduce what killed him with a post-mortem, and it maybe they'd search the house for clues, and of course take her laptop and iPad. None of those contained anything about Cohan, she'd made absolutely sure of that but she knew the clock was now ticking.

Please let them think it was an accident.

She quickly scribbled on the front of the package, *navy mini skirt size ten* and added the date, just as Teddy barged in. He never took any notice of the rule to knock before entering.

She handed the package to him, "There you go, I've wrapped it all. It's one of my old mini-skirts I don't wear anymore."

"Will they still wear mini-skirts in a hundred years?"

"They might do," she shrugged, "who knows?"

"I will," he said confidently, "I'm going to live 'till then so I can see it when it's opened again."

"I hope you do," she grinned, "Come on, let's get a move on."

Laura reached for her coat from the hall cupboard. Her mum came back from waving Teddy off to school, "Are you sure you're alright to go to work, you look a bit peaky to me. How's your headache?"

Physically she felt like throwing up the breakfast she'd forced herself to eat so everything appeared normal, and her movements felt jerky and awkward as if her family would guess any minute what she'd done. She had to get herself into work, even though the thought of getting behind the wheel of her car made her feel nervous.

"I'm fine, honestly." She pulled her jacket down at the front and made a conscious effort to control the tremor she still had in her sweaty hands as she buttoned it up. "I better get going. I'll be home a bit earlier tonight as I've got some time owing," she kissed her mum's cheek. "Bye, Dad," she shouted towards the kitchen.

"Bye, love."

Bless them both, they were going to get more bad news today. Not bad to her, but they'd be shocked because they saw Cohan as their kind, gentle son-in-law. It felt almost like a dream as she walked out of the house and down the drive.

Had it really happened? Was Cohan dead? She walked past her car and carried on down the drive. At the front gate, she stopped and reached in her bag to remove the empty Jersey milk cartons she'd crushed and placed them in the recycling boxes her dad had left out for collection that day. She pushed them down to the bottom and covered them up with the empty milk cartons the family used. All she needed to do now was dispose of the EpiPen in the receptacle for used needles and syringes at the station. They were incinerated and never opened.

The feeling of relief that she'd taken care of everything, eased her anxiety a little. All she had to do now was wait.

Tick tock.

She opened the door of her Mini and breathed out. They'd have a job proving she killed Cohan without any evidence. Although circumstantial evidence gained weight at a trial, invariably it was challenging to prove and convictions were rare. She'd read enough books on criminals and watched endless documentaries to know that.

As she reversed out of the drive a tiny voice in her head reassured her, *you're doing great.*

Chapter 38

LAURA

They were sitting at the kitchen table having just eaten dinner. Her mum checked her watch, "They'll all be waiting for the film to start, Teddy's so excited, he loves the cinema."

"Is it nine I've got to pick them up?" her dad asked.

The shrill of the telephone interrupted them.

"I'll get it." Her mum got up and moved towards the kitchen phone. Laura's instincts told her it was the call she'd been waiting for. Her head had been all over the place at work, and when she returned home, her mother and father were behaving normally, so they didn't yet know.

"The film ends just before nine, I think Mum said, so maybe go for ten to."

A loud screech confirmed what she already knew.

Her dad rushed up from the table. "What is it?"

Her mum's face had gone deathly white as she held out the phone, "I'll have to sit down." Her dad took the phone from her and Laura grabbed her arm and led her towards the chair where she'd been sitting.

"What's happened, Mum, who is it?" Laura asked injecting a level of fear in her voice. It reminded her of that dreadful night only weeks earlier when she'd come downstairs to the sitting room and asked exactly the same question about Danielle. But this time, she knew exactly what news the current phone call had delivered.

"It's Cohan's mother," she started to sob, "she says he's died . . . something to do with his nut allergy." She frantically shook her head from side to side, "I don't believe this is happening."

"Died?" Laura exclaimed in her best acting voice, "What do you mean died? He can't have."

Her mum started to shake, "I'm not sure how much more of this I can take."

"You're alright Mum, take some deep breaths, I'll get you some water."

She reached for the water jug in the centre of the table and poured some into her glass. Her dad put the phone down and came over to her mum wrapped his arms around her. She felt guilty for inflicting more pain on them both, but quickly dismissed it. She'd done what she had to, knowing Cohan would have no qualms about carrying out his threats.

"What's happened, Dad?" she asked, piling on the shock. His shaken expression caused her tummy to clench.

"It appears Cohan somehow had some nuts and, because of his allergy, it's killed him."

"Killed him?" Laura shook her head in disbelief. "Where did he have nuts?"

"At home, apparently," he indicated with his head to the back of their house. "It sounds like it might be something to do with the milk."

Her mum sobbed, "I can't believe it, Ian, not Cohan as well."

Laura had to get away so she could gather herself and let out the breath she was holding. Her insides ached with nervous pain. "I'll make some tea."

After a restless night tossing and turning and dreaming about being locked up in prison, the following morning, Laura was sitting with her mother and father at the kitchen table. She'd had to make a bit of an effort and try to rustle up some breakfast for them all as her mum couldn't. She must have had a terrible night, judging by her red eyes and pale complexion.

Laura picked at some scrambled egg, but food was the last thing she could stomach. Her inside were churning. Any minute she expected the police to come knocking, and her anxious eyes surreptitiously looked at the wall clock every five minutes. But even though she was messing herself thinking about it, she was prepared. She'd spent long enough planning in her mind not only the killing, but afterwards too. Every angle she had covered. It would come out about her and Cohan's affair, but she couldn't forewarn her parents of that. She would have to explain everything, and even though they'd be terribly upset, disappointed, and no doubt angry, he was gone now and couldn't hurt them anymore. What she'd set out to achieve, she'd done. Now she needed to just get away with it.

"I said we'd give Cohan's mother a ring back today," her dad said.

"We must, Ian. Poor, poor lad, he was . . ."

The doorbell rang. Laura's tummy plummeted instinctively . . . this was it. Her mum didn't have any idea though and feebly said, "Tell whoever it is, not now, love, would you? I can't face anyone today."

With heavy legs, Laura made her way to the front door. It felt like she was going to her own execution. The next few hours were going to be the hardest, but she'd got through the worst, she needed to keep her cool. She took a deep breath to steady herself and opened the door. Two uniformed police officers stood in front of her, one male, one female."

"Laura Foley?"

"Yes."

"I'm officer Bryan Forge, and this is officer Sian Mortlock. We'd like you to come down to the station with us now please to help us with our enquiries."

"What enquiries?" She put on her best puzzled face."

"We can discuss that at the station."

"Dad," she called anxiously, which brought her mother and father rushing from the kitchen.

Her dad took one look at the uniformed police officers, "Please come in," he requested politely, "what is it?" He waited expectantly while the officers stepped into the hall, "What's going on?" he asked.

"I'm sorry, but we're not at liberty to discuss anything with you, sir. We have asked your daughter to come with us to the police station. She may have some information that could assist our enquiries."

"Information about what? We've just had a bereavement that we only heard about last night so now isn't a good time for Laura to be going anywhere."

"I'm sorry about that, but I'm afraid this won't wait." The officer looked directly at Laura, "You can come voluntarily, if not we will have to arrest you."

"Arrest her!" her father barked, "What on earth are you talking about?"

Georgie girl's voice whispered in her ear, *turn on the tears. Now!"*

Laura's eyes filled up, "I don't understand. Can you at least tell me what it's about?"

"I'm afraid I can't, only that we think you may have some information that could assist us."

Her dad took her hand. "Don't worry, I'll get my coat and come with you."

Her mum was sobbing into a tissue. "What's happening? What do you want with Laura? I can't take any more of this, my other daughter's only just died."

Her dad put his arms around her. "Calm down, love. There's just been some sort of misunderstanding. We'll go to the station and sort this out and be back in no time."

"Please don't go," her mum pleaded, "I don't want to be on my own, I don't feel well."

"It's alright, Dad," Laura reassured, "you stay here with Mum. I'll give Ed a ring, I'm sure he'll come with me."

"Good idea," her dad agreed, "he's a decent chap, I'd be happier if someone was with you."

She looked at the officers, "Would it be okay to ask him my friend to come with me?"

They nodded so she headed for the kitchen to retrieve her mobile and handbag. She'd ring Ed on the way to the station.

"How long is she going to be, do you know?" her dad asked.

"As I said, sir, we're unable to discuss anything further at this point."

The pained look on her parents' faces tore her apart.

"I'm okay." She hugged her mum with genuine tears, she was scared. "I'll ring you as soon as I'm done," she reassured as if she was talking about a trip away and letting them know when she'd got there. Her dad's eyes were full as he stood protectively with his arm around her mum and watched her go.

They were good stoic people and she'd let them down.

Chapter 39

LAURA

As soon as Laura arrived at the police station, she was met by Tracy, the officer who she'd first related the account of Cohan Laity to. She'd been sympathetic at the time, and genuinely concerned about Cohan stalking her, but today she was more formal. Her first question had been to ask if she wanted representation during the questions they needed to ask. Tracy explained that they weren't obliged to provide legal representation as the interview was voluntary, but she had the right to request her own legal advice to protect her rights.

Laura rejected it in her best, *why would I need that* voice, eager to portray her innocence.

Tracy left her alone to wait for Ed, explaining as soon as he arrived, she'd bring him through. He must have driven across London as if he had a blue flashing light on his car such was the short time it took for him to get there.

He greeted her with a hug. "Are you okay? What's going on?"

Tracy stood watching them both so Laura needed to play dumb. "I'm not sure. I'm here to answer some questions. My sister's husband Cohan Laity has died, I'm thinking it must be something to do with him?"

"Oh, God, how awful . . ."

Tracy interjected, "If you'd like to come this way please, we'll make our way to the interview room." She spoke to Ed, "If you want to take a seat, I'll get someone to bring you a drink while you're waiting."

Tracy led her into a dingy interview room and took a seat opposite her at the table. "It won't be long, Detective Siddley's on his way."

They sat in silence waiting until Hawthorne Siddley came into the room and took the second seat next to Tracy.

I knew it would be you.

He put his papers down on the table and pulled in his seat before speaking. "Thank you very much Miss Foley, for coming in today. You've been offered your own legal representation?" he looked at Tracy and she nodded.

Laura cleared her throat, "Yes, but I don't know why I would need it," the nerves in her voice didn't require much faking, "why am I here?"

"First of all, let me explain about the process. You've been invited in for a voluntary interview to assist us with our enquiries. You are not under arrest and free to leave at any time, and the interview will be recorded. Do you understand?"

"Yes."

"Right, in that case, we'll put the tape on and identify ourselves and then we can begin."

They all said their names out loud for the tape.

"You're here today to assist us with some questions we have about Mr Cohan Laity. You are aware he died last night?"

"Yes, his mother rang and told us."

"Hopefully we won't have to keep you long, but we need to clarify a few things."

"I'm not sure I can help," she looked directly into Hawthorne Siddley's penetrating eyes, "you know about my situation with him."

"Yes, I do. And that's precisely why I've asked you here today." He looked down at his notes, "Can you tell us where you first met, Cohan Laity?"

"I've already told you that, at my twenty-first birthday party."

"But that isn't true, is it?"

Christ, what do they know?

"I'll ask again, when did you first meet, Mr Laity?"

Cohan must have told them when they interviewed him!

She took a deep exaggerated breath. "In Spain, when I was cat-sitting for a relative."

"So, meeting him for the first time at your twenty-first birthday party was a lie," his eyes narrowed, "yet twice you've told us that?"

Make up an excuse, quickly.

"I am sorry," she piled on the anxiety, "it was because I'd just lost my sister, I wasn't thinking straight."

He stared. He had the most penetrating brown eyes and a way of looking as if he didn't believe a word she said. And clearly he didn't as he'd taken no further action when she'd complained about Cohan.

"I see. When Mr Laity came to England and began a relationship with your sister, did you tell her that you'd had an affair with him previously?"

She shook her head. It was bad. She knew what it looked like. "Look," she rubbed her forehead, "I was going to tell her, and my boyfriend all about the affair and hope he'd forgive me, but when I got back, he told me he'd found a lump which turned out to be cancer so he had to have surgery. I didn't want to add to his troubles by telling him. Besides, I'd thought it was just a fling that I could put behind me, but then Cohan followed me to London."

"And when things began to get serious between him and your sister, did you not consider telling her about the two of you?"

"I did try and say something, but she wasn't interested. Said I was making it all up because I was jealous. And after that, Cohan started following me about and saying we should be together. He was always stalking me. I came to see you but you did nothing about it. I'm telling the truth, the man was unhinged."

"We have reason to believe his death is suspicious."

"Suspicious?" she repeated, "What do you mean? I thought it was to do with some nuts and his allergy?"

"That's correct. But there is another scenario and that is someone could have intentionally given him nuts. And if that had happened, and the person responsible was aware of his nut allergy, then that would be perceived as murder. Do you understand what I'm saying, Laura?"

She nodded, "I think so."

Act dumb! Just act dumb!

"But how could anyone have given him nuts, he was always very careful what he ate?"

"It doesn't have to be obvious. Someone could have injected some into his food, or even his drink. He wouldn't have had any idea until he consumed it and the symptoms started."

She nodded as if she was following.

"Where were you on Thursday night, Laura, between the hours of nine and ten p.m.?"

She put an incredulous look on her face. "Why?"

"We need to know where you were."

"I was at home."

"Would someone be able to verify that?"

"Of course, but why would I need someone to?"

"Procedure that's all."

"What, you think *I* gave him some nuts?" She shook her head incredulously, "I hate to disappoint you, but it's highly unlikely I'd be in his company giving him nuts. I loathed the man."

"So you didn't see him the night he died?"

"No. Why would I? I've spent the last three months trying to avoid him. I told you, he was stalking me, he followed me everywhere, why would I follow him?"

"Maybe you wanted something to happen to him."

Lay it on thick. It's too obvious the person that hated him would kill him.

"I'm not sorry about what's happened, if that's what you're asking. The man was mad . . . evil, he was just clever at disguising it. He had everyone fooled, even you. He's a storyteller; he fabricated stuff and was easily believed. I fell for it, my sister fell for it, my parents fell for it . . . we all did, even you." She widened her eyes, "Everyone's better off without him."

"Will your parents be able to confirm you were at home the night he died?"

"Yes."

"When did you last see Mr Laity?"

She thought for a moment, remembering to look pensive as she considered the question.

"At Carlton road health centre, about ten days ago, I rang you about it. He'd been making threats to my brother."

"And you haven't seen him since?"

"No."

"Have you ever been to Mr Laity's house?"

Tell them yes, they can't disprove it. If they did find any traces of DNA, they would be legitimate.

"Yes, not while he was there though. My sister invited me just before their wedding. She wanted to show me the house."

"I see. How many mobile phones do you own?"

She frowned, "One."

"Is it a contract phone?"

"Yes. Why are you asking me this, I don't understand?"

"Mr Laity told us before he died, you were communicating with him from a pay-as-you-go phone."

Bloody liar.

"Well, he was telling you a pack of lies," she put on the most disparaging face, "why would I? I came to you about him stalking *me*."

Hawthorne Siddley looked directly at her. If his intention was to unnerve her, it was working. And even though she was Frank Milton's daughter, and knew his mantra of *show no fear to anyone,* off by heart, she still needed to play a part.

She looked away.

He broke the silence. "I think that's all for now. Thank you very much for coming in and assisting us with our enquiries. We'll be in touch if there's anything else."

He paused the tape.

She stood up. No point in saying anymore. She needed to get out of there, quickly, and confidently. As if she was innocent.

Go Georgie!

Chapter 40

HAWTHORNE SIDDLEY

"So what do you think?" Tracy asked after seeing Laura Foley back to her friend and out of the building.

He blew out a breath, "Well, there's no direct evidence that's for sure."

"What's your hunch then?"

"I think she's capable. There's something about her." He pulled a face, "I don't know, I can't put my finger on it."

"Quirky?"

"Yeah, definitely quirky, and I suspect, much brighter than she appears."

"Does that make her a killer, though?"

"I don't know. Her father was a killer. I guess it depends on whether you believe the nature, nurture debate, or if you think it's programmed in the genes."

"Do you," she tilted her head, "think it's programmed in the genes?"

"There's plenty of evidence to say it can be. What did you make of her?"

"Gut feeling?"

"Yep, that will do."

"I don't think it's her." She scrunched her nose up, "I'm sure she wished him dead, but I don't think she did anything. It's too far-fetched her getting into his house and somehow putting nuts into the milk. Far more likely somehow the milk got contaminated at the factory. It sounds like he was extremely sensitive to nuts."

"Yes, but as the manager told us, it's more than their jobs are worth for cross-contamination to occur. The milk containing nuts in it is stored in a completely different part of the plant." He thought for a minute, "Unless we've got a random factory worker trying to sabotage milk and kill those with a nut allergy."

She widened her eyes, "Don't think I haven't thought of that. But if that was the case, someone would have come forward by now. There'd be a pattern and they did say there hadn't been any other incidents. So the question is, are we ruling Laura Foley out as a murderer, or ruling her in?"

Hawthorne considered for a moment, "Right now, I'm not sure. Find out if they've done the checks on that glass he drank the milk out of. Maybe she's not as clever as she thinks. Let's see if his saliva's present, and his fingerprints."

"Will do. What's your money on?"

"Who knows?" he shrugged, "One thing is certain, if she's been in the house before, they most likely will find her fingerprints."

"Yeah, I was disappointed when she said that. I'd have put money on her saying she didn't visit the house when she hated him so much."

"Ah, yes, but telling us she'd been in and actually being in are two different things. Sadly there's no one to corroborate her account."

He checked his watch, "Let's meet again after lunch. You'll need to visit the milk factory to ascertain if there is any way that milk could have been contaminated accidentally. I know what they said on the phone, but get them to show you around and see what you can find out. They'll have said no straight away to deflect any sort of focus from them."

"Okay, I'll see you later," Tracy nodded.

Hawthorne returned to his office. His back had been aching at his lower spine for three days and, as much as he tried, he couldn't help but worry he'd got a reoccurrence of cancer. He'd read all about secondary cancer, which could spread rapidly following surgery. He tried to weigh up his overactive mind against physical symptoms, and despite upping his analgesia medication, he knew something wasn't right.

He reached for his mobile and rang Pelo, tapping his fingers while he waited for her to answer. *What was taking her so long?*

"Hello," she answered on the fifth ring.

He didn't recognise the background noise. "Where are you?"

"At shopping mall."

"Don't tell me you've walked?" Pelo walked everywhere and the nearest mall was at least nine miles away. And it didn't sound at all like the noise was from shopping surroundings.

"I got bus."

"Did you? I didn't realise you knew which bus would get you there."

"I asked yesterday at newsagent when I got you paper. They told me."

He'd underestimated what a bright little thing she was.

"You should have asked me, I'd have taken you to town." Much as he hated shops of any description, he would have taken her if she'd asked. "Are you okay getting home, do you know which bus to get?"

"Yeah, I have it on piece of paper, 3X."

"I thought you said you were going to pot the hanging baskets today with the flowers we got from the garden centre?"

"I do that later. I home soon, on bus in fifteen minutes."

"That's good then. Okay, I'll let you get off. Ring me if there are any problems and I'll come and get you."

"Sure. Are you okay?"

"I'm fine, looking forward to getting home to see you."

He could sense her smiling. "Yeah, me feel same."

"By sweetheart."

"Bye bye."

He put the phone in his pocket. All his aches and pains would miraculously disappear when he got home and made love to her, but a sense of unease had crept in. He didn't like the thought of her going into town. If he was totally honest, he didn't want her doing stuff without him at all. It gave him an uncomfortable feeling he didn't like. A sort of dread, as if she might somehow break away, and he couldn't bear that.

He sighed. Instead of thinking about Pelo, he really should be concentrating all his efforts on the Cohan Laity murder, but he'd cracked that, in his head at least. As far as he was concerned, Laura Foley had done it. She'd switched the milk and given him the almond stuff and, nicked his EpiPens, so there was no hope for him. But proving she'd done that, and getting enough for the CPS was going to be a significant challenge. In his experience, they didn't do circumstantial. He reached for his bottle of water, *Keep drinking plenty to drain your lymphatic system* the colorectal specialist nurse had advised, but he hated bloody water. He took a mouthful and considered what he had. A man had died from a nut allergy. The contaminated milk could have occurred at the manufacturers with the labelling. Laura Foley had already said she'd been in the house previously so any evidence they found relating to her would be useless and easily dismissed by a brief. He was certain there would be Laity's fingerprints and saliva on the glass. So, he didn't have much, only his gut instinct she'd done it. He had hoped that getting her in informally would scare the shit out of her, but she'd seemed quite composed. Yes, she'd done a good job of appearing anxious, but he didn't buy it one bit.

He checked his watch, and decided to meet with Tracy after lunch and then head home early. He wanted to see Pelo. Her going to town on her own had unsettled him. They'd got another meeting coming up to try and extend her visa but the application was looking unlikely. She'd mentioned again getting pregnant which he'd dismissed telling her the usual spiel about not wanting children, especially since his cancer diagnosis, which wasn't a lie. The lie was he'd done something about fathering children years earlier and had a vasectomy. The last thing he'd ever wanted in his life was kids. And much as he loved her and desperately wanted her to stay with him, he couldn't have fathered a child. The thought of it sent a wave of fear galloping through him. She'd have plenty of time for kids when he'd gone, but for now, he advised she keep taking the pill and she was happy to comply. It didn't seem as if kids were high on her agenda, either, thank God. He'd just have to increase his efforts to come up with a way of keeping her here. Returning home wasn't an option as far as he was concerned.

Chapter 41

LAURA

Laura sat in the curved booth at a local café in Reigate. The noise of chattering echoed around and she welcomed normality after the oppressive police station. She'd telephoned her dad and said she was having a coffee with Ed and reassured him everything was okay, and decided on the way home she was going to pick up some flowers for her mum.

Ed came back from the counter and sat down with their coffees. "Are you sure you wouldn't prefer a pub? I reckon you need a stiff drink after the morning you've had."

"Do you know what, I couldn't face one right now. Coffee's just what I need."

Ed took a sip of his, "That's better. The crap they gave me at the station tasted like wallpaper paste."

"You've tried wallpaper paste before, have you?" she gave him a wry smile.

"You know what I mean," he grinned, "anyway, now you're here, spill. I want everything, warts and all. They don't invite you into a police station for nothing."

No point in holding back now. She'd known perfectly well the consequences of her actions would mean she'd have some explaining to do.

"You know I once told you I had a stalker."

"Yeah," he stared intently, "and I told you to tell the police."

"That's right, and I did."

It all came out then, every detail since she'd met Cohan. It seemed almost therapeutic being able to talk about it with someone. Ed patiently listened to her spewing it all out and didn't interrupt. She held nothing back, except her part in Cohan's death. He'd gently taken her hand when the conversation stalled; Danielle's death was the hardest to talk about and she couldn't control the stray tears. It thumped hard. She would always blame herself for allowing that monster into their lives.

Ed raked in his pocket and handed her a handkerchief, "Here, it's clean."

She swallowed the lump in her throat, and dabbed her eyes, "And just when things couldn't get any worse, they ask me in for questioning as if they suspect me of murdering Cohan."

He took a sip of his coffee and kept hold of the cup. "He's definitely been murdered, then?"

"I don't honestly know," she shook her head, "they don't actually give you details of what they think. But picking on me is ridiculous as I know nothing about his death. We only found out last night when his mother rang."

"I wonder what evidence they've got to make them bring you in?"

"God knows. I understand now why these people being interviewed by the police on the telly keep on answering, *no comment.* I tried to help by being honest, but everything I said sounded twisted." She sighed, "And I did lie and say I'd previously met him at my twenty-first, which they lost no time in reminding me about."

"Don't be so hard on yourself, I reckon it's perfectly understandable. I think you probably do need some sort of legal representation though if they want to see you again. Is there anything I can do to help?"

"Thanks Ed, but I don't think so. It's helped today just having you there."

"Well one thing I can do is insist you take some time off work, no arguing. I'll fix your leave card."

"There's no need, honestly. I'd rather be working."

"Nope, I insist. You hardly had any time off when Danielle died, so right now I think you owe yourself some, even if it's just a week."

Her tummy twisted with turmoil. She could be spending a lot of time away from work shortly the way things were going. Despite the provocation she'd been under, pulling off a heinous crime had been a gamble which still might not pay off. She'd got rid of Cohan so her family were safe, but at what price?

"Thanks Ed, maybe I will take the week off and see how things go," she agreed, "Mum and Dad could do with some support. I just hope the police come to their senses and realise all of this is nonsense."

"They will do, I'm sure. I reckon if they had any evidence he'd been murdered, they'd have arrested someone by now."

"I hope you're right because I'm not sure how much more of this I can take."

"Come here." He pulled her towards him and hugged her tightly. It felt good to be in a man's arms again. After a few seconds of savouring his warmth, he pulled away and stared at her face enquiringly. And then, totally unexpectedly, his mouth moved towards her and almost touched her lips.

She pulled away, "Don't, Ed."

Embarrassment coloured his face, "Sorry, I shouldn't have done that," his expression was pained, "the timing's not right, you've got enough on at the moment." He raised his eyebrow enquiringly as if he was expecting her to say something along the lines of, *maybe later*.

"I'm flattered, really I am, and I do care for you," she said, "but only as a friend. And I know Matthew and I are over, but I still miss him. I can't think about anyone else right now."

"Have you heard from him since you split up?"

"Not a thing."

"I don't mean this to come out how it's going to sound, but why did you tell him?"

"I didn't. Cohan told him after I'd reported him to the police for stalking and they took him in for questioning. It was his way of paying me back."

"What a bastard." He tilted his head, "Maybe when it's all blown over, he'll be back?"

"I doubt it. Matthew would really struggle with me being with someone else."

"He loves you though, anyone can see that. If he's got any sense, he'll try and work things out with you."

"I'm not so sure, I've really hurt him. I wish to God I'd never met Cohan Laity. He's brought so much darkness to the family, but it is all my own fault."

"Stop right there, you weren't to know he was a raving psychopath."

"No, I know that, but I still brought him into the family, even if it was indirectly."

"You didn't. He tracked you down."

"Which he wouldn't have been able to do if I hadn't had an affair with him and openly told him things, making it easy for him to find me."

"Hey, don't be so hard on yourself. He's gone now so you need to put him out of your mind and move forward."

"I can't though, Ed. He murdered my sister, I know he did . . . and all to get back at me."

"Well, if that's so, then he got what he deserved. Anyone can see that."

"Try telling Hawthorne Siddley that."

Ed frowned, "Hawthorne who?"

"Hawthorne Siddley, a bloody unfortunate name, isn't it? He's the detective in charge of the case and believe you me, he's as geeky as he sounds. It's him that interviewed me and asked all the questions. Well, him and his sidekick."

"That's a weird name, isn't it?"

"Yeah, it is."

"Anyway, maybe they'll leave it now. If they haven't got any evidence he was murdered, and you were at home at the time, I don't know how they can even try and pin it on you."

"Trust me, they make it clear just by their looks that they suspect something."

"Yeah, but speculating and actual evidence are too very different things. My guess is they'll give up soon. They can't keep questioning you. Just sit tight."

"Easier said than done. I have dreams at night about being locked up in a prison cell and not being able to see Mum, Dad and Teddy."

"They're just dreams, that's all," he squeezed her hand, "it's because you're stressed. You've had so much on with that piece of shit. Not only has he stalked you, he went and married your sister, and then she dies. Anyone would have trouble sleeping, I know I would."

"But what if I do get locked up? You hear so often of wrongful arrest. What if I go to court and I'm found guilty? I'll get a prison sentence then."

"That isn't going to happen. You didn't kill him, he died from his allergy," he reassured, "and you were at home the night he died."

"I know, but they're probably questioning that. They'll be asking Mum next if I was in bed that evening, you'll see."

"She'll say you were, though?" he took the last gulp of his coffee.

"Course she will. I had a horrible headache and went to bed early. But knowing Mum, she'll say she didn't check on me and then they'll be implying I could have crept out of the house."

"So? They can't really be thinking you hopped over the back wall to his house, gave him some nuts to eat, then left him to die?" He pulled a face, "It's too far-fetched to be credible."

"But is it? It could be done, I suppose."

He widened his eyes, "So what are you saying, you did it?"

"No, of course not, we're speaking hypothetically."

"Well, I'd be careful about what you do say, or before you know it, you'll be talking yourself into imagining you did do it. And that would give Mr Hawthorne bloody Siddley plenty of ammunition."

"Yeah, you might be right. Anyway," she glanced at her watch, "I'd better be making a move. I've now got to go and confess all to my parents. I should have invited them here then I wouldn't have to repeat it all," she said sarcastically. "They are going to be devastated when they hear everything. I'm dreading what they'll think of me."

"I'm sure they'll be fine, and from what I've seen of your parents, they'll support you. You've been through more than enough having to keep all this bottled up. And he was a complete arsehole to you. Would you like me to come with you while you tell them?"

He was such a support, but she needed to see her mum and dad alone. They hardly knew Ed. And much as she was dreading telling them everything, there was a part of her that would be relieved. Yes, they'd be devastated, but it had to be done. She still could well be charged so they needed to know. She'd prepared herself, knowing this day might come.

"You've been great, Ed, but they're likely to be upset so I'd better do this on my own." This time, she reached for his hand and squeezed it, "Thank you, I'm lucky to have you."

"Hey, that's what friends are for. You were a good friend to me when I needed one, so I'm here for you, now."

Chapter 42

HAWTHORNE SIDDLEY

He sat with Pelo in the small dingy room they'd been
taken to while they waited to be called in for an
interview regarding the extension of her visa
application. It was a repeat of months earlier when
they'd managed to get an extension for her to stay
while he was recovering from the cancer. At that time
the bloke that interviewed them seemed to just want the
interview over. He clearly had some sort of problem as
he'd been sweating profusely, and evidently not
listening as Hawthorne had explained that Pelo was
supporting him through his surgery and was acting as
his carer. Hawthorne deduced he'd been on the sauce as
he rushed through the interview at speed with glazed
eyes and few questions, and days later a letter arrived
for Pelo granting her three more months in the UK. He
was doubtful they'd get the same bloke again, he'd
most likely have lost his job by now, but he willed they
would and that he was equally as lenient.

He squeezed Pelo's hand, "Don't forget, just answer
the questions you're asked. We stand a better chance of
you getting another extension now that Aziz from the
newsagent has agreed you can have some paid hours
working in the shop."

"Yeah, but you no want me to work in shop."

"I don't, but if it means you get to stay with me,
then it's okay. We can work out the finer details later if
we can convince them you will be working and paying

contributions, and I'm going to try Angela one more time and see if she'll give me a divorce."

"But she already say no."

"Yes, but I've been thinking of other ways of persuading her."

"Like what?"

"Don't worry your little head about that, just leave it to me."

He was thinking of offering Angela money. She most likely would give it to the church, but if it got him what he wanted, then so be it. One thing was certain, there was no way he was having Pelo working in the corner shop. Her place was with him at home each night. He'd spent far too many evenings on his own with only a bottle for company.

The door opened. It was the same bloke as before, but he appeared much fresher than previously with his hair styled and gelled, and looking like a shop mannequin in his navy suit with precise creases down the trousers. More like the kind of civil servant you'd expect.

"Miss Atilia," he extended his hand towards Pelo and she took it. Even that made his abdomen twitch. He didn't want Pelo's hand in anybody's but his.

"I'm Ed Hurst. I see from our records I interviewed you last time." Pelo nodded, but she'd have no idea who they saw last time.

Ed Hurst extended his hand toward him. He took it, "I'm Hawthorne Siddley, I accompanied Pelo at the interview."

"That's right, you did, I remember your distinctive name, it's very unusual."

He must have got that from the notes as Hawthorne was certain he'd been too bloody wrecked to have remembered the time of day.

"Yes, it is, I get that all the time."

"Right," he nodded, "if you'd both like to follow me, this shouldn't take long."

They were taken to the same interview room as before and took their seats as indicated. Ed Hurst opened the file and glanced at the notes in front of him. Hawthorne would wager his last ten pounds there weren't any details from their previous meeting. As far as he could recall, he looked desperate for a hair of the dog rather than writing anything down.

Ed Hurst looked directly at Pelo and smiled. "I've read through your application, Miss Atilia, and note you have been offered permanent employment in the UK. However, I do need to stress you are in the country on a Tier 2 Visa currently, and that prohibits you from entering into a period of paid employment as your visa is about to expire." He smiled sympathetically, "I understand your desire to remain in this country, and our records show your visa has already been extended," he opened the file again, no doubt checking the date it would run out, "but it's now close to the time it expires." He looked questioningly at Pelo, "You have received a letter with the date you have to leave?"

Pelo nodded and Hawthorne sensed her tears before he saw them.

"Yeah. I been caring for Mr Siddley, but he no need me now he better."

Oh, I do, sweetheart, more than anything.

Ed Hurst nodded kindly, "I wonder, Miss Atilia, would you mind taking a seat in the waiting room again while I speak to Mr Siddley alone please. It won't take long."

Pelo looked anxious and Hawthorne nodded reassuringly to her despite having no idea whatsoever why Ed Hurst would want to speak to him alone. He doubted it would be to extend her visa.

Ed Hurst waited until Pelo closed the door behind her before speaking again. "I wanted to speak to you alone, Mr Siddley, on a private matter," he paused to clear his throat, "it's about Laura Foley." *Christ. How the hell did he know Laura Foley?* He continued, "I was with her at the station when you questioned her, so I wanted to speak to you on her behalf . . ."

Hawthorne interjected, "I need to stop you there. I'm afraid I'm not at liberty to discuss any sort of police business with you," he pressed his palms on the table as if to hoist himself into a standing position, "I came here today to support Miss Atilia with her visa application."

"Of course," Ed nodded, "but if you could indulge me with a minute of your time, I'd be grateful. It won't take long."

Hawthorne eased himself back into his chair. *Where the hell was this going?*

"Laura's been under an enormous amount of stress and I feel someone has to speak up for her. She really wouldn't hurt a fly, and all of the questioning she's had to go through has really taken its toll."

The cop in him couldn't resist, "What's the nature of your relationship with her?"

"I'm her boss, nothing more than that."

A pain shot through Hawthorne's head. It had escaped him that Laura Foley worked at the Home Office and he didn't like the fact he'd forgotten that. Chemotherapy seemed to have lost him his sharpness.

"I see."

He'll be shagging her, no doubt, she seemed to put it around.

"She's a bright girl and I'm confident one day she'll be doing my job."

"Good luck to her, then. As I said, I'm unable to discuss anything relating to police business with you."

"Yeah, I get that. But could you listen to what I have to say and consider it, you don't have to say anything?"

Hawthorne stared at him.

"If you are able to indulge me for a moment, this might be helpful to Miss Atilia's application."

That had his attention. "Go on."

"First of all, let me explain a little about the responsibilities I have in this role. Here at the Home Office, we receive thousands of applications from people who visit the UK and wish to remain here. Some we permit, but we can't of course allow every application. There are thousands of undesirables who want to live here, so there has to be a filter system. What I have to do is weigh up all the facts about each applicant. For example, will they contribute to the UK economy by way of employment, will they integrate, do they speak the language . . . you get the drift, this list goes on. There's a great deal to consider with each application. So, both your job as an investigating officer of crime, and my job as an investigating officer of people, both have an element of judgement to them."

Hawthorne gave a slight nod of his head, sensing where the conversation might be going.

Ed Hurst continued, "Once I identify a person that is illegally in this country, and I mean by that, those that have had a visa to stay but it may have expired, I then instigate them being deported if necessary. Or," he looked directly into Hawthorne's eyes as he continued, "in some circumstances, I'm able to grant what is called a period of stay."

He got the gist. He could help Pelo, but there'd be a price.

"I see." Hawthorne's interest was piqued, "I would imagine it's a demanding job making decisions like that?"

"Yes, quite."

"And as interesting as your job seems to be, I'd appreciate it if you cut to the chase. I really do have more pressing business to attend to right now."

"Yes, I'm sure. I'll try and be as frank as I'm able about the situation as I see it. I would very much like my friend to be left alone so she can get on with her life, and you would like your friend to remain in the UK so she can get on with hers. I feel we can help each other achieve our aims. You'll be familiar with the expression about scratching backs?"

"I am familiar with that expression, Mr Hurst, and on that note, I think it best we terminate this meeting right now," he raised an eyebrow enquiringly, "otherwise I could deduce you might be trying to bribe a police officer."

"Bribe?" Ed Hurst widened his eyes in fake astonishment, "not at all. I'm only concerned about a colleague of mine who is struggling at the moment. I know she had nothing to do with a man's sudden death, but if I'm totally honest, even if she did, hypothetically speaking of course, I think he probably got what was coming to him. He's been an absolute bastard to that family, Laura even believes he murdered her sister. What's the saying my grandmother always used, *You'll get your just deserts.*

"Yes, well, I'm not in the habit of listening to old wives' tales, my job is about working through facts. And you are referring to police business, which, with respect, is not any business of yours. So, I'd appreciate it if you could work on Miss Atilia's application, and to reiterate again, that's why I'm here today."

"Yes, of course, and I'll certainly be considering that in the next few days. I've got all the information so I don't think there's any need to bring Miss Atilia in again. If you could tell her I'll write to her in due course when I've made my decision. But just to add," his expression was patronising, "between you and I, it isn't looking favourable. However, anything could happen in the next week or so. I'll consider her application along with the others I have."

"I'd appreciate that," Hawthorne stood up, "now if you'll excuse me."

What a condescending bastard.

"Of course. Can I just add that Laura has no idea I'm speaking to you today. I'd like it to stay that way."

"As you haven't brought any information to a police enquiry, I see no reason to discuss this with her. And as we are unlikely to be meeting again, I'll say good day to you."

Ed nodded, "Thank you," and reached out his hand. It was a firm handshake.

They walked in silence to the room next door where his love was waiting with anxiety written all over her beautiful face.

"Good day to you both." Ed Hurst nodded, and Hawthorne led Pelo towards the exit, deep in thought about the dilemma that had now presented itself.

Hawthorne had returned to work after dropping an anxious Pelo home. He'd run out of words to console her; he wasn't a words man. He stood at the window of his office clutching a bottle of water and taking two more tablets to ease the pain radiating from his lower back to his leg. It seemed to be easier standing than sitting. He reached up and closed the window which had been creating a draft. Since his surgery and subsequent treatment, he felt cold on a daily basis. It was a new experience for him, he never used to feel it at all. It wasn't weight loss either, as with Pelo's delicious meals he was back to his pre-surgery weight.

Tracy tapped on the door and came in. "Hi boss, how did the meeting with the super go?"

Hawthorne had met with his boss about satisfactorily completing the phased return, and then answered his barrage of questions about the Laity case.

"Fine. I'm now officially back on full pelt as of next week."

"That's good to hear. And the Laity case?"

"He's not eager about us pursuing murder with zilch evidence. Said nothing we don't already know about the CPS."

"So are you any closer to a decision?"

"Nope," Hawthorne replied wearily, "I'll sleep on it tonight, but it's becoming increasingly unlikely the CPS would go for what we have without any evidence. It is all supposition."

"Then maybe we are barking up the wrong tree?" Tracy suggested.

"Nah, I don't think we are. The PM suggested there wasn't enough of the almond milk for it to have been a labelling issue. You either have almond milk or none-almond milk. And the amount of almond in a carton is a specific amount, and Cohan Laity didn't get that much. The carton that was in his fridge only had minute traces. I'm ninety-nine percent confident that that young woman added the almond milk to his regular milk, nicked his EpiPens and phone, and waited. His death was almost instantaneous without the rescue pen such was the severity of his allergy. You checked with his doc that he had two EpiPens, but we never found the other one. It had to be somewhere near, yet despite searches of his house and car, we didn't find it."

He stifled a belch, *bloody tablets*. He took another swig of his water before continuing. "We can't place Laura Foley at the scene of the crime. Her mother says she was in bed asleep that night, although she didn't check on her."

"Yeah," Tracy agreed, "she was most indignant that she hadn't checked on Laura in bed since she was fourteen. That does make the alibi tenuous to say the least, though."

"It does, and we've no forensics, everything was clean."

"We've got his saliva and fingerprints on the glass so it seems he did voluntarily drink the milk . . . but we're still pretty stuffed. I guess there's always the tiniest possibility we could be completely wrong and the milk was contaminated at the factory?"

Hawthorne reached in his briefcase for some indigestion tablets. "Yes, there's still that to consider. You could well be right."

She wasn't though. He'd been a cop long enough to be able to sniff out when someone was guilty. And Laura Foley was guilty. But right now, despite his lower back throbbing with pain, and his head aching intolerably, he had more to think about. Ed Hurst's inference that if he stopped pursuing Laura Foley he'd favourably look upon Pelo's application to stay, created an inner buzz. The question pending was, could Detective Inspector Hawthorne Siddley persuade the CPS to charge Laura Foley with Cohan Laity's murder on the circumstantial evidence they had? Or should Hawthorne Siddley, the recovering cancer patient with a prognosis that most certainly meant eventual death, keep the love of his life close by for however much time he had left?

It was without doubt a dilemma – integrity versus love.

Chapter 43

HAWTHORNE SIDDLEY

He felt a tear from Pelo's cheek roll onto his chest. He'd just made love to her and they were cuddled up together in bed. Her beautiful petite body and soft skin were warm from their lovemaking and he savoured her in his arms. Their time together was almost up and she would have to return to Thailand. The very thought of it constricted his chest.

How was he ever going to manage without her?

"I no want to leave you," she whispered.

"I don't want you to either," he kissed her head, savouring the lemon freshness of her shampoo.

"When I go," she sniffed, "you come see me soon?"

His breath caught in his throat, "Now I'm back at work it makes it harder to get time off."

"I scared you no take care of yourself. You say you do, but I no think so."

He leaned up on his elbow and tilted her head with his hand. "I promise you, I'm trying my best to sort something out. I'm seeing Angela when she's back from her holiday. If she'd give me a divorce, we could marry, and even though that doesn't guarantee permanency here, it would definitely help."

"You good man and do your best. I love being here to look after you."

"And you've done that so well. I don't know where I'd be without you."

She started to sob.

"You mustn't cry," he wiped her tears with his fingers. "I've got some other ideas if Angela says no again."

"What idea?" she sniffed.

"I'll tell you if it comes off, but I promise you we are one step closer to you being able to stay."

"You fake papers?"

"Don't be silly. I'm a police officer, I don't do criminal things."

"Why you no tell me then?"

"I will if it comes off."

"When you know?"

"Soon, I promise. Come on now, you get some sleep. I'm just going down for a nightcap."

"You wan me to come?"

"No, sweetheart, you stay and keep the bed warm. I'll be back shortly."

"Will you know what you do when you come back?"

"I think I already know. I love you very much, you know that don't you?"

She nodded and snuggled into him. "Hurry back."

He kissed her and grabbed his boxers to make his way downstairs.

He poured himself a large one, adding a bit more for measure, and savoured the heat of the first mouthful travelling down his chest. Should he let Laura Foley off and keep Pelo? However long he had left, he wanted her with him. The way he was feeling the last few weeks since returning to work, he guessed he wouldn't make the five predicted years. Why shouldn't he have the woman he loved by his side for however long that would be? She'd still be young enough to make a new life after he'd gone, and she'd have money. If he could somehow persuade Angela to divorce him, he could marry Pelo and then she'd have his police pension. So keeping her with him was not entirely selfish. He knew trips back and forth to Thailand weren't an option. The insurance alone with his medical condition would prohibit that. And the thought of her going back to servicing blokes filled him with horror.

But letting Laura Foley literally get away with murder was totally abhorrent to him. He'd joined the force at nineteen and loved every aspect of his job. He had an inbuilt barometer for justice and abiding by the law. Promotion had given him the chance to use his razor sharp brain to solve often the most complex cases. The law had been his life. To compromise on that was unthinkable.

He drained the last of his whisky. The irony wasn't lost on him that he'd been given the crystal glass as part of a set from the force to mark his twenty-five years continual service.

The bottom of the glass stared back at him.

He had to make a decision.

Chapter 44

LAURA

The whole family were sitting in the lounge waiting nervously for Hawthorne Siddley to arrive. He'd telephoned the house and said he would be calling at five that evening but had given no explanation as to why. Her dad had let on he'd telephoned him days earlier, wanting to know why the police had dismissed her stalking claims and were now pursuing her as if she was some sort of criminal.

Initially, when Laura had spoken to her mum and dad explaining the whole story between her and Cohan, they'd both been horrified. Exactly as she'd expected, they'd chastised her about Cohan, but once they got over the shock, they were exactly the same as they'd always been towards her. They'd been terribly disappointed that she'd had the affair in the first place while she was with Matthew, but not once did they berate her for Cohan coming into their lives. Neither of them believed Cohan would have done anything to Danielle, they'd been emphatic about that, therefore she'd hadn't pushed her views onto them. It was still hard for her to think about Danielle's terror in her last moments, and her parents' had enough to contend with coming to terms with the fact that Cohan didn't love Danielle as much as she did him. They believed she'd been happy before she died and it wouldn't be fair for her to ruin that.

Laura cringed when her dad had insisted they had a joint prayer of forgiveness, but joined in as she felt it was the least she could do. The two loving stalwarts didn't blame her and they had every right to.

"I wish he'd said on the phone what's going on," her mum said flicking the net curtain back from the bay window and peering out, "my nerves are in tatters waiting around."

"He isn't going to come any quicker with you stood watching, love," her dad said."

"I can't just sit still like you. Do you think if he comes in a police car, then we have to assume Laura will be arrested?" Tears threatened, she could see her mum swallowing them down.

Laura's tummy churned. She couldn't be arrested . . . she just couldn't.

"I'm sure if they were going to arrest Laura, they wouldn't have waited until the end of the day. They'd have done it already." Although the reassuring words came out of her father's mouth, for once they didn't sound quite so convincing.

"Do you think so?" her mum looked optimistically at her dad, "I hope you're right. I've lost one daughter already, I can't face losing another." A sob broke out, her dad rushed to put his arms around her and she cried even more with her head buried in his shoulder. He patted her back as if comforting a child, "You need to calm yourself. I've told you before, it's no good speculating about anything. If you're going to get bad news, wait until you do. Assumption does nobody any good, now come on, how about a nice cup of tea?" He looked towards Laura, "Can you manage one, love?"

Tea? She could be arrested, taken into custody and charged with murder. Didn't he realise, right now, tea wasn't going to cut it?

"I'm fine, Dad, thanks, I've got water."

"Well, I'd like one if nobody else does. I'll go and put the kettle on."

The doorbell rang. Laura was close to combusting. It wasn't possible to use the toilet anymore, there was nothing left. She remained glued to her chair while her mother went to answer it.

The clock on the mantelpiece caught her eye. Teddy would be on his way home from school and if she was going to be arrested she didn't want it in front of him. He'd be upset.

A familiar voice sounded in the hall. One she'd been longing to hear since they'd parted. The door opened and her beaming mum came back into the lounge with Matthew following closely behind. Laura hadn't seen him since he'd asked for her engagement ring back. He'd lost weight and was pale. He looked as awkward as she felt.

"Hi," he smiled nervously.

"Matthew," her dad greeted, and got up from his chair, "How are you?"

Matthew shook his outstretched hand, "Not too bad."

"Did you mention some tea, Ian," her mum said, "I'll come with you and help."

Her dad got the message, "Oh right, tea, yes, just the job. We'll go and do that now."

Her mum ushered her dad out of the lounge and closed the door behind them, leaving her and Matthew alone. He looked weary and his hair was in need of a good cut. "Can I sit down?" he asked.

"Of course."

He sat on the chair in the window rather than next to her. "God, Laura, you've lost loads of weight. You look awful."

She wanted to laugh at the irony of the situation. What did he expect? A full face of make-up when she was likely to be arrested? And, yes, she had lost weight, she could barely eat.

"I know that, I've been under a lot of strain."

He nodded sympathetically as if he understood, but how could he? How could anyone know? Only her and Georgie girl knew the truth.

"I expect you're wondering why I'm here?" he shuffled in his seat uncomfortably.

"I am a bit, yes." *Was the cancer back?*

"I've kept in touch with your mum and she told me about today." The eyes she loved so much stared kindly into hers, "I wanted to be here for you, whatever happened."

She shook her head, puzzled. "I don't understand?"

"I don't either," he shrugged, "I just needed to be here."

"Yeah, but why?"

He lifted an eyebrow, "You said everyone's entitled to one mistake."

She took a deep breath in, "I know I did, and as pleased as I am to see you, your timing couldn't be any worse. I might be arrested and carted off to a police cell any minute now. I'm messing myself thinking of what might happen to me."

"You didn't kill Cohan Laity, the police will know that."

Her heart contracted with love. Only Matthew could have so much faith in her. She didn't deserve it after the way she'd treated him, he was worthy of much better.

"They must have something though . . ." she faltered . . . "I'm really scared. I don't want to go to prison and leave Mum, Dad and Teddy," tears threatened but she held onto them, "I can't bear the thought of that."

He moved from the chair and sat on the sofa next to her. He smelled familiar . . . like Matthew. He reached for her hand but the shrill of the doorbell stopped him saying what he'd been about to.

Her mum called out, "I'll get it."

She tried to move her hand from Matthew, but he held on tightly. His strength gave her strength. She'd been such a fool. Laura that is, Georgie girl had done what she'd had to.

Hawthorne Siddley followed her mum and dad into the lounge. "Please, take a seat," her mother offered, "Can I get you anything to drink?"

"No thank you, Mrs Foley." He sat in the chair Matthew had vacated and her mum and dad took the smaller sofa.

Laura's heart thumped and her breath caught in her throat. *Would she be leaving with him?* It felt like a comedy scene playing out in front of her. Her dad was glaring daggers at Hawthorne Siddley, her mum was smiling at him hopefully, and she was clutching Matthew's hand and crapping herself.

Siddley cleared his throat and looked directly at her mum and dad, "I'll come straight to the point. We're satisfied that Danielle's death was accidental despite Laura's allegations."

She glared at him. *No it wasn't.*

"And we've concluded there isn't sufficient evidence to suggest that Mr Laity was murdered."

"So what does that mean?" her dad interjected, "that his death was accidental?"

Hawthorne Siddley stared menacingly at her. It was as if he could read her mind. "I'm saying there isn't any evidence to warrant further investigation. Of course it's for the coroner to establish the exact cause of death, but we won't be pursuing anyone in relation to it."

A little voice whispered in her ear, *See, I told you I could do it.*

She stayed silent, she daren't allow herself to think she'd got away with it. It could well be a trap. Her dad continued, "Well, that's a relief. As I said on the phone, my daughter has been under a great deal of stress . . ."

"Ian," her mum interjected, "I think we should leave it now. We've all been under a great deal of stress. Have you spoken to Cohan's mother, Mr Siddley?"

"Yes, we have."

"Good, I'm pleased about that. It's hard for her living so far away. I'll call her later and see how she is. And we do appreciate you coming round and telling us face-to-face."

Hawthorne Siddley nodded, "I don't normally, but in view of the allegations about Danielle's death, I wanted to speak to you personally and reassure you that we have looked into things carefully." He rose to his feet, barely glancing her way. "Anyway, I'll make a move if there's nothing else."

Laura held her breath, willing him to go.

"No, I think that's it," her mum nodded, relief written all over her face, "we'll show you out."

The lounge door closed behind them and only then did she let out the breath she was holding. Matthew opened his arms and she went into them willingly, clutching him as if she'd never let him go.

"Thank God," he breathed.

Chapter 45

HAWTHORNE SIDDLEY

He was eager to leave. The last thing he needed was thanking. Every nerve in his body was on end and a huge dark cloud hovered over him. As sure as eggs were eggs, Laura Foley killed Cohan Laity. He knew it. The success he'd made of his thirty plus years in the police force was down to his instincts and never giving up. He could sniff guilty and in all the cases he'd been involved in, he'd always managed to find that extra something. Not every case ended up with the culprit serving time, some of the courts found the men and women he'd tried to bring to justice, not guilty, but that was more down to the skills of a good QC rather than him and his team not doing their job. He never lost sleep over that, though. As long as he'd got them charged and to the courts, he was satisfied.

He closed the wrought iron gate behind him and moved towards his car, impatient to get away. A young lad of about fifteen approached him with a girl about the same age. "Hello," the boy gave him a beaming smile, "have you been to my house?"

He deduced it must be the young brother, Teddy, the one with Down's syndrome Tracy had mentioned.

"Yes, I've been speaking to your sister and parents."

"Are you a policeman? Mum said a policeman was coming today."

"Yes, I am."

Teddy turned his attention towards his car. "Why haven't you got a flashing light on your car?"

"I don't drive one of those. They're for the policemen in uniform so they can get to places quickly. I don't need to get anywhere fast."

"Why?"

Hawthorne smiled at the boy, "Because my job is more office based."

The girl with Teddy spoke for the first time, "The flashing lights are for night-time, you don't need them in the day?"

"No," Teddy argued, "they are for anytime. I've seen them in the day. Aren't they?" he asked.

The last thing he needed was to be talking about police sirens. He wanted to get home to Pelo. Now he'd done the deed, he had something to celebrate.

"Yes. Now, you'll have to excuse me, I must get to another appointment."

Teddy seemed oblivious to his keenness to leave, "Do you have to go out in the night when it's dark?"

Hawthorne shook his head, "Not often. I used to years ago."

"I like night-time best," Teddy said, "I watch things at night with the binoculars my dad got me. There are some foxes that live at the bottom of the garden. Dad says they come from under the shed."

The girl giggled. "Your dad told you to stop doing that. He said you had to stay in bed at night and sleep. You'll get into trouble if he finds out."

"Well, Laura will as well then, 'cause she creeps out at night."

"What for?" the girl asked, "does she feed the foxes?"

"I don't think so," he screwed his face up, "I don't know where she goes. I only saw her once. She climbed over the wall at the bottom of the garden into Cohan's."

Hawthorne Siddley's chest tightened. He knew without even asking what night Laura went over the wall. It was the piece of evidence he'd been looking for. Laura Foley had left the house the night Cohan Laity had died, she'd not been in bed all night as she'd said. He knew it. He'd always known it. He should be overjoyed . . . he had a potential testimony that could place Laura Foley at the scene of the crime. The proof he needed to put her behind bars. His heart was racing furiously. The same way it always did when he'd cracked a case.

He needed to think. "Right, well, it's been nice to speak with you both but I really must be off. Goodbye."

Teddy and the girl smiled and walked away and he got into his car. The lad would have no idea of the bombshell he'd just dropped. The question now for Hawthorne was – what was he going to do with the information? Would the brother be able to stand up in court and swear which night Laura went over the back wall with a jury watching him? He'd inadvertently grassed on his sister having no idea of the ramifications. But once he knew exactly what that snippet of information could do, he'd probably clam up. He wouldn't want to incriminate his sister. And Laura Foley was full of tricks. She'd somehow get to him and he'd change his account.

He stared out of his windscreen and sighed. Hadn't he already made his decision? There was no point in reneging on that now. Not when it meant Pelo could stay with him.

He started the engine.

"Fuck!" the copper in him spat out loud as he moved away.

Chapter 46

LAURA

Laura's mum came into the lounge and rushed forward to hug her, and then she hugged her dad.

Her dad's emotion was evident in his voice as he held her, "Thank goodness they saw sense." She sobbed and he held onto her tightly. "You've nothing more to worry about now, sweetheart, it's all over."

The door burst open and Teddy came in followed by his friend, Sadie. "Dad, they have blue flashing lights on police cars in the daytime don't they?"

"Yes, of course they do," he replied blowing his nose. "They have to catch criminals in the daytime as well as at night."

Teddy turned to Sadie, "Told you."

He spotted Matthew, "Hiya Matthew. Have you come back?"

Her mum dabbed her eyes, "Tea anyone?"

"I think we deserve something a bit stronger than tea," her dad scoffed.

Her mum smiled, "Sounds good to me. Come on then all of you," she led Teddy and Sadie towards the door and gave her dad a *let's leave them alone look*. He took the hint and followed, closing the door behind him. Laura could just hear Teddy's voice fading, "Can I show Matthew my new postcards?"

She rolled her eyes at Matthew, "Subtle or what?"

"I've missed them," Matthew took her hand, "and you."

"I've missed you too, so much. And I'm really pleased you came today, I guess it could have gone either way. I know how it looked. I'd been kicking off about Cohan stalking me, and then he dies. I was really scared after they interviewed me."

"I should have been with you. I couldn't bear it if they'd taken you away. I know you're no killer. If they had accused you, I'd have fought for you alongside your mum and dad."

"Would you? After all that happened . . . after I'd let you down so badly?"

"Yeah, even after all that. I still love you and I want us to move on." His eyes were full of so much love, "It'll take a while but I want us to have that life together we planned, to go and travel and eventually settle down and have those kids we promised ourselves."

"Oh, Matthew," tears threatened, but this time, they were happy tears, "you don't know how much I've wanted to hear that. I love you too, very much. I always have done and I'm going to spend the rest of my life proving that to you. I'll never let you down again, I promise."

"I know that," he nodded, "but we need to also remember, it might not all be plain sailing with me. We have the cancer to think about. It could come back."

"And it might not. The consultant said many patients go on to lead a perfectly normal life and not have any reoccurrence. Remember that footballer we googled with his wife and kids? He's fine ten years on from his surgery."

"Yeah, I supposed we just have to stay positive." He pulled a face, "I've got a confession, though."

"What?"

"I've started smoking since we split up."

"Aw, no, you haven't."

It hurt that she'd driven him to it. He'd done so well quitting in the first place. No point in berating him though. "Well you've stopped before, so you will again. I'll help you."

He leant forward and kissed her. It felt so good. He reached in his pocket and produced her precious engagement ring. A tear trickled down her cheek as he placed it on her finger. "Now," he caught the stray tear with his thumb, "how about you go and wipe those mascara eyes, and we'll start again from the beginning, shall we?"

"Yeah," she swallowed, "let's do that." She kissed his hand, "I'll be back in a jiffy, go find Mum and Dad, I'm sure he'll have a cold beer for you."

"Okay," he stood up, "I'll have a drink with them to celebrate, but after that, can we go somewhere on our own, we've got a lot to talk about?"

"Course we can," she smiled lovingly at him, "I'll just wash my face, we'll have a quick drink with them and then we're out of here."

Laura closed her bedroom door and breathed in deeply as her heart-rate steadied. She'd feared the worst and believed she was going to prison.

She pressed to call Ed on her iPhone and waited for him to answer. "Hi, Ed, just a quickie, I had to ring and let you know. The chap that's dealing with the case, Hawthorne Siddley, has been round and says they're treating Cohan's death as accidental, so there won't be any further investigations and the case is closed."

"Thank God, that's brilliant news, anyone could see he was barking up the wrong tree."

"Yes, I can't believe it's all over, I've been worried sick."

"I know you have. What exactly did he say?"

"Just that they'd investigated thoroughly and there was no evidence to point to it being murder. He was almost human after all the questioning."

"And so he bloody should be. You should never have had to go through all of that."

"I know. And I've got another bit of good news."

"What's that?"

"Matthew came round to support me. Mum contacted him and told him the police were coming."

"That's brilliant, I'm really pleased for you."

"That means such a lot to me. I've been worried since . . . you know . . ."

"Hey, don't be daft. It was a one off, workmates comforting each other. Forget about it, I have."

"Thank you, I will. See you on Monday?"

"Yep, hurry back, my filing's gone downhill."

"When has it ever been uphill?"

"Cheeky. Make the most of the weekend celebrating."

"I will do. Thanks Ed. Bye."

Chapter 47

LAURA

Laura sipped the sparkling wine her dad had given her, and could hear her mum in the hall on the phone to Cohan's mother. She couldn't stop looking at Matthew sitting in the chair opposite, attentively listening to her dad's ramblings about graffiti on the door to the church annexe, while patiently looking through Teddy's latest drawings he'd slapped on his knee. He was a good man and she loved him for his gentleness towards Teddy. Now they'd had the obligatory drink, she wanted to be on her own with him.

Her mum coming back into the room was a timely interruption, "Right, I think it's about time we all had something to eat."

It was the cue Laura needed. "Did you say earlier something about us going out for a pizza, Matthew?"

"Yeah, I did." He glanced at her mum and dad sheepishly, as if he didn't want to interrupt things, "If that's okay?"

"Oh, that'll be nice," her mum smiled, "you two do that. It'll be lovely for you both to have some time together."

"Can I come?" Teddy asked.

"Not tonight, Teddy," her dad said, "I need you to help me move some things around in the garage, they're heavy so I need someone strong to help me. We can go for a pizza at the weekend."

"Aw, but I want to go now," he pulled a face, "I haven't seen Matthew for ages."

Laura jumped up, "I'll just get changed, I won't be five minutes." As she left the room she heard her mum trying to pacify Teddy. There was no way he was joining them, much as she loved him, tonight was about her and Matthew. She rubbed her thumb along her engagement ring checking it was still there.

When she reached the bottom of the stairs, she paused at the ornate hall mirror and stared at her reflection. Every single time she looked in the mirror, she saw the nine-year-old girl with the pale skin and greasy hair staring back at her . . . but not this time. It was Laura's adult reflection she saw. Georgie girl seemed to have gone, but not before she'd taken care of everything, just as she said she would. Cohan couldn't hurt her anymore; her family were safe, and Matthew was back. All was well.

Laura's lips twitched and formed a sly smirk as she mounted the stairs. A little voice in her head whispered, *So, who's smiling now?*

Acknowledgements

I remember when *Who's Smiling Now?* first came together. My husband and I chatted one evening over dinner in our favourite spot, Keswick in the Lake District. I had published four other romance novels and wanted to try something different. I chatted on about the idea of two sisters and how one would commit a murder and get away with it. I wanted a detective to know how she'd done it, but needed an Achilles heel for him so he had to let the case go. Hawthorne Siddley came to fruition and my husband's suggestion of there being immigration issues fitted well. After that, all I had to do was write it!

I am extremely lucky to have a wonderful editor, John Hudspith who made the story better in every way. His editing skills are second to none and, because of him, I am continually improving as a writer. And it's not just the editing, I rely totally on his suggestions, guidance and advice which have without doubt, attributed to my other books being successful. Thank you, John.

Praise must go to the talented Jane Dixon-Smith (JD Smith Design) for the beautiful cover she designed for *Who's Smiling Now?* – I absolutely love it. Jane mocked up four designs for me to consider and each one was unique and stunning, so the dilemma was choosing which.

Thanks also to my diligent beta readers, Sally Warr and Sallyann Cole for their input. I love how you spot the mistakes I make. Clearly I read the novel how I *think* I've written it, so I rely on your expertise to point out how I actually *have* done, therefore your beady eyes are vital. Thank you!

To my friends whose encouragement is immeasurable. Thank you! You are always there for me (most often than not with an alcoholic beverage in front of us!) and I sincerely appreciate your support. What a dull place it would be without you in my life.

To the readers who have purchased this book, a massive thanks to you all, and for those of you that have recommended it to friends and colleagues, I'm indebted. Many of you have kindly spread the word about my previous books and that means the world. If you would like to get involved in a wider conversation about any of my books and feel able to leave a review on Amazon/Goodreads, I would be eternally grateful. I love hearing what readers think about my stories, and if you would like to contact me directly, my email address is joymarywood@yahoo.co.uk.

Finally, heartfelt thanks to my devoted husband who takes care of everything so I can write. You are such a star, John and I'm so lucky to have you. Love as always X

Other Books By Joy Wood

April Fool

Chanjori House

Knight & Dey

For The Love of Emily

All available on Amazon

Lightning Source UK Ltd.
Milton Keynes UK
UKHW010336280422
402152UK00002B/155